BY TWO AND TWO

ALSO BY JIM SCHUTZE:

My Husband's Trying to Kill Me!

Cauldron of Blood: The Matamoros Cult Murders

The Accommodation: The Politics of Race in an American City

Preacher's Girl: The Life and Crimes of Blanche Taylor Moore

BY TWO AND TWO

The Scandalous Story of Twin Sisters Accused of a Shocking Crime of Passion

JIM SCHUTZE

WILLIAM MORROW AND COMPANY, INC.
New York

It is the policy of William Morrow and Company, Inc., and its imprints and affiliates, recognizing the importance of preserving what has been written, to print the books we publish on acid-free paper, and we exert our best efforts to that end.

LIBRARY OF CONGRESS CATALOGING-IN-PUBLICATION DATA

Schutze, Jim.

By two and two : the scandalous story of twin sisters accused of a shocking crime of passion / Jim Schutze.

p. cm.

ISBN 0-688-12871-8

1. Murder—Alabama—Huntsville—Case studies. 2. Wilson, Betty, 1945– . 3. Wilson, Jack, Dr. 4. Lowe, Peggy. 5. White, James Dennison, 1951– . 6. Trials (Murder)—Alabama—Madison County. I. Title.

HV6534.H89S38 1995

364.1'523'0976197—dc20 95-6764

CIP

Printed in the United States of America

1 2 3 4 5 6 7 8 9 10

First Edition

BOOK DESIGN BY PATRICE SHERIDAN

For Amy,

my literary niece

ACKNOWLEDGMENTS

My beloved wife, Mariana, listened to what I had to say when I came home from Alabama and told me it was a far better story for the way it had turned out. Bob Mecoy at Avon Books agreed. Which, frankly, amazed me. My intrepid, brilliant, and suave literary agent, Janet Wilkens Manus, was able to make it happen (she always does that). My stern but humane editors—Tom Colgan, Liza Dawson, and Doris Cooper—whipped it and me into shape.

After all that, the mere writing of it seemed like a relatively small thing. And a pleasure.

For the sin ye do by two and two ye must pay for one by one.

—RUDYARD KIPLING, "Tomlinson"

BY TWO AND TWO

ONE

IN THE MORNING, THE SUN ROSE OVER THE BIG BRICK house at 2700 Boulder Circle in Huntsville, Alabama, and the human beings inside awoke to a busy day, spiced with the anticipation of pleasant things ahead. Trey had come into Jack's room early that morning to tell him he was not going to Santa Fe with them after all. He had decided to take off early with some friends for the Florida beaches. Jack went back to sleep, and by the time he and Betty awoke, Trey was long gone, on his way to celebrate the end of exams in the land of sun and surf.

For Jack Wilson, the morning of Friday, May 22, 1992, was an opportunity to spend time at his beloved office, doing what he loved most, treating his patients and working with his staff, with one exception from the usual Friday pattern. Normally on Fridays he sent the staff home at noon and then departed himself for a gantlet of eye surgeries, often stretching into the late evening. He scheduled the surgeries together on Friday afternoon so his patients could get their recuperation out of the way on the weekend and not miss work. But on this Friday, there were no surgeries scheduled. He would send the staff home as usual and then go home to see if Betty needed help getting ready for their departure Saturday morning for Santa Fe. Since Monday was Memorial Day, the office would remain closed until the following Tuesday.

. . .

Betty had more errands ahead of her, but the important things, such as tickets and reservations, were already arranged. The things left to be done were light duties, all pleasant enough—picking up a new pair of tennis shoes and perhaps a few more things to wear. She needed to take the money from the political fund-raising party the night before and deposit it in the bank.

Trey had been understanding and perfectly good-natured about being disinvited from the Santa Fe trip. He certainly had not failed to notice, in his time in the house with them, that Jack and Betty's relationship had its ups and downs.

Setting out on her round of errands, Betty thought about it. It had been such a strange process—their relationship. There had been times in Betty's life—quite early, when she was still a girl—when she had assumed that marriage, domesticity, family life, parenthood, were not places where she was invited to go. In the moments when her father's shadow fell across her memory, she felt chilled and alone, terribly hungry. She felt as if she would be lucky to grab a moment of intensity with whatever man was handy and wash it down with a belt of good booze. In the other moments, when the memory of her mother's strength and tenderness lighted her way, she yearned for a safe, stable nest of her own.

Then there was Jack—funny, odd little Jack, the tiny frail lad behind the pop-bottle glasses, pale from long afternoons indoors watching television and daydreaming alone, reading books under the bed, locked up in a succession of cracker-box houses with loony old Wirta, who told people his stage name was Dean Stockwell. All that while, the little boy had savored the words of his dead stepfather, Bill Wilson. Strive for the light. As soon as he was able to get out the door on his own two feet, still a boy by most people's measurement, he had done just what his stepfather had told him, with ferocity and tenacity. Tender, profoundly insightful, he had almost no idea how to carry out the small rituals of polite behavior.

How did they ever get together, she wondered? How did they

stay together through her alcohol and drug problems, her affairs, his Crohn's disease, their profound emotional insecurities? The terrible scene in the bedroom. But then, who else would have stayed with either one of them? In a world that could be Hell, perhaps their marriage was made in Heaven, after all.

Jack came home for lunch. He helped Betty put a small selection of leftovers on the kitchen table.

When they were seated, she said, "It's just the two of us, you know."

Jack said, "Just the two of us, eh?"

She nodded, then rose with her plate, turning away a little shyly.

Betty went back to the mall, bought some tennis shoes. She thought of more clothes she might need and drove to a small dress shop. She remembered she needed to go to the pharmacy. She was rushing to make a 5:00 P.M. Alcoholics Anonymous meeting. As usual when she was facing what she feared would be a difficult personal experience, she was feeling especially anxious about drinking. She would probably attend several meetings this evening.

Jack lingered in his office for hours, unable to leave. His practice occupied twenty-five hundred square feet of space on the ground floor of the Whitesport Center building, a three-story brick complex behind tall white pillars. The building was a short distance from Crestwood Hospital and was occupied mainly by medical practitioners, many of whom were already gone for the holiday weekend. Here, rambling in the half dark from station to station, machine to machine, Jack walked the decks of his own ship, making sure it was battened down for the long weekend.

A few minutes before five, Betty was working her way toward the end of her round of errands. She would just make it to her meeting.

At some point between four and five, David Williamson, a short, burly man with a butch haircut, walked out of the bar at the Ramada Inn where James White was staying. In his boxy suit and heavy black shoes, Williamson looked like a plainclothes cop, but in fact he made his living selling sports photographs. He had been in the bar trying to hawk some Alabama-Auburn football-game photos.

James White was in the lobby, drunk and stoned, shivering with tension. He thought he recognized Williamson, even though he had never seen him before in his life. He jolted toward him, put his own red, twisted face inches from Williamson's and began jabbing at Williamson's chest with his finger.

"Hey, bud," Williamson said, "do I know you?"

James muttered and snapped at him, but Williamson could not make out what he was saying at first. When Williamson backed away, James pursued him, which made Williamson angry.

"Listen," Williamson said, "you need to get away from me, or I'm going to go out in my truck and get my gun."

The mention of a gun seemed to penetrate the haze. James stopped following and jabbing with his finger. Williamson backed away and then headed toward the door. He decided he wanted to go get his gun anyway. Just as he was turning to go out to his truck, James muttered the only words Williamson was able to understand.

"I'm going to make that bitch pay for what she done to me," he muttered. "I'm going to show her what lonely is all about."

At 5:00 P.M., Betty realized she had forgotten to bring the light-blue bank bag in which she had stored all the checks from the fund-raiser. She made a mad dash back home to pick it up.

James was in the house.

He had headed up through the woods behind the house. Three eighth-grade boys from the neighborhood were practicing golf swings in the yard next to the Wilson home. Because they were there and would see him, James had been unable to go around to the front door, even though he would have found it unlocked. He had gone into the garage instead and tried the door there. It was also unlocked. He found his way quickly up to the top floor of the house.

In his first several statements to the police, James White insisted that he did not really know why he had come to the house. He was angry, he said, and he thought perhaps he wanted to get inside, "ramble around a little," see if there was something to steal and perhaps wreck the place, destroy some things, hurt the house somehow. He told police afterward he had been drinking heavily for several days. At the time he entered the Wilson house, he was very drunk on beer and was also taking lithium, Darvocet, and handfuls of caffeine tablets.

He was not carrying a gun. He was carrying a knife. It might or might not have been the brown-handled Sharpe lock-blade knife that he always carried. He had brought a ski mask with him.

The staircase opened onto one end of a broad central hallway running parallel to the front of the house. When James rounded the railing and walked down the corridor, the first two doors he came to were Jack's bedroom, on his left, and, directly across from it, Betty's. James walked into Jack's room, looked around bleary-eyed, then sank on Jack's bed and tossed the ski mask to one side. He rose and walked to the window at the end of Jack's room, looking to the side yard. He saw the boys below, playing golf. He looked around the room. A cheap answering machine and a battery charger sat on a table, neither one hooked up.

James froze.

The front door was opening downstairs.

Huntsville is set at the very end of the Appalachian Mountain chain, with a flat-topped peak above it and a broad fertile plain rolling out below. The city's modern history and local economy have been dominated by military research, high finance, a major medical center—the sorts of things that bring people in from all over the United States, from all over the world. It is one of the Southern cities Southerners think of as Yankee.

The hardwoods on the mountains make a brilliant display of

color in the fall. In the late spring, the huge white blossoms of the magnolia trees give the thoroughfares a lavish elegance. It is a place between places. It's one of the first places you go if you grow up in a small town in Alabama and you are black, or gay, or poor white, or whatever, and you yearn for a place where you can be anything you want to be.

That was really Betty Wilson's story. She came here years earlier to get away from Gadsden, Alabama, where she had grown up. Now she was more or less what she had dreamed of being as a girl. Rich. Prominent.

She was an attractive woman of middle age—short, trim, with lively blue eyes, fine features, and black hair streaked white on one side of her bangs. Before she married a doctor, she had been a nurse, and before she became a nurse, she had worked in one of Huntsville's first commercial health clubs. She had never lost her appetite for training and fitness. Even during the worst of her years with booze and cocaine, she was always sharp, fashionable, and very pretty. She put herself under the knife for all of the available cosmetic surgeries, from minor facial adjustments to major reconstruction.

Later, when she was better and had sorted out her feelings about her twin, she realized she had probably never needed any of the painful operations she had endured in order to make herself more beautiful. But Betty's life was always much easier for her to understand in retrospect than in the moment. When it was happening, everything was headlong, hungry, fierce, odd, wonderful, terrible. There was never serenity.

She was born Betty Woods on July 14, 1945, in East Gadsden, originally Hoke's Bluff, a part of the city of Gadsden on the Coosa River in northeastern Alabama. Gadsden was a tough town in the forties and fifties. During the war it had been a munitions and chemical manufacturing center. Between 1930 and the end of the war, the city's population had doubled, to 56,000. After the war there was a quick transition to peacetime manufacturing, bolstered by a huge federal government program to develop the Coosa for commercial uses, but the end of the war and return of the soldiers were more than the local economy could handle. In the late 1940s and early '50s there were massive layoffs in the steel mills and the rubber plants in Gadsden, and many families suffered the hardest times they had known since the Great Depression.

Later, trying to remember that far back, some people said that the Woods family had been poor. But that was not true. Oscar and Nell Woods were of very modest means but never poor. When other families were losing their homes, Oscar Woods moved his family out of the wartime apartment blocks in what was called Goodyear Village and bought a tidy little brick house on Hoke Street, at the far eastern end of town in a neighborhood that had been a log-cabin homestead only a generation before.

Oscar Woods was a city of Gadsden policeman. It may be difficult for people who weren't alive then, even for people living in the Gadsden of today, to imagine what it meant in the years right after the war to be a police officer in a small city in Alabama. This was hard country—the part of Alabama where, in the 1960s, citizens armed with guns and ax handles would burn the freedom buses. People who run the city of Gadsden today, especially people who run the police department, sometimes allow a little shiver to escape when they talk about the way it was back then. No one would want it back.

The police were paid a pittance, nowhere near enough to support families and decent lives. They made it up in corruption. Like a lot of the South, the area around Gadsden had remained dry after the repeal of Prohibition. Most of the police were in the pay of the bootleggers. Most of the bootleggers were firemen.

Race was a biting, grinding canker in the mouth of the city. No one was more fiendishly obsessed by it than Gadsden Police Officer Oscar Woods—a tall, dark, handsome man who had started out on a motorcycle and worked his way up to detective. Everyone called him Wormy.

Wormy Woods took a rookie out in a patrol car for a drive through the African-American part of town one afternoon. He saw a middle-aged black man walking down the sidewalk. He said to the rookie, "Now I don't know this particular nigger here from Adam, which means I've got to get out of this car and go introduce myself, which pisses me off."

He got out of the car smiling genially, walked up to the man, and struck him in the nose as hard as he could with his fist, sending him sprawling. The man lay on the ground, a hand to the bloody pulp of his nose, and stared up silently at Officer Woods, whose hands were at his hips, sweeping back the jacket of his natty blue suit to show the protruding black butt of his service revolver.

Back in the car, Oscar Woods said to the rookie: "That's how I handle niggers."

Wormy took money from the bootleggers and used it to keep mistresses across town. He worked for the union busters. It was generally believed that he knew what had happened to a number of people, black and white, who had disappeared from Gadsden. And the truly frightening thing, from today's perspective, is that most people who knew Gadsden back then probably would agree Wormy Woods was not all that unusual a cop. One of the things the civil rights movement and the turmoil of the 1960s accomplished was to free everyone, white and black, from the Wormy Woodses of the world.

During the day while he made his rounds, Wormy Woods drank. He drank with his women. He drank at the illegal establishments he helped protect. He drank at the stills where some of the stuff was made and at the warehouses where the rest of it was hidden. He drank in the police car. He drank in his own pickup truck. By the time he came home at the end of the day, his condition was somewhere between fairly drunk and stinking.

The daughter of Mr. Pruett across the street remembers seeing him pull up in the pickup behind the little brick house one thundering rain-lashed night. He pushed the truck door open brusquely, sat motionless, then rolled slowly out the door and onto his face in the mud where he lay for several hours, rain pounding his back. The neighbors who saw him in that condition shook their heads and prayed for the family inside that little brick house.

On some nights he came into the house in a rage. In court, Peggy, Betty's twin, recaptured a memory from very early childhood—her father towering over the twins in their beds in the middle of the night, waking them by shining his police flashlight in their eyes. He made them eat Ben-Gay ointment. That was all she remembered.

From the time the girls were tiny, Peggy was always the peacemaker and accommodator. She drew Betty aside with her into the bathroom and shut the door. The two little girls whispered intently to each other for hours, while Peggy tried to talk Betty into doing whatever was necessary to keep their father at bay.

On occasion he sobbed drunkenly about what he had done to people. When Betty was eight years old, she crouched at his shoe, clutching his knee with her face buried in his trousers.

"Please, Daddy, please," she cried, "Jesus can help you. You have a disease. You can turn to Jesus, and he will help you stop drinking."

He shook his head violently, tears streaming down his face. "No, no! It's too late! It's too late for me!"

Decades after she was no longer young, Nell Woods, Betty's mother, was still remembered with a certain awe by men of her generation. In her twenties and thirties, she was a woman so beautiful that she made men stop and catch their breath. She dressed well. She worked long hard hours in a factory making hangers for dry cleaners. The plant was barely heated in winter and was not air-conditioned during the long sweltering summer. Nell Woods worked in blue jeans and a short-sleeved blouse, with her hair tied up in a bandanna. But each night before she began the long walk home, she went to her locker and changed into the clean blouse, skirt, and pumps she had worn to work that morning. Betty once asked her why she changed her clothes just to walk to and from work, and she said, "I've got my pride."

Nell's two other daughters, GeDelle and Martha, were eight and ten years older than the twins and were more or less independent by the time the twins were well into grade school. Most of what Nell earned she spent on the little girls. Every Friday night, she walked them a mile to the movie theater. The three of them laughed and played the whole way there. Each girl was able to buy one candy bar and one drink for the movie. One Saturday each month she led them on a longer walk to a clothing store in town, where each twin was able to pick out a new outfit.

On Sunday afternoons she would say, "Get the brick," and the girls would squeal with delight, rush to the closet, and retrieve the special brick they used for crushing pecans and walnuts. The rest of the afternoon was spent in the kitchen, cooking up batches of fudge.

Nell Woods never complained—never said anything to imply that her life was anything but normal and pleasant. It was an approach to life that would make modern family therapists cringe. But the fact was, it gave the little twins a window on what life could be. The dark terrifying times when their father came home drunk and raging were not the only reality. There were also the moments of warmth and comfort they knew with their mother.

Of the two, Peggy was the one who opted most clearly for her mother's world. Betty tended to be more complex. She hovered atop a wall of irony, between the world as presented by her mother and the world as it was when her father came home.

They were fraternal, not identical. Both were pretty little girls, but it was Peggy who had inherited the very best of each of her parents' very good looks. She was a beauty. By her teenage years, Peggy's body was at once slender and sensuously full. Her voice was clear and fluting; her mother had taught her to speak with the pleasing, gracious Alabama accent of the middle and upper-middle classes. She was gregarious and had manners, always perfectly in control of herself.

In later years the men who had been boys with her in school always remembered the eyes first—huge almond-shaped blue eyes that seemed at one moment to be looking down demurely and at the next to be strangely direct and piercing. Peggy, they all agreed, was a heart-stopper.

Social lines were drawn harshly in Gadsden and had everything to do with money, of which the Woods family had none. But Peggy's good looks and pleasing manner earned her entrance into the company of the prestigious high school clique. She was chosen for literally every honor offered by Gadsden High School in any way linked with physical beauty, and there were many—sophomore-class maid, junior-class maid, homecoming queen, other crowns and other occasions for pictures in the Gadsden newspaper.

In the course of her adolescent career, Peggy developed the stagy, overly theatrical, earnest persona of a Southern girl who has often spoken to audiences in school and at church—a bulletproof sweetness that manages to assert without ever being overt.

It was just the ticket. She was invited to join a high school sorority whose other members were mainly girls from wealthy families. As she did whenever she gained acceptance into any new circle, the first thing Peggy said was, "And now, I know you all probably haven't had time to think of it yet, but we must remember to make sure my twin sister, Betty, is invited to join, too." And she was.

But if Peggy was the sun, Betty was the moon. Shy, awkward, bookish—a little peculiar to most eyes in Gadsden—Betty might have preferred to be left alone, but Peggy would not hear of it. In the troubled little brick house on Hoke Street, where Detective Woods raged and staggered at night, Peggy was the family hero. Her twin, Betty, was going to enjoy some part of each and every honor that fell on Peggy's perfect ivory-smooth shoulders, whether Betty liked it or not.

It was Betty who was probably a bit more active with the boys. There was a devilish streak in her that enabled her to do things Peggy would never have dreamed of doing—skipping school, coming home late in cars with boys who had been drinking, pulling the wool over the eyes of teachers, defying parents and other authority figures.

For a while after high school, the twins' lives continued to be linked and parallel. Both married after graduation, without going to college. Both had babies right away. Each stayed married only a few years. Betty left her young husband—a good man and good father to their three little boys—because he wanted to tell her what to do, what makeup to wear, and how to act, and she discovered that she could not stand for a man to rule her life. She set off for Huntsville. Her husband agreed to keep the little boys until she got settled, which was never.

Peggy left her husband because she disapproved of the way he behaved. She left him for Wayne Lowe, the handsome young choir director at Calvary Baptist Church, just across Hoke Street from Goodyear Village where Peggy had lived as an infant. Wayne was married, too, and had to divorce in order to marry Peggy. He took immediately to Peggy's little girl and boy and became their true father—the one they would still call "Dad" when they were adults.

Wayne and Peggy moved eventually to a remote wooded subdivision on Logan Martin Lake, five miles outside the stock-car–racing town of Talladega and barely thirty miles from Gadsden.

Wayne taught school and became choir director in a church in the nearby hamlet of Vincent, and he sold household items door-to-door evenings and on the weekends. Peggy went back to school and completed a teaching degree. She taught at the elementary school in Vincent with Wayne and often worked at second jobs. They always dressed well and drove nice cars, but they lived within their means. By scraping and doing a lot of the work themselves, they built an attractive new house high on a bluff above the lake. By 1991 the house was nearing completion. Angie, their eldest, was twenty-three years old and married, with a baby of her own; Blake, twenty-one, was completing college; and Stephanie, thirteen—the child Wayne and Peggy had had together—was within two or three years of becoming the same heart-stopping teenage beauty her mother had been.

In one area alone of Peggy Woods Lowe's life was there restlessness. As Peggy had been the hero of the little brick house on Hoke Street, so she felt compelled to reach out and fix things for other families whose bad luck cast a shadow on her path. On several occasions she informally adopted unwed teenage mothers—simply had them leave their own unhappy homes and come live with her, her husband, and her own children—for however long it took to resolve the matter. One young woman stayed for over a year.

She found a homeless family living in a dump, sleeping in their car and eating garbage. There were several very young children, all filthy, their skin raw from insects bites and scratching. So she brought them home, all of them, bathed and fed them, and then she and Wayne found them housing and work.

The rest of the family never objected, even when Peggy loaned money from the family's scarce accounts to various panhandlers and importuners who came her way. The way Peggy Lowe staved off the darkness was by reaching into it and fixing things first, before the darkness could overcome her. If a person had to have a vice, it was the kind to have.

From the moment Betty left Gadsden for Huntsville, her life swung wide from Peggy's path. As close as they had been, it was nevertheless a relief for Betty to be free of her twin. In some ways, all of Peggy's relentless fixing and tending had kept Betty from doing what she was inclined to do on her own, which was have a good time.

She worked two and three jobs but spent most of what she earned on clothes and cars. She never did manage to bring her three boys up from Gadsden, but their father was a good man, and she visited often. In Huntsville in the 1970s, alone and on her own in a fashionable singles apartment complex, Betty Woods was enjoying the heady experience of being noticed by people, especially by men.

She drank hard. She fooled around with cocaine. She led what she felt was an exciting, fast-lane life. When it got ahead of her, she retreated to a pile of books in her apartment or drove south to Gadsden to see the boys.

In the early 1970s, a few years after she had come to Huntsville, the city was abuzz with talk of a major new commercial hospital being built in the once-staid medical district on the flats below Garth Mountain. The addition of the new hospital to the district was an important factor in elevating Huntsville to the status of a major regional medical center. Young doctors were coming in from all over the country, some to join or buy existing practices, some to start their own new practices from the ground up.

A woman whose husband was a major investor in the new hospital belonged to the health club where Betty worked at night. She said to Betty one evening, "You're too smart and pretty to spend your life doing this stuff. Why don't you go down to the new hospital and apply for something with a little more meaning? Use my name."

Within three years Betty had completed most of a curriculum for nurses at the University of Alabama and, more important, had discovered a new truth about life—that she, too, could be needed, that she could make a difference in life-and-death struggles, and that she could be adored and fawned over for her role. She could be a hero, too.

It was a happy but unstable time for Betty. She developed an expertise in kidney dialysis for which there was a great demand in the hospital. She worked long hours, enjoying the work with a passion. She played hard away from work. Her life was driven by both self-indulgence and selflessness—and all of it intense and intensely addictive.

And then one day in 1976 a nervous ophthalmologist administered a commonly used drug to an elderly female patient in the middle of surgery, a normally ordinary and straightforward procedure, but in this instance the drug caused the patient to go into renal failure. Surgery had to be halted, and the patient was rushed to another room, where Nurse Betty Woods immediately began an emergency kidney dialysis.

Betty was intent on her work and her patient and did not notice at first when the ophthalmologist came into the room. He was a little man, thirty-three years old, with shiny black hair, huge brown eyes, and a long aquiline nose. Even in his preoccupied distress over his patient's condition, there was something elfin and faintly mischievous in the way he shot around the room, holding his head, sighing, shaking his head, groaning: "Oh my

God is she going to be O.K., how is it going, are you getting anywhere, oh my God, this is terrible, I had no way of knowing, I've used that stuff a million times, she's such a dear lady, I told her this would be so simple and now look, oh my God, how is it coming?"

"Leave me alone, Doctor," Betty said.

His voice was funny, with a high-pitched, almost feminine timbre. "Sure, I'm sorry, please, do what you're doing, I've used it a million times, I've never had a problem, I just can't believe this, she's such a dear woman, I just love her, she's one of my favorite patients."

He was dancing around her.

"Doctor, will you stop it?"

"Yes, certainly. How is she?"

"She's fine. She's doing very well. She's going to be just fine, unless you keep bothering me, in which case I might decide to shut this goddamned thing off."

He stopped. He peered intently into her eyes. He put one delicate finger to his long nose. "Do you see this nose, Nurse? You do that, and I'll suck all the air out of this room with one breath."

"Doctor. Get out."

Jack Wilson left the room. She checked him out from behind as he left.

"There goes the cutest little thing I have ever seen in my life," she thought.

The path by which Jack Wilson had come to be a medical doctor with a promising practice in Huntsville, Alabama, was long, tortuous, bizarre—a tribute to the American way and proof that you can never tell how things will turn out. He never knew who his biological father was, and no one even tried to give him a name or description. He told a few trusted male friends in Huntsville that it could have been anyone and that his real mother was probably a whore.

His siblings remember it differently. They say Carolyn English, his real mother, was a young, attractive single woman at the end of World War II who ended up with a married man for a lover instead of a husband of her own. She worked hard as a waitress and had children out of wedlock whom she was not able to support. Hers was not a respectable life, but it was not exactly street prostitution, either.

It was Wirta who always told Jack his mother was a whore. And that was after Jack was ten years old and had figured out that Wirta wasn't his real mother and Carolyn was.

Wirta Wilson used to stuff pillows in her dress and walk around Villa Park, a little suburb due west from downtown Chicago, telling people she was pregnant. Then she would leave for a few days, saying she was off to the hospital in Chicago, and she would come home to her little working-class bungalow with another baby, adopted by informal means from someone who couldn't take care of it.

Jack was the youngest of Carolyn English's children. Wirta had adopted his two older sisters from Carolyn, his real mother, and she had adopted younger twins from another woman. Wirta was so cold and indifferent with all the children, once she had possession of them, it was difficult to divine why she had ever been so eager to acquire them in the first place.

Carolyn visited whenever she could. She was pretty and affectionate, very unlike Wirta. Her relationship to the children was never explained to them—part of the deal with Wirta. But it was always much sadder than it should have been when she left on the train again, sadder than the departure of a mere family friend. Finally, at the end of a visit when Jack was ten and already a talent on the piano, Carolyn sat with him on the bench, laughing and hugging while he played and they both sang "Bye Bye Blackbird" together.

The little boy, impish and bright, funny and sad, turned his face up to Carolyn, smiling with tears in his eyes, and said very softly, "Are you my real mother?"

She looked back helplessly over her shoulder at Wirta, who stood watching grimly from the kitchen door with her hands on her hips. Carolyn turned back and told him quietly. "Yes, Jack.

I am your real mother. But Wirta has given you a home, and I have not."

Wirta was not about to leave it at that. As soon as Carolyn was gone, she started in on him. "She's a whore. She walks the streets of Los Angeles. Half the pickaninnies in California are your brothers and sisters."

The great love of Jack's childhood was Bill Wilson, Wirta's husband—a warmhearted, intelligent, literate man who adored the bright, funny, tiny little whip of a child he always called Jackie-Boy. Bill Wilson had worked as many things—a newspaper man, an editor of books—but life had not been easy for him in his later years. Most of the time Jack was growing up, Bill worked as a cook. He came home tired, with throbbing feet and an aching back. But he never turned his back on the little boy. The boy brought the spark of life back to Bill Wilson at the end of a long bleak day. Little Jack's laughter, his pranks and jokes, his wonderful prowess on the piano, the zany stories he told about his adventures, most of them wildly untrue—these were what kept Bill Wilson's heart alive.

And it worked both ways. The reason Jack made up stories was that very little really happened. He went to school, which he loved. But he was so small for his age and seemed so odd to other children, his brown eyes hugely magnified and swimming behind the thick lenses of his glasses, that he was unable to play normally in the neighborhood. He was the butt of jokes and the target of bullies. He came straight home from school each day. Wirta was usually absent; she spent her afternoons in movie theaters by herself, watching the same films over and over again. Jack spent his afternoons watching television, reading books, playing solitary games of make-believe, and daydreaming. In the early evening, when he was especially tired and lonely, Jack would crawl under Wirta's big bed and read books by himself.

In some of that miasma of television, daydreams, long hours thumbing through the cheap set of encyclopedias Bill had purchased a volume at a time from the grocery store, the magical chemistry by which an adult personality is formed was taking place in the little boy's mind and soul.

"Janey," he whispered to his older sister, "when I grow up, I want to leave this world a better place."

When Bill came home in late evening it was like a curtain call for Jack. He sprang to his feet and began spieling off the funny routines he had imagined and practiced all day, basking in Bill's fond laughter. They were a pair.

At some point his teachers told Wirta they thought Jack was more than simply bright, that he might be a prodigy in certain areas. Wirta began to take a new interest in him, in her own very odd way. She snatched him by the hand and trotted him downtown to a radio station in Chicago to audition for a quiz show. The producers chose him instantly and put him on the air. He was funny, quick, answered all the questions correctly, and won a puppy.

Bill built a little house and dog run for the puppy, and the puppy became Jack's dearest, closest companion. He ran home to it after school and kept it at his side every moment. Two years later, when it was struck by a car and killed, Jack cried for days. When Bill came home at night, he took him in his arms and whispered over and over again, "The only way out of it, Jackie-Boy, is to look for the sunshine. You have to make yourself get up and go look for the sunshine again."

Wirta, meanwhile, announced to friends and neighbors that Jack had been signed to star in the movies and that he was going to make a lot of money. Later, when Bill moved them to Los Angeles, Wirta told people they were going to California because Jack had been signed by a big studio and that, from now on, he would be using the stage name Dean Stockwell.

Wirta would have seemed funny to Jack, had she not also had a mean, dangerous streak. Jack learned early to navigate a wide path around her eccentricities and to go along with whatever she said. If she said he was Dean Stockwell, he was Dean Stockwell.

For some reason, she stopped beating Jack early, perhaps because of the trouble it might have made with Bill, but she continued to whip the hapless little boy and girl twins who were younger.

Then she hit on an even more sadistic plan. Jack was always

protecting the twins, sticking up for them and telling them how to avoid trouble. In their eyes, he was the family hero. So why not make him do the beating? By then the older siblings had left home.

Jack took the cowering little boy and girl into the bathroom, brandishing Wirta's leather strap until they bleated in fear. He slammed the door, making many more loud threats, and then he leaned down and whispered into their ears: "Every time I slap my leg, you scream."

Wirta, who was not clever, never figured it out. The twins, at Jack's prompting, screamed loudly. It was a charade they used many times.

Bill knew what was going on and approved. He told Jack that Wirta had suffered, that she could have been many things but that life had been a great disappointment to her. He said she was a good woman who had given a good home to Jack and his sisters.

Bill died of cancer when Jack was fifteen. For weeks, the boy was paralyzed by grief and despair—by sheer terror of what life would be without Bill Wilson. He went to school, because it offered relief, but the rest of the time he lay under rumpled blankets in his tiny bedroom and sobbed quietly to himself, alone in the house while Wirta was off watching movies.

Then one evening he came out of the bedroom and said to Wirta, "I am going to get a job to help you with money."

He came home two days later with good news. He had charmed and bamboozled his way into an afternoon job doing bookkeeping and filing chores for a trucking company. His employers took to him immediately and began right away expanding his duties and giving him raises and little bonuses.

A few weeks later, he came to Wirta with quite a bit of money. While she sat at the kitchen table and counted it, he said, "I had to get a Social Security number. My birth certificate says my name is Jack English. You only called me Jack Wilson all these years. It's not my legal name. I am going to have my name changed legally to Wilson."

She looked up suspiciously from her counting.

"Why?"

"Bill was the only father I ever had. The best father anybody could have. And you gave me a good home."

Jack Wilson was admitted two years early to nearby Occidental College, where he began a lifelong habit of ruthless study. He worked at his bookkeeping job, he continued helping to support Wirta and the two younger ones, and he studied. He studied with an intensity that blinded him to all the rest of life, even to himself. His wardrobe was always mismatched, rumpled, often old and absurdly childish for a young college student. He assumed he was invisible to women, and he was.

Nothing mattered but study. He studied, he told Betty later, because he wanted to be somebody. Because he wanted to make money. Because he wanted to be respected. He studied because he was fascinated by what was in his books and by what his teachers said in lectures. He was especially intrigued by the workings of the eye and all the deformations and diseases that caused people to see poorly, as he had always done. He was fascinated by the thought that poor vision, rather than being a fact of life, was a condition that he himself might be able to cure.

But the main reason he studied was that study was the way to the light. It was the way out of his dark, crabbed life, alone in the house with the encyclopedia, the television, and the endless daydreams.

After he had finished his classes, completed his duties at work, and checked in at home to see if Wirta and the twins needed anything, he headed straight to the Mary Norton Clapp Library at Occidental, where he worked until the early hours of the morning. In his solitary childhood, with a mainly absent father and a distracted mother, Jack had never learned many of the small, ordinary behaviors associated with daily life, such as sitting properly in a chair. He climbed around on his chair in the carrel, sat perched with his legs folded lotus-style underneath him, or crouched on the balls of his feet on the chair, leaning over on his elbows over his books, or lay sideways in the chair with his books held up over his face, clambering and wriggling around like a monkey, but always with his mind fastened ferociously on the book before him.

His dietary habits were horrible. He stuffed candy bars in his mouth, drank Cokes and ate potato chips whenever his hunger became noticeable enough to distract him. It was during this period, and later when he was enrolled in the University of Tennessee Medical School in Memphis, that Jack began to confront the fact he was suffering from Crohn's disease.

Named for Burrill B. Crohn, the American gastroenterologist who identified the disease, Crohn's is a disease of the ileum, which is the third portion of the small intestine. The cause is unknown. There is some evidence it may be identified with high-achieving personalities, but there is a chicken-and-egg debate over which comes first.

The symptoms of Crohn's are fever, diarrhea, cramping and abdominal pain, and weight loss, all of which Jack had suffered on and off, in some degree, since childhood. But in medical school, the Crohn's got worse for a while. It tends to afflict its victims in cycles. The only known cure for a severe case is the surgical removal of the ulcerated portions of the ileum.

The disease is thought to be associated with stress, but in Jack's case it began to abate when he entered his hospital internship, normally a time of great stress in a young physician's life. Of course, in Jack's case the opposite was true. For him, internship was a time of bliss and untold wonder.

For one thing, little Jack Wilson, the funny kid who never had a friend, who had to run home in order to avoid getting picked on by the other kids, strode the halls of Charity Hospital in New Orleans and was thrilled to the bone every time someone addressed him as "Doctor." It was an impossibly distant and glorious daydream, which he had wrought into the stuff of real life through the sheer force of his own determination. He felt like a magician.

But then there was the other thing—the dream he had never even dared to entertain.

When he was still at the University of Tennessee, he forced

himself one evening to attend a mixer with some co-eds from Memphis State University. At the small party, without planning it at all, he happened to say something that made a girl at the other side of the room laugh. He looked up quickly but then looked away. She was one of "them"—the pretty people, the normal people.

But she approached him and spoke to him. And he made her laugh again. She continued to talk to him, although he wasn't sure why. Then she said to him, "You know, Jack, when you take your glasses off, you have the most beautiful eyes."

So he asked her out.

Her name was Julia Kelly, and she was a junior at Memphis State. She was from New Albany, Mississippi, and spoke with a soft, graceful accent. And she really was very good-looking—small and dancerlike, with a delicately chiseled face, bright brown eyes, and a luxuriant brunette mane.

By the time Jack arrived at Charity Hospital to begin his internship, Julia was his wife and they were expecting their first child. She was teaching school, they were impossibly poor, and Jack Wilson was walking two feet off the ground every day of his life. He continued that way for the next ten years, through his internship in ophthalmology in Birmingham and well into the first years in Huntsville, where he went in 1968 to establish a practice.

The Crohn's swept back down on him during the final years of his ophthalmology internship—this time with a vengeance. He had to do something about it, or it would stop him. Reluctantly, he agreed to an operation by which the ulcerated portion of the ileum was removed and the remaining part was sutured to the opening of the large intestine. As soon as he could, he plunged back into his work, the magical balm that healed all wounds.

In 1976 when Julia left him, after they had had two sons and adopted a third, Jack was as shocked, bewildered, and shattered as he had been during those dark days in boyhood after Bill Wilson's death. He continued working incredible hours as usual and then retreated each night to a barren apartment with dust balls on the floor, his only furniture a mattress slung on the beige wall-to-wall carpeting in a corner of the living room.

Before his marriage failed, Jack had never had any handle on what it was to lead an ordinary life. There were the bleak little houses he had shared with Wirta and the twins and then there was the joy of medicine, his dream come true. But he did not know—because he had never been around it—what it was for people to lead more or less ordinary lives, with healthy relationships, a balance between work and leisure and time left over for intimacy.

When he sat on the mattress in the cheap apartment with the dust balls and thought it all through honestly, he began to understand incredible things about himself. He was a success only in medicine. He was a failure in other parts of his life—important parts. He had been a lousy parent to his boys, almost never at home with them, cranky and exhausted when he did see them. Between medicine and the recurring bouts with Crohn's, he had failed to provide Julia with even meager bonds of companionship, let alone a sex life.

Slowly he pulled it all together and into focus—the demons of childhood, the glory of his medical practice, his failure as a husband and parent. He was never given to self-pity. He wanted to figure it all out, and, in a rather detached and intellectual way, he did. He was not resentful toward Julia. He held her to a legal separation and for two years refused to give in all the way to the notion of divorce—until he met Betty. But during that entire time, Jack and Julia remained friends.

Walking off down the hall that day from the dialysis room where Betty was reviving his patient, he felt something quick and very pleasant in his heart. He liked that nurse. A lot. She wasn't all sweetie-pie and deferential like so many. She seemed bright and tough. And she was very good-looking. Was she single? For the first time since he and Julia had split up, Dr. Wilson thought seriously about asking out someone new.

The day before the murder, a man friend called Janine Russell on the telephone. Her boyfriend, Bunky, was off somewhere, possibly with James and James's brother. She wasn't sure. It had been a rough week of drinking. After her husband had died in a dune-buggy accident five years earlier, Janine had stayed sober for a long time, but lately she and James and Bunky had been doing a lot of drinking together. The last time she had seen James and his brother and Bunky, the three of them were up in James's trailer with the door locked. She had peeked in the window. They were all three passed out on their faces on the floor. Janine's house was just up the hill from James's trailer.

The friend said that he needed to drive his daughter's car twenty-five miles west to Alabaster, a small community on the freeway south of Birmingham, to get it worked on. He had undergone surgery on his leg recently, and he couldn't drive far by himself.

In her mid-thirties, Janine looked as if she could be in her mid-fifties. She was short, heavy, with a pockmarked complexion and long, stringy blond hair. Life with babies in a cramped dirty little house was not easy. She was always up for a road trip.

On the way over to Alabaster in her friend's car, she talked about how wild James White had been all week. He always talked wild when he was drunk and high, but this week he was especially crazy. He kept raving, foaming at the mouth almost, about some woman, a schoolteacher down at Vincent Elementary who had a twin sister up in Huntsville who was rich. He had been ramming around in his truck, driving up to Huntsville and back. He had called Janine that morning from a motel in Huntsville, screaming and rambling on the telephone about the twin, who was a rich-bitch doctor's wife. Apparently this woman had cussed James out over some work he was supposed to do for her. Janine couldn't get straight what he was talking about.

Earlier in the week James had called Cheryl, his last ex-wife, who had left him for his best friend and still lived in a trailer near his. Cheryl called Janine and told her about it. James had told Cheryl he was going up to Huntsville to star in a pornographic movie.

But this morning he said things to Janine that sounded as if he intended to kill someone up there, a rich person or something like that. He was in a rage, one of his bad rages.

Janine's friend, who knew James, said that if James was crazy and really talking like he meant it about killing somebody, maybe Janine should talk to somebody to cover herself.

She was afraid to trust anyone. If James found out, he might kill her. The friend said he knew a man in Alabaster who was in the Volunteer Fire Department. Maybe while the car was getting fixed, they could go talk to him.

When they got to town, they hunted up the volunteer fireman, who steered them to a Shelby County sheriff's deputy he knew. Janine poured out her halting, confusing tale to the deputy. She told him about James, his drinking, and the nonsense he was talking about this schoolteacher back in Vincent, how he was having sex with her and she loved him and she was going to leave her husband for him, but she had a twin in Huntsville and she was supposed to pay him for some work, and James was angry about something that had happened in Huntsville and he was going to get even. Janine couldn't remember the teacher's name.

The deputy took some notes, appraising both the story and the storyteller. After Janine left, he made some calls, including a call to the Madison County sheriff in Huntsville. It wasn't the sort of information that gets a lot of attention in a busy police agency: the drinking companion of a local rumdum in a little town in central Alabama had reported that the rumdum was talking about going to Huntsville and hurting somebody, a relative of an unnamed schoolteacher in Vincent, possibly the wife of a doctor, but it wasn't clear who it was or why the guy was saying all this or whether he had really said it at all or whether, if he did say it, the guy meant it.

Had the deputy attempted to interview the rumdum himself?

Nope. Too far. Too busy.

The Madison County Sheriff's Department passed on the information to the Huntsville Police Department. The matter was then forgotten and lost in a sea of more urgent business.

That day, the day before the murder, the day before James entered the house, while Janine Russell was pouring out her halting, unconvincing story to a deputy in a county one-hundred miles away, James was in Huntsville stalking Betty and her son. He was hiding in the woods outside the house on Boulder Circle, following them to the mall, drinking heavily, eating pills by the handful, and all the while the eyes were flickering back and forth and the narrow wet lips were stammering behind a matted beard, muttering and nattering, saying the prayers of a killer. Only James knows now if he knew he was there that day.

James White lived in a small rusty house trailer, perched at a slight list on the rim of hills above the little town of Vincent. Next to the trailer was a small frame house, unoccupied, with the roof cracked in at the center of the ridgepole, windows shot out, yard so thick with crumpled beer cans it glittered.

James and his friends used the front porch of the empty house for drinking, on old wooden chairs and the backseat of a car. In the part of the year when the leaves were off the trees, they could sit up there and look down the hill through the woods to the roof of the First Baptist Church.

First Baptist was a tidy brick church with pillars in front, in the center of a beautifully tended lawn. On some Sunday mornings, when all of the monied townspeople gathered on the parking lot below, driving new cars and wearing new clothes, James and his crew were already gathered above them on his porch, cackling and screeching like crows.

Of the little set of folks living in trailers and broken-down houses in the woods at the top of the hill, James Dennison White was more or less the leader. He was good at what he did.

In a long line and a tradition stretching back into the mists of the Southern frontier, celebrated in literature from Twain to Faulkner, James White was of a species, a type. Anybody who grew up anywhere near a small Southern town could have spotted James White a country mile away. He was a dirty, rascally, smirking, hat-in-hand, yes-ma'aming and yes-siring, backstabbing, booze-sucking, white trash rodent, of the sort for whom quaint nineteenth-century epithets like jackanapes and scalawag were still somehow especially apt.

Every life has a logic, and given the scheme of his own life, James had done rather well that year, notwithstanding a rough start. A bad chapter with the drink had led to a problem with the authorities. James was forced to confess that he had sexually molested his eldest daughter, the child of one of his earlier wives. The confession was part of an arrangement that allowed James to split some of his time between jail and a mental hospital. No stranger to either place, James always felt more at home in mental institutions, when there was a choice.

While still in jail, before he got himself transferred to the mental hospital, James got into a bit of trouble over a sodomy charge. Later in the mental institution, he was diagnosed as schizophrenic. The doctors there said he heard voices and couldn't tell the difference between truth and lies—pretty much the same thing they had said when he was kicked out of Vietnam over twenty years earlier for stabbing an officer. In James's particular circle of friends, hearing voices was more likely to be taken as a reflection of one's weird powers than as a handicap, and getting the shrinks to say you were crazy—well, that was simply a matter of survival.

If he was crazy, he was certainly doing well at it. Early in the year, he had pulled down $16,000 in a workmen's comp settlement for an injury to his knee. Then in October he had raked in another $21,000 for an injury to his ankle. It had been easy. Once a week he had to wrap his leg in an Ace bandage, dust off his crutch, drive down to the unlucky company that had hired him, and walk around looking lame. Next thing his friends knew, James was counting greenbacks.

James White knew how to do things.

He hit the local bank in nearby Childersburg for two loans, one for a pickup truck and the other for a house trailer—a fairly incredible feat, seeing as how James could have served as the National Poster Person for Unbelievably Bad Credit Risks. He never had the slightest intention of repaying either loan, of course.

James used part of his wealth to buy a "pink ice ring"—cheap jewelry with a semiprecious stone—for the daughter he had molested.

In the meantime, James could always grab a couple of his rogue companions, go out into the country and talk some old lady at a convenience store into letting him pour asphalt on her parking lot for four or five thousand dollars. Of course, he always needed a substantial amount of the cash in advance, for materials.

He dealt drugs on a small scale.

At the time he met Peggy Lowe, James was probably pulling down between $75,000 and $100,000 in annual income. He spent it all as fast as he could get it on booze and drugs. But what else was a country bum's life for?

Peggy and Wayne Lowe together, teaching all day and doing odd jobs at night, couldn't come close to the money James White saw in a good year of rascaldom. He and his friends sat on the broken porch of the wrecked house that was semi-attached to his trailer, drunk in a yard carpeted with beer cans and whiskey bottles. They looked down through the treetops on the hill at their feet, down to where the middle-class people were gathering in their Sunday finery for services at the First Baptist Church of Vincent, and they snickered. It was a deep wheezy snicker of a sort that only generations of class division, alcoholism, and a shrinking gene pool can produce—the low growl of submissive malevolence.

TWO

THE EARLY PERIOD IN JACK AND BETTY'S RELATIONSHIP was very on-again, off-again. Betty took Jack for an amusing new interest but nothing more. At the same time, Jack was making the one effort of his life at being macho. It was, Betty said years later, "his cowboy period."

In all the getting mad and getting over it, the forgotten dates and the late-night reunions, a real chemistry began between them. Betty was doing a good deal of social drinking but none of the serious solitary stuff that she would save for their marriage. Jack was still working furiously at his practice, but he was also beginning to listen to the women who worked for him, his only real friends at that time, when they told him he absolutely had to stay away from the office on weekends and whenever possible at night.

Jack and Betty had fun. They went out, to shows and dancing, on trips and to parties. Jack's practice had grown marvelously under his relentless nurturing. He was popular with his patients and among other doctors. He was becoming something of a figure in Huntsville.

Betty still had a tendency to pull back sharply from social contact, to be overwhelmed by her old sense of social awkwardness and by the feeling that she was different and did not really fit in. It was a trait that tended sooner or later to cut short her relationships with men.

But those were the moments when Jack came after her. When he talked to Betty, early on a Saturday morning in her apartment, he was able to say things to her, to see things in her that others could not see. Of course she was different and unlike other people. It might be a fragile straw with which to make the bricks of marriage—a common status as eccentrics. But the fact was that Jack could tell Betty important things about herself, things that rang true. He was the one who told her to ask, next time she visited her mother in the little town of Boaz north of Gadsden, to see baby pictures of herself and Peggy.

She sat on the sofa in her mother's house, staring at the old fading color photographs in amazement. "Mother, I was cute! I was cute as a button."

"Cuter than a button, Betty. You both were."

Jack knew things about darkness. Some were the things Bill Wilson had taught him. Some things he had learned on his own. Darkness is a place, he said, not a puzzle. You don't solve it. You go the other way. Out of the cave to the light.

There were things Betty could see in Jack, too. His failures as a parent, still very painful to him, had to be weighed against what he had accomplished—the little ninny with no friends, now an important man in Huntsville and viewed by his patients as a blessing.

From the moment he had hung out his shingle, Jack Wilson had always taken a completely crazy approach to the business side of his practice. His own experience with poverty made it impossible for him to withhold treatment from anyone who could not pay, and, in the years when Medicare and Medicaid were still new and just cranking up, there were lots of people with bad eyes who couldn't afford to see an ophthalmologist. And Jack loved to practice medicine, and he loved his patients. They were his fans and, in many ways, his family. He often said to Betty, "I hope the patients never figure this out, but I actually would pay them to let me do this stuff."

Since he knew he was never going to turn them away, Jack Wilson simply made a joke of it. When one woman told him sheepishly that she wasn't sure whether she could afford his care,

Dr. Wilson turned to his bookkeeper and said, "Put this lady on our hundred-year plan."

He even reached out for poor patients. He lobbied city officials to install a shelter at the bus stop in front of his building so that patients who traveled by bus would not have to wait in bad weather.

It was during this process, when a fellow doctor asked him why he wanted to encourage "those people" to gather in front of his office, that Jack Wilson shocked the doctor by telling him, "I think I probably have a lot of half brothers and sisters among the people you call 'those people.' "

Betty shared Jack's feelings about racism: It was an ugly, vile poison in the old culture of the South—a thing that reminded her, every time she heard it, of her father when he was drunk, braying about black people, spraying spit from his twisted lips and staggering over the furniture. She hated it, and so did Jack.

You don't get to be perfect, she told Jack. You get to do the very best you can, and you have. You are a fine doctor and a good man.

Jack had never raised his rates because none of the other ophthalmologists raised their rates, and medical treatment was, at that time, a very price-sensitive commodity. The last thing Jack Wilson wanted to do was anything that would tend to discourage patients from seeing him.

Government insurance changed all that. All of a sudden, everyone could pay, at least for certain procedures. Not only that, but the government came back each year and asked the physicians in Huntsville what their "customary fees" were and whether those fees were going up at all. New fees, set according to the prevailing rate for the region, would be established each new year by the government.

Over coffee in the hospital cafeteria, the doctors quickly figured out that it was in their mutual interest to raise their fees in concert. It didn't hurt the patients. They weren't paying. And the only way any of them could get more from the government was if everybody's fees went up so that the regional prevailing rate would appear to escalate.

And there was even more to it than that. The new government insurance paid for only certain procedures. A doctor who was a psychiatrist was stuck because he had only one procedure he could perform. But ophthalmologists and doctors like them were in a much more favorable position. They could fill their offices with technicians performing a host of procedures—the ones Medicare and Medicaid paid for—and run all of their patients through the mill.

At first there was a fairly innocent sort of "adjusting" that went on. If poor old Mrs. Wright couldn't pay for Procedure A, and the government wouldn't pay, then the doctor might put down Procedure B, for which the government would pay.

In the years ahead, when Jack Wilson started grossing as much as a million dollars a year from his practice, the business of fleecing Medicare and Medicaid became much more sophisticated. Clever staff members took over the computers that Jack understood so little and rearranged the billing process so that virtually every conceivable penny was wrung from the government insurance programs.

As it happened, one of the people who understood and excelled early at the business of government-paid medical services was Betty. She saw it as a game of cat and mouse and delighted at finding her way through the maze of regulations to the pot of gold.

Kidney dialysis, her field, was especially expensive, and, when dialysis was added to the realm of procedures Medicare would pay for, a great deal of money began to sluice back and forth between government and private accounts. Betty was very good at seeing to it that the sluice worked in the hospital's favor.

So good was she, in fact, that a new private concern asked her to leave the hospital and come to work in Atlanta as an administrator, helping set up dialysis clinics around the South. By this time, Betty was serious about Jack and wanted to know his intentions.

He urged her to take the job. She balked. In fact, she realized that Jack's answer was not what she had wanted to hear. Did it mean his feelings for her were less serious than hers for him?

No, he said, we'll continue our relationship by long-distance commute. He told her he would come to Atlanta and pay for her to come back to Huntsville for visits. They would talk on the telephone. She needed to do this, he said. She needed to achieve success and recognition in her own right. Only then would she be ready to accept the full-time commitment of marriage.

What Jack said made sense at a certain level. He was so smart. And he seemed able to look right into her soul. But beneath the surface of his compassionate intellectualism, there was a cleverness in Jack. He talked and talked, and he always made sense, but he was also always trying to make things come out his own way.

There were things about Jack's manner that irritated and even appalled her. They were waiting in line to buy a baguette at a French bakery in Huntsville one day, when Jack sat down suddenly on the floor. She tried not to stare at him while he sat spraddle-legged in the middle of the floor and pulled off both cowboy boots, then both socks. When he started picking things from between his toes, she hissed at him:

"Jack! Jack! What in God's name are you doing?"

"I get some kind of stuff in between my toes with these boots, and it's just been bothering me all day."

She turned to the woman behind her and said, "He's a doctor."

But even when he was at his most eccentric Jack could also be very appealing.

Their sexual relationship had reached an interesting point—a place where Betty had never been before with a man. Jack, she had discovered early in the relationship, was shy and even childish about sex. He loved to make love, once he got started, but it was always up to Betty to do the starting.

It was a job she found she rather enjoyed. She would trap him on Sunday mornings when he was getting dressed in his own very odd way, standing naked before the bathroom mirror spending as much as half an hour adjusting his baseball cap—the only stitch on him—before hastily throwing on the rest of the day's clothes. If she didn't police him, he often picked his clothes up from a pile of dirty laundry.

She slipped up behind him wearing only her bathrobe, which she allowed to fall open. She folded her arms around him and pressed herself against his back.

"Betty please," he giggled. "I'm trying to get dressed."

"You're putting on a baseball cap. That's not getting dressed."

"Well, I have to do this first. Betty, please."

He tried to wriggle free, but she cornered him against the shower with her arm posted against the wall in front of him. He gave her a wild look, like a trapped cat, then sprang underneath her arm and sprinted for the living room, naked as a jaybird except for the cap. She ran after him.

With a breathless shrieky giggle, he leaped from the sofa to the floor and over a chair to escape, but she pursued him, grabbed him by the shoulders, threw him down on the sofa, and made love to him. By the time they left the apartment it was dusk and they were hurrying ravenously to their favorite Italian restaurant.

Betty knew he was right about the Atlanta job. In many ways, she did need to do something challenging and exciting with her life. Jack had helped her a great deal already in her need to come out from under the shadow of her twin—a shadow she had imposed on herself.

But Jack also kept things hidden. He hung back. He was thrilled with their relationship, as he had been thrilled with Julia, as if all of this were an entirely unexpected windfall, something he had neither worked for nor, perhaps, desired very strongly. Betty suspected that for all Jack's talk of striving for the light, he also had learned as a child to shield himself from darkness and disappointment by telling himself he didn't need relationships.

She took the new job. The company was thrilled with her. She was extremely effective at seeing to it the government would pay the full freight for new dialysis centers almost as fast as the company could acquire the real estate and the equipment to build them. Jack was good about getting on the plane almost every week to come see her. He called her every morning.

She waited hungrily for his calls, even though he called early and mornings were becoming a bit difficult for Betty. She was dating other men occasionally at night, with Jack's knowledge and irritating approval, but for the most part she was not interested in other men. She wanted Jack. Somehow. She wasn't yet sure on what terms. Most days ended alone in her fancy new apartment in Atlanta—just Betty and the bottle of booze she told herself helped bring sleep.

The job continued to improve. She moved to bigger and more lavish offices. There was a bar in her office, fully stocked with liquor, which she never touched during the day. She traveled a good deal, often by company jet.

One day a young male assistant said, "Betty, you really look wonderful in that dress."

When he had left the room, she walked to an ornate mirror at the back wall of the office and regarded herself carefully. Then she started to laugh out loud.

"People are kissing my ass!" she thought.

Jack's call came in early 1978, just as Betty was up for yet another promotion. His voice was curiously flat and somber, with none of his usual ticklish wit.

"I can't make it with the Crohn's anymore, Betty."

"What are you going to do, Jack?"

"The operation, I think."

Betty silently threw her hand to her mouth and bit her finger. The operation. She and Jack had never really discussed it.

But they were both medical practitioners, and both knew exactly what it meant. If Jack was finally conceding that his Crohn's disease had gotten ahead of him, then it meant he was ready for an ileostomy—the removal of most of his intestine and the short-circuiting of the ileum to a stoma, a surgical opening in his abdomen. For the rest of his life he would wear a bag to collect his feces.

But he kept talking.

"I've been thinking about it, and with the operation and all, this traveling back and forth to Atlanta is just going to be too much."

"And?"

"So I just think you ought to come home, and we'll get married."

She sat on the edge of the bed for a long time after hanging up. "What a proposal," she thought. "God, what an asshole Jack can be."

She flew to Huntsville that weekend, and they talked. The good thing about Jack—the strange thing, given his emotional furtiveness on many scores—was that he could always talk directly and straight to the point on the big issues.

"I'll be a mess. I won't be easy to live with."

"Yeah," she said. "I know. You won't. Good thing I'm a nurse."

She quit the job, closed down her apartment, and moved everything to Dust-Ball Manor—Jack's apartment in Huntsville. She was extremely nervous about the decision. Then Jack hit her with a new complication.

"I have been working on some projections for my income tax, and I can save between five hundred and six hundred dollars if we put off the wedding seven more months, until after the first of the year."

Betty shrugged and went on about the business of trying to clean up Jack's apartment. She dumped stacks of old newspapers into garbage bags, scrubbed spots in the carpeting, hung pictures on the wall, called the landlord to demand that drapes be replaced. The more she worked, the angrier she became. Jack had already confided that he was now earning several hundred thousand dollars a year in personal income. She had quit her job, given up a career, returned to him in spite of the medical trials he and she both faced in the months ahead. He knew that she was worried about whether or not he really loved her as deeply as she loved him, and now he was going to put the whole thing off half a year to save six hundred bucks! Without ever asking her what she thought!

But just when she thought she would explode, Jack was in front of her with his hands on her shoulders and those huge brown eyes peering intently into her face. "Sorry," he said. "I don't know what's wrong with me. I'm stupid about things. Let's get married right away. Right?"

She gazed back at him with tears in her eyes. "Right."

"Hey," he said. The old twinkle was back in his eyes for the first time since he had told her about the operation. "What's six hundred bucks between friends?"

The night before they married, they sat at a little wrought-iron and glass table on the balcony of Jack's apartment. Jack was quiet for a long time, staring off toward the stars above Garth Mountain. Betty watched him. There was a bottle of booze on the table. He wasn't drinking, because of the Crohn's. She was putting it away at a good clip.

"Jack," she said, "I'm not exactly Miss Mental Health of 1978. I still have a lot of problems. Things that bother me a lot. I guess I'm what you would call needy."

"Yes," he said quietly. "You are."

"I don't know if you're going to be able to support me emotionally."

"No," he said. "I don't think I will."

They were married the next day. The only guests and witnesses were Betty's elder sister, GeDelle Cagle, and her husband, Euel, who lived in Huntsville.

The following Sunday morning, Betty heard Jack in the bathroom and went to him. He was standing in front of the sink in his bathrobe. He looked pale and drawn. She tried to slip her arms around him from behind, but he took her forearm in his hand firmly and pushed it away.

"Betty, we're married now. Married people don't carry on like that all the time."

There was no humor in his voice, no twinkle in the eye. Jack was sick and in a great deal of pain.

The fairy-tale ending, for Jack and Betty, would have been a gradual process of surrender, love, and support, in which each came to understand and accept the other's weaknesses, learning to see and cherish the strengths more. Perhaps that is what was happening, finally, just before the murder. Perhaps not. Either way, their marriage did not look like a fairy tale. It was made of all the rot and wonder, the stench and the awe of very real life.

The operation was much harder for both of them than either had imagined, even though Betty was a nurse who had spent years tending to blood-soaked and incontinent patients, holding them to her breast to help them overcome the pain, humiliation, and sheer terror of illness. Her professional experience was not enough.

Jack could not face sex, at first because the ileostomy had made him even more painfully self-conscious than before, and later because the surgeries and the drugs he was taking seemed to render him physically impotent.

Betty could not get her mind around the idea of life without sex. Sex had always been the place in life where she had found reassurance that she was desired and therefore real. Betty was a complicated and often difficult person. When she drank, she convinced herself Jack was not really impotent but was feigning it to hold himself aloof from her.

Such an idea never occurred to her when she was sober. But the drinking had become much worse. By then they were living in the big house on Boulder Circle, and they were a wealthy and prominent couple in Huntsville. Shy little Jack Wilson had blossomed in the glow of attention and respect his status earned him. His sly wit made him a favorite at parties. His reputation for generosity and humor was legend in the city. Radio talk show hosts called him at the office to chat about this and that. The Wilsons were on the social A list.

It was never a life that came easily to Betty. When she headed up a long azalea-bordered driveway toward her first medical auxiliary reception, she was half drunk at ten in the morning, terrified of the women inside, whom she thought of as "rich bitches." On the worst days, her social fear made her defensive and unpleasant. She spoke coarsely to shock people. If someone said, "We think so much of your husband," Betty might say, "He's an asshole."

She was suffering alcoholic blackouts often. It was not until five years after Betty had joined Alcoholics Anonymous and stopped drinking that Jack was able to make himself tell her about the blackouts. She would storm into the bedroom at three in the morning, rip the bedclothes off him, and scream at him: "You horrible little impotent shitbag! You have ruined my life! I hate you, I hate you!"

The next day, Betty would remember nothing. Even though Jack was a physician, he did not understand that she was having alcoholic blackouts, and neither did Betty. Jack wondered how she could be so cool and collected the next day, as if nothing had happened. In Betty's mind, nothing had.

Jack disguised his wounds well, but there were times when he was overwhelmed by the sheer pain of it all. On those occasions, his composure imploded. It happened suddenly: He was detached, humorous, and above-it-all one moment and sobbing and suicidal the next.

One day in the kitchen, Jack collapsed into racking little-boy sobs in front of Shirley Green, the big, red-haired, raw-boned country girl they had hired recently as housekeeper. He asked Betty, "Why don't I just kill myself, Betty? Would that make you happy?"

But the little-boy-lost act had exactly the wrong effect on Betty, who remembered nothing of her blackouts or the abuse she had handed him. Instead, when Jack cried, Betty saw Wormy Woods towering over her in the tiny living room of the house on Hoke Street, drunk and sobbing, sloppy with remorse. The sight filled her with anger.

"I'll go upstairs and get the gun you gave me, Jack, if you want it. You can just go ahead and do it right now."

Betty was too much a mess herself at this point to have room for Jack's pain. She was having brief sexual flings with men she met at parties, always when drunk. She sometimes let Jack know, and on those occasions he retreated deep into all the defenses and the self-insulation he had learned as a boy.

"It's just sex, Betty," he would say, in his most intellectual and patronizing voice.

"That's right, Jack. You're right. It's just sex."

In the circle of wealthy doctors' wives she met in the Huntsville medical community, Betty's discerning eye quickly picked out the daytime boozers, the cocaine users, and the good-time gals. They became her boon companions. They all complained about the hours their husbands worked and reinforced in each other the feeling that medicine was a mistress. They quarreled with each other, and sometimes their disputes—usually having to do with drugs and sexual partners—turned into venomous feuds.

Betty became more and more jealous of the time Jack spent at the office and hospital. Jack plunged ever deeper into his practice. He floated in and out of the house on Boulder Circle late at night and early in the morning, sloppy in the hand-me-down clothes he collected from his grown sons, looking like a little tramp seeking shelter from the cold.

Betty tried to launch a business of her own—a small string of expensive clothing boutiques. The business enabled her to visit New York often, which she loved. But the liquor and her state of mind prevented the business from ever really catching fire.

High summer, 1986, was the very bottom, the nadir. Neither one of them believed they could go on. Neither one could leave.

One of Betty's sons by her first marriage, Dink, had left his new baby, Alan, with her for the afternoon one very hot day. She had errands to run. She and Jack had agreed that she would drop their BMW sedan off at the dealership for repairs at noon and that he would meet her there to give her a ride home. But he never showed up. The baby was squalling, and she couldn't stay in the showroom with him, which meant that she had to stay outside on a bench in the sweltering heat. She had a terrible hangover headache.

When the car was repaired, she put the baby in his infant seat in the back and drove straight to Jack's office. Two of Jack's employees, a technician and a newly hired bookkeeper, were just getting back from a late lunch. The technician saw Betty roll onto the lot. She took the new bookkeeper by the hand and said,

"C'mon, I want you to meet Betty, Dr. Wilson's wife."

But before she could begin the introductions, Betty shrieked at her: "Where is that goddamned Jack Wilson?"

The technician said, "I don't know, Betty. I'm just getting back, but I know he was still at the hospital when I left, having some kind of complication with a surgery."

"Well, when that little son of a bitch gets back, tell him I was here, and give him this for me."

She stuck her arm out the window and jabbed up and down several times with her extended middle finger. Then she gunned the car and roared away.

Jack, who had pulled up moments before and parked quietly at some distance, witnessed the entire scene. When Betty was gone, he got out of his car, went inside, and sat at his desk staring at his hands folded before him for a very long time. The technician watched him through the open door. He did not take calls or get up out of his chair.

That night Jack came home early. Betty was in the kitchen with Shirley Green. Jack stopped just inside the front door, as he did every night when he came home, and took off his shoes. He removed his watch and pulled his billfold out of his trousers. He laid both things down on top of his shoes. It was a ritual repeated each and every time he returned to the house. Jack could not be comfortable until he was stripped down to the PJs and socks he had grown up in.

He walked into the kitchen and said, "Betty, I want you to pour yourself a big drink."

"What?"

"Pour a big drink and come with me. We are going to have a talk."

He led her to a glass table on the deck by the Olympic-size swimming pool behind the house. It was summer dusk, warm but no longer oppressive, not unlike the evening before their wedding day when they had sat on the porch outside Jack's apartment and talked about the future.

She sipped her drink and looked across the table to try to

gauge his expression. He looked very determined, but not angry. If anything, there was a regretful calm at the edges of his mouth and in his eyes.

"You want a divorce," she said.

"No."

She was surprised.

"What, then?"

"I just want you to know something, Betty. It's doing us both too much harm for me not to say it and for you not to know it."

"What, Jack?"

"I love my medical practice, Betty. I love it. I love my patients. If you make me choose, I will choose my practice and my patients. It means everything to me. Betty, it is what I am.

"I love you, Betty. I love you more dearly and more deeply than I have ever loved in my life. But if you make me choose, I will choose the practice, and I will go on without you."

She had never heard him speak this way. She stared at him, then looked off toward the electric lights dancing on the rubbery blue surface of the pool.

"I see," she said.

A month later, she came to him.

"Jack, I want to stop drinking."

He took both of her hands in his. "I will do anything I can to help you."

"Oh, Jack." She began to cry, and then to sob. He took her into his arms and held her gently.

"Jack, will you send me to a hospital? Somewhere out of town?"

She went first to a hospital in Birmingham, where she dried out. Counselors there told her she needed to disabuse herself of two ideas: one, that she was going to hide her problem or her recovery from anybody back in Huntsville; two, that anybody back in Huntsville was paying all that much attention. The first thing she did when she came home was join Alcoholics Anonymous.

The first meetings were very tough. Betty went to the podium in a mink coat and told long dramatic stories about how difficult it had been growing up in the shadow of a more beautiful twin sister. People in the audience shook their heads skeptically and said, "It doesn't sound that tough to me."

She went on at length about Jack's rejection of her sexually, but people in the audience said, "Hey, give the guy a break, will you? You said he had an operation!"

She cried, and they came up to the podium and put their arms around her.

"You may think you have a big problem getting over booze," one man said, "but you've got a bigger problem getting over bullshit."

Gradually, it worked for Betty. She did not start drinking again—the most important thing. As she grew accustomed to looking at the world through sober eyes, she saw how different it was. She really wasn't the center of attention. Other people were not planning their days around her. Gradually, her fellow members in A.A. prodded her toward a vision of her own responsibility for her own life. Sometimes the prodding was gentle, sometimes rough. A.A. was a world of well-intentioned and often very imperfect souls, working to help each other up out of hell and back into the excitement and wonder of real life again.

She had been dry eight months when she found herself sitting idly on a bench in the anteroom of the hall where her A.A. meetings were held, waiting for a meeting to begin. She wasn't thinking about anything in particular. And suddenly, as if from nowhere, a moment of great clarity came to her.

"Jack has done nothing to hurt me," she thought. "My sister has done nothing to hurt me. My father, God rest his poor soul, turned his own life into a hell. But he wasn't trying to make my life miserable."

Even with the drinking behind her, sex continued to be a terrible problem. Jack couldn't even talk about it, let alone do it. Betty simply could not hold herself together without it. Even though her recovery seemed to be going well, she still felt very wobbly inside. She found herself faced with a new type of temptation in the man department. A number of the men in Alcoholics Anonymous were very attractive. The process of the meetings tended to strip away pretense. It opened vulnerabilities and created a whole new dimension of intimacy and trust.

Betty was especially attracted to a man named Errol Fitzpatrick—a tall, urbane, self-possessed man who was director of risk management for the city of Huntsville, meaning that he was in charge of seeing that all of the city's various departments, including police and fire, were either covered by insurance or self-insured. His duties included telling each department which practices would have to change in order for the department to remain insurable. It was a very responsible post, sometimes involving friction and politics, and it called for an unflappable personality. Once Errol Fitzpatrick got his drinking under control, he was the perfect man for the job. Married, with two young children, he was viewed as a rising star, both in Huntsville and nationally in the profession of urban management.

That he was African-American was not especially important to Betty, one way or the other. She had had other black lovers before Errol. She had been down that road at least far enough to get over the thrill of the exotic. She was drawn to Errol, she told a friend, "because with him you can have sex—you can have great sex—and you don't have to pretend it's anything else."

Jack made a great study of looking the other way, which Betty found infuriating. She began inviting Errol to the house during the day, while Jack was at the office. By that point, Jack and Betty had separate bedrooms—his a plain box-shaped affair on the second level at a front corner of the house, hers the entire back half of the second level. Betty's personal quarters were divided into three areas—a spacious bedchamber, a walk-in closet as big as most bedrooms, and an enormous bathroom that looked like a set for the nightclub scene in a 1930s musical. She and Errol made full use of the entire space, while Shirley Green angrily rammed the vacuum cleaner around downstairs.

There were even social occasions when it was quite natural for Betty to invite Errol to the house while Jack was there. Errol was not the type to flaunt anything—in fact, he was more the type to dread indiscretion—but he did show up, and he chatted amiably with Jack on those occasions. Shirley Green watched from the kitchen door with steam coming out of her nostrils.

Jack's refusal even to try to have sex with Betty was literally driving her around the bend. His unspoken tolerance of her affairs did nothing to comfort her. She wanted him to care, to be angry and to fight for her. She had dried out from alcoholism, but her frustration over sex often reached the level of frenzy, so that she achieved none of the serenity people normally seek in Alcoholics Anonymous. It was an aspect of her life and personality that none of the other A.A. members failed to notice.

A.A. members are taught that they cannot control their alcohol problems without controlling all of their weaknesses. One serious defect of character, uncontrolled, is the leaky hole that will sink the boat, probably in a sea of booze.

Betty's problems with Jack and with sex continued to haunt her, and following the dictates of A.A., she discussed those problems candidly with her fellow members.

Betty confronted Jack one night in his bedroom. He looked up from his perch on the side of the bed, where he had been reading a medical journal. When she entered the room, he rose and put the journal down.

"Jack," she whispered. She reached her hand out to his arm. He turned his head and moved a foot away.

"What is it?"

"Jack . . ."

Tears were forming in her eyes.

"Betty, I don't think . . . what is it? What's wrong?"

She drew up her hands and allowed him to step a few feet farther away.

"What are we, Jack? What are we? That's all I want to know."

Jack peered at her from behind his enormous glasses, with his head cocked back. He held his hands out in a shrug. His voice was cool and ironic.

"We are adults, Betty."

She stared at him, lips quivering.

"Betty," he said, "I need to get some sleep tonight. I'm sorry about whatever it is that's bothering you. But I've got to get to bed. I have surgery tomorrow."

She wheeled and stalked out of the room. Just as she reached her own bedroom door, she shrieked, "Fuck you, Jack! You little asshole!" She slammed her door shut hard behind her.

The next day Betty was seething, nervous, distracted. Mary Ann Lau, who was her protégée at the time in A.A., could tell that Betty was offcenter that day. As always when she was like this, Betty ranted and didn't listen to what other people said. As usual on such days, she had a terrible mouth.

"He's a short little shitbag," she said at lunch. "The house stinks because he won't take care of the goddamned thing."

Mary Ann, an attractive blonde in her early forties, had come to Huntsville from her native Iowa to become assistant to the executive director of the Humana Hospital. She had joined A.A. soon after. She wore her hair in an immaculate bun and was stiffly formal both in dress and manner. Her drinking problem had been an enormous humiliation to her. Without booze, she was self-conscious in social situations.

As always when Betty used foul language, Mary Ann winced. "Betty, I hope you don't say things like that to Jack's face."

Betty was staring off into space. "I had a dream," she said. "I dreamed Jack careened off a cliff in his car and died."

"How terrible," Mary Ann said.

"Yeah, I guess I'll just have to be patient."

"Betty, what is the matter with you?"

"The matter? Hey, I'm dry, I'm doing great. Why do you think something's the matter, Mary Ann?"

"Why do you have affairs with all of the men in A.A.?"

"You don't?"

"Why don't you just get a divorce?"

"Ha! And give up my life-style? Fat fucking chance."

Mary Ann looked around quickly to see if anyone had heard. Blushing, she said, "Betty, honestly."

Because A.A. addresses each member's moral life in totality, each member's private life is everyone else's concern. What might be mere gossip in another situation could be vital information among people who are watching each other like hawks for something that might mean a member is about to fall off the wagon.

Betty kept up with the news better than most, but she sometimes used what she knew shrewishly, in her own defense rather than to help someone else.

One night after a meeting, while everyone was gathered sipping coffee before saying good night, Betty very clearly and obviously arranged an assignation with Errol Fitzpatrick. Later, in the parking lot, just as she was about to get into her BMW, another woman member approached her.

"Betty, I'm sorry, but this is not just me, it's how everybody feels," the woman said. "A lot of people feel like the way you carry on with the men in the chapter is destructive."

"Is that right?" Betty asked. She moved away from the car and approached the woman. "You wouldn't have Errol in mind in particular, would you?"

"Well I do think you kind of throw that in everybody's face."

"Right. Well, I appreciate your concern."

"I'm worried about your sobriety."

"Dear, you couldn't possibly fucking be worried about something else, could you?"

"What are you talking about, Betty?"

"I'm talking about you and Errol and a motel room after the last Round-Up. I guess you didn't get asked back, eh?"

The woman leveled a cold eye at her. "You are a very hurtful person, Betty Wilson. And I do not believe that you are recovering."

"Excuse me," Betty said, turning her back. "Right now the only thing I need to recover from is you."

The only other refuge in Betty's life, aside from A.A., was exercise. She was famous among her friends for being a Jazzercise fanatic. For one thing, she was convinced she needed to exercise in order to keep her many cosmetic surgeries from sagging and bagging—a Dorian Gray horror that woke her up at night. For another, strenuous exercise smoothed her out emotionally and helped her fend off the temptation of drink.

Mary Ann Lau stayed closer to Betty than most of the other women in the chapter, but it was not easy. Mary Ann believed one of the things most alcoholic women need most to get under control is their relationship with men. She was distressed when Betty told her she had reacquainted herself with an old high school friend at a class reunion and that the relationship had become torrid. The new lover lived in another city, and Betty said she was commuting, telling Jack she was making buying trips for her small dress shop in Huntsville, by then on its last legs.

One day Betty asked Mary Ann to take her to Huntsville International Airport. Betty got out of the car at the curb to show the skycap her luggage in Mary Ann's trunk. Then she came back to the car, walked around to the driver's side, and signaled for Mary Ann to lower the window.

"Honey, I need a favor. This trip is a little bit last minute."

"What do you mean?"

"Well, it's a spur-of-the-moment thing." She smiled and rolled her eyes devilishly.

"Do you mean that Jack doesn't know you're going?"

"That's what I need the favor about."

"What, Betty?"

"I need you to call Jack and say I decided at the last minute to go down to Birmingham to meet Peggy for some shopping."

"Betty . . ."

"He doesn't give a shit . . ."

"He won't believe me . . ."

"He doesn't give a shit. Just do it. O.K.?"

Betty started to follow her bags into the terminal. Mary Ann hurriedly shut off the car and got out, chasing her. She caught her by a sleeve.

"No, Betty."

"Mary Ann, what is it?"

"I won't do it. I won't lie to Jack for you."

Betty shrugged. "Fine. Thanks a bunch." She turned again to go into the terminal, but Mary Ann pulled her back.

"Betty, you had no right to ask this of me. It's wrong. It's bad. You know me, you know what I've been through. I guess you can be like this, but I can't. I'm not tough like you. This is . . . it's wrong, morally, and it's destructive. You hurt people, Betty, you hurt Jack. . . . "

"How is that any of your goddamned business?"

Betty spoke loudly, and heads turned.

Mary Ann looked around.

"Betty," she said quietly, "I just . . . I cannot afford to be your friend anymore. I'm sorry. This is bad for me. You had no right . . . you shouldn't have asked me. I'm sorry I even brought you out here."

Betty shrugged. "O.K., Miss Goody Two-shoes. You go your way. I go mine."

"I'm sorry, Betty."

Betty turned and shrugged, nodding toward the long bank of busy airline ticket clerks. "I'm not," she said.

In these bitter years, Jack and Betty managed to stay together, and one of the things that may have helped them do it was their grandchildren. Betty baby-sat every day with Dink's children, Alan and Casey, and, in spite of whatever hardships her duties caused her, she loved every minute of it—looked forward to their coming each day and felt sadness every evening when their parents took them away.

For her, the time with the grandchildren was a second chance—time she had lost with her own children.

Jack came home to see them, even if it meant he would have to return to the office or hospital afterward and stay until late at night. He lavished on them the same kind of playful attention he had received from Bill Wilson at the end of Bill's long painful days as a short-order cook. Doing so seemed to set something right deep in Jack's heart.

When Jack came home, the ritual was always the same. She

would tell the grandchildren, "Pop is coming!"

The children ran squealing through the house, straight to the kitchen where they hid under the table, clutching each other, gasping and giggling.

Jack took off his shoes at the door, removed his watch and wallet, and laid them on top of the shoes, then came high-stepping and prowling like a daddy longlegs into the kitchen.

"Betty," he would ask in a stage whisper, "where are Al and Casey?"

"Oh, I think they got tired of waiting and went on home by themselves."

"Oh, good. Then they won't mind . . . if I just bend down . . . and look . . . UNDER HERE!"

When they ran out from under the table, Jack would take them by their tiny hands and skip with them to the stairs and up the stairs to his "Adventure Closet," filled to overflowing with helmets, nineteenth-century plumed hats, tin swords, velour capes, fake beards, and a jumble of cheap wigs. He caped the children and draped them in long wraps, wigs, and swords, and then they all went off down the hall, around the house, and into the yard, Jack singing in his high little voice, "Let's go off adventuring, adventuring, adventuring!"

When they were tired, he took them where he had often gone at the end of his own solitary childhood days. He crawled under Betty's huge four-poster bed with them and read them stories until their parents came.

One morning in early 1991, Jack called another of his landmark meetings at the table in the backyard. This time neither one of them was drinking. Betty had been dry for more than five years.

"Betty, this is all very hard for me. Very hard. But I love you, Betty, and I don't want to lose you. I think I am losing you. There are things that have happened that . . . I know I act like I don't care, like I can handle it, but . . ."

"Like what, Jack?"

For the first time, he told her about the blackouts when she used to wake him up and call him a little shitbag and rail at him for his impotence.

"Jack," she said, shaking her head slowly through tears, "do you know that I was blacked out?"

"Yes, I do now. I didn't then. I didn't know anything about such things."

"It's not an excuse, Jack, but . . ." She pushed her hand across the table and took his hand.

Then Jack told her something that filled her with fear. With great effort and over a period of a year or more, Jack said, he had brought himself to the point of being willing to try again.

"Try what?" she asked.

"Sex."

"Sex?"

"Yes. Sex."

"Well, Jack, that's wonderful . . . but how?"

He had been watching the research on a relatively new device, just released to the market in 1987, which created an artificial erection without a surgical implant. It consisted of a sheath of soft silicon, like a condom, to which plastic tubing was attached. When hooked up to a small electrical vacuum pump, the device created a vacuum around the penis, which held the penis erect as long as the pump was running.

It had been a few years since Betty had seen Jack naked. In that time, Jack's habitual sloppiness about everything, his own grooming especially, had extended to his care of the ostomy bag. On one occasion when she had tried to speak to him about a mess the leaky bag had left in his bed, he brushed her off airily, which threw her into a rage. She rushed downstairs to leave the house. As she passed Shirley Green in the kitchen, she said, "Don't touch his room! If he doesn't care if he's covered with shit, then neither do I."

No sooner was she out of the house than Shirley Green stormed upstairs and changed the sheets.

But on this occasion, with Jack so vulnerable and yet so gallantly willing to try again, she felt she had to force herself to repress her feelings about the bag. She had to do what she could to help in the experiment.

And an experiment it was. They went to Betty's bed, where Jack stripped and then installed the sheath on himself. Betty took off her clothes and waited for him. He started the humming little pump motor, and the device achieved the intended effect more or less instantly. In better days, they might even have laughed at themselves, but on this occasion there was far too much at stake. Years of pain and injury had been allowed to accrue between them, and in this one terribly awkward moment they were attempting to breach that wall. They were two adults as lost and uncertain as frail new adolescents.

They began to have sex, and the process seemed to be working out fairly well. Betty put her hands on Jack and lifted him slightly up and to one side, in a habit recalled from the subliminal past of their earliest sexual relationship. But the movement caused the tubing from the vacuum device to tangle in the ostomy bag. The bag pulled loose from its fitting, just as a rush of excrement was leaving the bowel. The feces splattered out over Betty, hitting her in the mouth and eyes and covering the bed with spatters.

Jack was lost in the act and unaware. She put both hands on his chest and pushed him away.

"Get off, Jack! Get off! Don't you see what happened?"

He rolled away suddenly, tangled in the tubing and the bag.

"Oh, my God, Betty! I'm sorry! I'm so sorry!"

She lifted herself, rolled off the bed and stood shaking herself and shrieking. "Oh! Oh! Oh, how disgusting!"

Jack stood before her, the vacuum sheath still erect. He was covered with smears and spatters. "Betty . . ." He reached out toward her.

"No! No! Don't touch me! You're covered with shit, Jack! Look at you! Oh, God, so am I. Look at this! Get away! Don't touch me!"

Jack shouted: "Betty! Please, Betty!"

She rushed to the bathroom and turned the shower on full-blast and piping hot.

In the high-pitched shrieking voice of an angry child, Jack shouted after her, "I will never . . . never! . . . ever! . . . never touch you again, Betty!"

Shirley Green stood at the landing halfway up the stairs, listening to the shouts.

Jack stayed at the office that night until the last staff member had left, then drove to the hospital where he had nothing in particular to do. It was well into the evening when Betty found him, a tiny little figure slumped at a table at the back of the cafeteria, his glasses gleaming green beneath the fluorescent light like the eyes of a fly. He was alone, poring over a medical text. She sat down across from him.

"Oh, hi," he said mildly. "Is something wrong?"

"No. I just came to check on you."

He barely nodded, staring at her briefly, then looked back down at his book. "I'm just about ready to come home."

"Good," she said. "I have a nice dinner ready."

"Oh. That's nice."

He folded the book shut and looked up at her quizzically.

She said: "I'd like us to go to Santa Fe."

"What's in Santa Fe?"

"Oh, Jack, you don't know anything. I've been reading about it. It's in the high desert in New Mexico, and it's all adobe architecture. It's supposed to be very spiritual and artistic. I thought we could go there, just the two of us, and have a romantic interlude."

He peered at her. "A romantic interlude?"

"Yes."

She reached across the table and took his hand. They both laughed, but they were both crying.

"What do we do between now and the interlude?" he asked.

She sighed and shrugged. "I think I'm finally going to get that horrible kitchen remodeled."

The town of Vincent, Alabama, was a portrait of the past—a pretty little village cradled in a deep green elbow of Highway

231 where it ran north along Logan Martin Lake toward Gadsden. Like most of the small towns in America, Vincent ceased long ago to have an independent local economy of any kind. By 1991 it had become one of the farther-flung outposts of Birmingham—a bedroom community for people who didn't mind commuting an hour in order to escape the inconveniences of urban life.

A few commercial buildings still stood on the old main street of the town. Most of the business activity had migrated farther downhill to the highway. The people who called Vincent home and sent their children to the public schools tended to live either on old farms in the country nearby or in new subdivisions that had sprung up in the woods.

In August 1991, James White landed a little job doing some work for Melanie Little, who taught his daughter Kelly Renee. Vincent Elementary was in a one-story, rambling brick building just off the highway.

It was a modest building, built a wing and a room at a time on tight small-town budgets. If a teacher didn't like something in his or her room, he could repair or build it himself during the summer months or get someone else to do it. The chances of the district paying for professional remodeling were slim.

James's involvement was ambiguous at first, as always. His daughter's teacher needed to have some shelves built, and in this case, Calvin Smith, the principal, had agreed to supply the lumber if Melanie Little could persuade a parent to do the work. James appeared to be volunteering to do the work for nothing. He did a nice job, but by the time he had finished explaining this personal problem and that personal problem, Melanie Little felt she needed to do something to help him.

Just down the hall, Peggy Lowe was getting her own first-grade room ready for the onslaught. Her husband was working on his room. Wayne and Peggy brought their pretty teenage daughter, Stephanie, to the school with them to help each day. At noon the family gathered for lunch in Peggy's room.

When James had finished building Melanie Little all the shelves she needed, he continued to hang around the school, suggesting that he needed help with his problems. Melanie Little, in effect, handed him off to Peggy Lowe by suggesting that Mrs. Lowe might also need help with her room.

He appeared in the doorway, stooped slightly forward at the waist, eyes downcast, kneading his grimy baseball cap in his hands and stuttering nervously, addressing Peggy Lowe as "Mizrus"—a Southern courtesy title freighted with class distinction. He spoke quickly, in a wet stutter, his terrible brown teeth flickering behind a matted beard.

"Mizrus Little said you might need some hep with some shevs, and I done finished working for her, but I was still looking for some work to do, and I can do shevs pretty good, if you wanted to go look at what I done in Mizrus Little's classroom, which I just finished, but she don't need no more, so I was wondering if there was anything I could do down here."

Wayne was skeptical, but Peggy agreed to go look at the shelves in Melanie Little's room. Wayne returned to his own room. In the moments it took for Peggy to walk down the half-lighted corridor with James, he began spinning his web of woes.

"You're Kelly Renee's daddy, are you not, Mr. White?"

"Yes, Mizrus Lowe, I sure am, that wonderful little girl, she's the most precious thing in the whole world to me, her and her sister and brother, and it's why . . . it's why . . ."

He faltered.

She stopped and looked into his face. He stood bowed before her, cap in hand, tears in his eyes. She was especially fond of his daughter whom Melanie Little taught, who was pretty and extremely bright. It always sawed at her heart to know a child first and then meet a parent like this.

"It's why it just bothers me so bad not to be able to support those chid'run, Mizrus Lowe."

She gave him work building shelves in her own room.

Every minute he was in the room, the brown teeth flickering behind the beard, he spat out his odd, singsong, nattering song of suffering. "I thought this last time I got married that all my problems was behind me, especially since I got dried out from drinking and drugs, and I met Cheryl, and she had her own kids plus she and me had a child, and my wife from before was having troubles getting a job, so I brought those chid'run back to stay with me so I could look after them."

"Well, that was good of you, Mr. White," she said.

He smiled sweetly, basking in her approval. Stephanie, watching from a distance, grimaced and turned away when James's smile caused him to show his teeth.

"I was only trying to make up to them for all the bad I done before, because I knowed I was bad, and I wanted to do better for them than I was done. My parents wasn't even married. In fact, I never knew who my real daddy was. I thought the man who lived with my mother when I was little was my daddy, and I took his name till I was fifteen, but then he told me he didn't have nothing to do with me being born, and my mother said it was true, so I took her name, which was White."

He humped and scrabbled around the room, dragging boards and cutting them across chairs with a wheezing handsaw, his knee as a brace, his face always cloaked by the beard, sidelong eyes shadowed by the bill of the dirty baseball cap.

"I joined the army when I was seventeen. They sent me to 'Nam. I was over in Germany awhile. There was a German girl called me Cookie, and that name just sort of stuck, so that's what everybody called me."

He grinned broadly, and Stephanie looked away.

"I married a girl in Lawrenceville, Georgia, after I got out, but then I caught her in a van with seven or eight guys."

"Stephanie," Peggy said, "why don't you go see if your father needs some help."

"One of the things that really gets me," he said, "is that one of my ex-wives, the guy she's with, he's a child molester. What would you think of somebody like that?" He stopped and watched her carefully.

"Oh, that's terrible," she said.

He turned back to his work. Banging away with the hammer, nails in his lipless mouth, he told her how his second wife had broken his heart by running around on him. " 'Course, back then is when I had some pretty bad drug and alcohol problems, so I can't blame her all the way. She was havin' a hard time with me, too, I guess."

His third wife, sadly, had been faithless as well. But the one who had really broken his heart and turned him completely against women—who had shut out all hope for love itself—was his fourth wife, who had left him for his best friend.

All of James White's stories were intersticed with mentions of his dire financial straits and the hardships imposed upon his children, including the one in Melanie's class.

Finally there were no more shelves that could be built in Peggy Lowe's classroom. She and Melanie Little had told James they couldn't afford to pay him cash for his work, but they had been cooking hot meals at home and bringing them to the school for him to take home to the shifting population of children who stayed with him off and on in the trailer on the hill.

James, of course, was after more than food. Peggy went to Calvin Smith and persuaded him to hire James to build some risers the school needed for a choral group. Smith agreed to hire James and pay him some money.

For James, all of this activity came under the heading of business development. In the evenings, when James was drinking with his buddy Alvin; with Janine Russell and her boyfriend, Bunky; and the rest of the trailer-house crowd, he began to ramble on incoherently about Peggy Lowe, what a fine-looking bitch she was, how he had her wrapped around his little finger, how she wanted him, a real man who could give her some sex, not that pussy-looking husband of hers. They would laugh, and James would laugh, too, but everyone understood that somewhere just beneath the surface of his maniacal giggle, James was building up a story that he himself would soon take for truth. Then it would be dangerous to laugh.

By the time the work at the school had run out and the school year had started, James was putting the serious bite on Peggy Lowe. He sent his little boy Josh, a student at Vincent Elementary, to waylay Peggy in the corridor. The little boy handed her a scrawled note. One of James's children had been in the hospital recently, the note said, and James was in great despair over his inability to provide proper care for the child. So depressed had he been, the note said, that he had attempted suicide. For better or worse, his very good friend Alvin had stopped him at the last moment. Was it possible that Mizrus Lowe and her fine husband, Wayne, might have any work at all for him at their beautiful new house on Logan Martin Lake?

The issue was less complex for Wayne. Very strong religious principles, and his visible position as the music minister in the First Baptist Church of Vincent, might have seemed to require him to extend a helping hand to a wretch like James White. But Wayne Lowe was also an experienced man. He could have sent James packing in a New York minute, had it been up to him.

But for Peggy, James's stuttering, self-pitying chatter was a window on a dark place that evoked difficult memories. James persuaded Peggy to hire him to work on her home on the bluff above the lake. Wayne resisted, but there was a great deal of finishing work that needed to be done, and, given Wayne's schedule, he was never going to get to it himself. Mr. White had done a good job at the school, Peggy said, and he seemed to be willing to work on the house at very reasonable rates.

James figured he had landed a live one. He persuaded Peggy and Wayne to hire him to do several jobs—painting, tacking trim pieces on the outside, running some shoe molding along the baseboards in some of the rooms—each job at a separate price. Then, barely having begun any of the work, he went for the cash.

On a chilly fall evening, Peggy and Stephanie were in the kitchen, talking happily across bubbling pots, trading chatter about their day, when the doorbell rang. The front of the house faced the steep hill running down through trees to the lake. The bell was at the back, where a long winding dirt driveway ended at the back door of the house, next to the garage. Peggy pulled open the door and found James White and an older daughter, Tara Maria.

He said he had come to measure some of the rooms again before buying materials. Peggy told him to go do what he needed to do. Stephanie immediately called Tara over to the stove to have her taste what was cooking. Stephanie made small talk about events in the middle school both girls attended, and Tara responded, awkwardly at first and then more cheerfully.

Peggy became aware that James was standing in the hallway making a motion at her with his head. She stepped out to speak to him.

"What is it, Mr. White?"

"I was wondering, Mizrus Lowe, if you would mind stepping out on the deck with me for a minute. I got something I need to tell you."

The wind was snappy and cold across the wooden deck at the front of the house, high above the lake. Peggy shivered and rubbed her uncovered arms.

"What is it, Mr. White?"

He pulled a soiled and rumpled utility bill from his pocket. "I got behind on my electric, ma'am, and they done shut me off."

"We have been paying you money, Mr. White. We have paid you in advance for a lot of work you haven't done yet."

"I know that, Mizrus Lowe, and I feel just . . . I been so down on myself lately, I almost got back to drinkin' for a little bit. I got off that idea again, but now . . . they shut the electric off, and, man, it's cold already, and I just feel so bad, because those chid'run are with me now, and they're just freezing to death in that trailer at night."

Peggy gazed inside the house. The plate-glass window at the front of the house looked in across the living room and over the counter separating the living room from the kitchen. Behind the counter was her own beautiful daughter, laughing and doing what she could to put poor Tara at ease.

"How much do you need?"

"To get it turned back on would be a hundred and fifty dollars."

It was a substantial sum—enough to make an awkward hole in the Lowe family budget for the month.

"Come inside," she said. "I'll write you a check."

Of course, it was chickenfeed for James—barely a good

night's boozing. But it was much more significant for what it represented—his first serious bite of the apple. He was into her. He was into her good.

In the months ahead, James relentlessly inched up the ante. He persuaded Peggy to persuade Wayne to agree to more work around the house. He even persuaded Wayne to persuade his own mother to allow James to pour a driveway for her for several thousand dollars.

At night when he drank with his friends, James's boasting about his hold over Peggy Lowe grew wilder. James interpreted any act of kindness extended to him as an indication of his own power. The more money he squeezed out of Peggy Lowe, the more delicious was his sense of sway over her. And in her mid-forties Peggy Lowe was a very attractive woman. Inevitably, James's boasts began to project more and more toward a day when he would get a lot more than money out of her.

He was now calling her almost every day on the telephone, sometimes several times in a day, maundering over his long list of woes, his need for more money, his excuses for not doing any of the work the Lowes had paid him for. Peggy Lowe walked around her house dusting and making beds with the cordless telephone wedged beneath her chin like a violin, often not speaking herself for half an hour at a time while James prattled on about his problems.

He called her one time and said that his anxiety about money had become so great that he was considering suicide again. She counseled inner strength and resolve. He called another time, with his children making noise in the background, and told Peggy that if things didn't improve, he was afraid he might go back to drinking full-time. There was real alarm in her voice as she urged him not to do that.

Bingo.

THREE

NOW THE THREATS TO GO BACK TO DRINKING STARTED coming fast and furious. Peggy began to suspect from his manner and speech that it was a threat James had already acted on. The problem was that there simply was no money left—no margin, no extra, no slush fund—that she could use to make James go away. The incessant phone calls had become a huge emotional burden. But even at that, Peggy Lowe was unable to simply say, "Mr. White, stop calling me."

And so, at some point in the second week in May 1992, when he had called her to threaten both suicide and a return to drinking (in unspecified order), Peggy Woods Lowe said to James Dennison White, "Mr. White, I just can't help you with any more money, and I don't know what to do about your drinking, but my sister Betty, who lives in Huntsville, is a recovering alcoholic, and she might be able to help. She's married to a doctor, and they are doing a lot of work on their house right now. She's having her kitchen remodeled. Maybe Betty could help you get involved with Alcoholics Anonymous, and she and her husband might be able to give you some work, too."

"She's your sister?"

"She and I are twins."

When James met his friends that night, he was stuttering faster than usual, drinking harder, if that was possible, and talking even more wildly.

By the time the sun was down, all the crowd out in front of the broken little house next to the rusted trailer at the top of the hill were good and drunk. Amid cackles and staggering speeches, there was a lot of jabbing and needling about whether or not James had made it into bed with Mizrus Lowe yet and whether she was supporting him in the style to which he was accustomed.

Gradually the crowd figured out that James basically was being fired by Mizrus Lowe without ever having made it to first base, which elicited cackling howls of delight from everyone but James. The howls were even more shrill when James announced testily that Mizrus Lowe had a twin sister who was even richer than she was and that he was going up to Huntsville to work for her.

"Shit, James, if that don't work out, maybe they'll turn out to be fuckin' triplets."

James took it at first and then was drunkenly apoplectic.

"There ain't no bitch make a fool out of J.W.," he muttered over and over again as he slipped slowly into unconsciousness.

In the days ahead, James nagged Peggy relentlessly about when he would be able to go to Huntsville to work for her sister. Peggy called Betty and said she was trying to help a handyman in town who needed work in order to keep his children fed and clothed. Betty agreed to hire James, whom she had never met, to do part of the work being carried out in her kitchen. She already had a reputable carpenter working almost full-time on the job, but this was not the first time Betty had decided to divvy up the work in her house in order to help out a person in need. She had tried to do the same thing with the housework, offering to hire back a former housekeeper who said she regretted having left Betty's employ. Betty's plan was to give her one of Shirley Green's days, but it was the last straw for Shirley Green, who walked out the door never to return. The contrite former housekeeper got all the work.

In this case, Bobby Brooks, the carpenter/contractor doing the work, was in high demand in Huntsville and had lots of other work to keep him busy. He said it was all right with him if Betty parceled out part of the job to this man her sister had sent her.

Part of the deal, as far as Betty was concerned, was that the little man with the drinking problem whom Peggy had shipped her way was going to get involved in Alcoholics Anonymous. If anything, Betty's radar told her it was not a good sign that this person was not already in A.A. But she decided she would withhold judgment and give the man a chance, all of which was in keeping with the creed of Alcoholics Anonymous.

But it was one chance. One chance only.

At some point in the process of negotiations over the work he would do in Huntsville, James was supplied with a map to Betty's house. From that moment forward, he began making nervous drunken loops back and forth from Vincent to Huntsville in his pickup truck, driving the eighty miles drunk and high and talking to himself.

He made the trips even though Betty had not actually agreed yet on a specific time for the work to begin. He may have been attempting to show up in order to start the work anyway, then turning back after arriving in Huntsville, because he realized he was too drunk to start work. He himself may not have known exactly why he was making the trips. His friends said later it was just how James was, especially now that his fantasies about Peggy Lowe were falling apart on him. With a couple of cases of Budweiser on the truck seat next to him, the floor jumbled high with crumpled empties, smoking dope and swallowing handfuls of caffeine tablets to stay awake, he roared and rattled along the narrow wooded Alabama back roads at night, staying off the Interstate to avoid nosy state troopers. He prattled and stuttered to himself, dreaming God knows what.

He went to the house but did not knock. He may have parked outside on the street in the late night to look at the house. He may also have parked his truck farther down the mountain, on Chandler, and walked up through the woods to view the house from behind.

From the back, at the right angle, he would have had a clear view across the pool deck into the windows on the main floor, which would have appeared to be the second level from the back, above the basement level. He would have seen a busy life inside the kitchen window. Jack and Betty were hurrying through informal meals, trying to get ready for a long weekend trip they had planned to Santa Fe over the Memorial Day holiday.

Betty's son Trey, a college student who was living with them, was preparing for final exams. He and Jack got along well. Trey had all the qualities Jack admired in a young man. He was studious and serious about life without being dull. He was good-looking and socially adept. When the pressure of school and work weighed on him, he could unwind by grabbing a baseball bat from his closet and heading off to a batting range to swat at balls from an automatic pitching machine.

In other words, he didn't do drugs and he did stay in school. He was a comfort instead of a disappointment.

Obviously none of those inside—Jack, Trey, or Betty—could have imagined James Dennison White out in the woods watching them, his fingers twisting in meaningless gesticulations at his sides, the brown teeth moving behind the snarly beard, eyes flickering back and forth beneath the baseball cap. But James could imagine anything he liked. James was beginning to hear the voices.

On the weekend of May 16 and 17, the regional Alcoholics Anonymous organization held its regular annual retreat, called the Mountain-Top Round-Up, at Lake Guntersville State Park, a six thousand-acre refuge high on a hill above an enormous man-made lake on the Tennessee River, midway between Gadsden and Huntsville. Dominating the park was a huge lodge, built in 1974.

Betty had originally hoped Peggy would come up to stay with her at the lodge during the Round-Up. Alcoholics Anonymous had become very much the center of Betty's social world, and she enjoyed having her beautiful twin come meet all of her A.A. friends.

But Stephanie was beginning a protracted bout of mystery illnesses, possibly connected with adolescence. She had fainted at school one day that week. Peggy called Betty to say she would be staying at home with her daughter over the weekend.

In the middle of all this, James called Peggy with yet another long rambling tale of urgent distress.

"I was supposed to have my child'run this weekend, but Cheryl said some people told her they seen me drinking, so she won't let me see the kids. I'm just so . . . Mizrus Lowe, I cain't take it. I'm here by myself, and there's nobody here to stop me, and I got a gun, and I'm just about made up my mind to just put a damn bullet in my head and be done with it. I'm sorry I bothered you. I just called to say good-bye."

"Mr. White," she said, "please stop talking like that. I just can't . . . we cannot afford to employ you full-time, Mr. White. Listen, my sister is attending an A.A. convention at Guntersville State Lodge this weekend; I'm sure if you went up there she could help you, and it might be good for you to be around the A.A. people right now."

"Well, I don't have no money for gas."

"She may be able to help you."

"O.K. How do I get there?"

Peggy called Betty, and told her what was going on.

"Will you help him?"

Betty was silent for a while and then sighed. "You know I will. Tell him to come on. At least that way I can see him around some A.A. folks and see what he does in a meeting before he comes to my house to work."

Betty had made reservations for herself and Peggy for the weekend, beginning Friday. When Peggy canceled, Betty decided not to drive down to Guntersville until Saturday morning. When she arrived on Saturday, she was infuriated to learn that the lodge intended to charge her for the room she had not used the night before, because the reservation had been guaranteed by credit card.

Was the lodge full on Friday night? Didn't they have lots of empty rooms, since the convention hadn't started yet?

No, the clerk said, the lodge was completely filled for the entire long weekend. The desk had turned people away Friday night who would have taken that room. But Betty didn't like the idea of paying for a room she had not used. She demanded to speak to the lodge manager. The manager appeared and was polite but firm. Mrs. Wilson would have to pay for the room for Friday night, even though she had not used it. Betty put on a fairly loud show of her displeasure—enough to make some of her A.A. friends uncomfortable.

"Come on, Betty," one said. "You can afford it."

"That is not the point!" she said excitedly. "That is not the point!"

In the end she had to pay for Friday night. She was still shaking with anger when she got to her own room and began unpacking for the weekend.

Peggy called her room to tell her Mr. White would be arriving later that morning. She explained again that Mr. White looked bad and would be uncomfortable. She also mentioned that he had no money and was extremely self-conscious.

"Well, I can't get him a room here, Peggy."

"Where will he stay?"

"Guntersville is full of motels. He can stay anywhere and then come here during the day for the meetings."

"He has no money."

"Oh, shit. So he wants money. O.K., fine, tell him to come find me, and I'll advance him some money to tide him over if he needs it."

"I'm afraid he won't want to go walking through all those people in the lodge looking for you, Betty. He's very self-conscious."

"Well, Peggy, what in the hell do you want me to do, stand out in the road and wait for the asshole?"

"I'm sorry, Betty."

Betty composed herself. "No, I'm sorry. It's all right. That's typical with these birds. Look, you tell him I'll leave some money for him in my car. It's the big BMW. Tell him what it looks like. He can find it. I'll park it out in the open."

"Where in the car?"

"In the car, Peggy. On the seat. There's a library book still in the backseat of my car. I'll put it in there. He can go get the money, and then he can go get a room and call me from there."

James was to show up at Guntersville late Saturday morning, when the weekend's events would be under way. But, of course, he didn't arrive until late Saturday night, and he showed up drunk.

A park road ran down a steep course from the lodge three and a half miles through the woods to the main park gate on a two-lane highway below. At the gate was a small wooden guard shack, painted gray, and in the shack each night was a single guard whose job it was to tell people they could not enter the park after closing unless they could show they were registered guests of the lodge, with a key to prove it.

The guard that Saturday night was Keith Tucker, a muscular young man in his early twenties, who wore a very thin brown mustache and his hair in bangs beneath a guard cap.

It was almost 10:00 P.M. when James rolled up in a thunder of unmuffled engine noise.

"I done tole you," James argued, "I am supposed to meet Mizrus Betty Wilson up there at the hotel or whatever it is."

"And I told you, sir, the park is closed to nonregistered guests."

"Well I got to get in touch with her. I drove a long ways, about a hundred miles to come up here, and I'm out of money, and I don't have no place to stay."

"You can't go in, sir."

"Can't you call up there?"

"No, sir. I have no phone here."

"You got a two-way radio, don't you?"

"Yes, sir, but I can't use it for that."

"Well, man, what in the goddamn hell am I supposed to do? This is the shits, man. This is the shits!"

James was out of the truck stamping around in the dirt like Rumpelstiltskin. Keith Tucker decided to be more helpful.

"There's a Conoco gas station that's a convenience store right back up the highway in Guntersville where they've got a pay phone on the outside wall. Maybe you can call up to the lodge from there. Here's the number."

When James found the pay phone, he called Betty's room several times but got no answer because Betty was attending a poolside meeting. James then called Peggy in Vincent and made the call collect.

"Mr. White, where are you?"

"I'm at a pay phone, Mizrus Lowe. I just got here, and they won't let me in up there."

"Well, why are you just getting there now? You were supposed to be there this morning."

He told her all that had transpired. Peggy sighed and agreed to call the lodge, have Betty paged if she was not in her room, inform her of Mr. White's dilemma, and see what could be done. She instructed him to return to the guard shack and wait.

When the call came to the front desk, the staff all remembered Betty Wilson—the one who had pitched a fit over having to pay for Friday night. Two security guards in the lodge were detailed to go from meeting room to meeting room, from lounge to lounge, through the lodge's several restaurants, the main lobby and smaller lobbies on other levels, through the crowds of many hundreds of people, paging Mrs. Betty Wilson at each stop along the way.

They never found her, but someone in the crowd heard them asking for Betty Wilson. That person went to the pool, where he had just seen her, and told her she was being paged to come to the front desk. Just as she arrived, one of the guards was returning to report he had failed to find her.

A portly young man with a pockmarked complexion and small close-set eyes, security guard Robert Hawkins was usually willing to do whatever was asked of him, as long as it wasn't expected he would do it quickly.

"This is Mrs. Wilson," the night manager explained to Hawkins. The manager told Betty that a Mr. White was waiting at the gate, apparently because he was supposed to pick up a package of some kind.

"He's supposed to get something out of my car," she said. "I'll have to take it down to him."

"Oh, no," the manager said, "we wouldn't want you to have to go down there at night. I'm sure Mr. Hawkins will volunteer to take it down."

Robert Hawkins stared blankly at the manager for a moment, then smiled suddenly and said, "Oh, yes. I volunteer."

"It's a library book in the backseat of my car," Betty said. "I'll walk out with you."

"Ma'am, I need to go get my truck. It's pretty far down to that gate. I'll meet you at your car."

When Hawkins pulled up next to the BMW in his pickup, Betty handed him the book and said, "O.K., give this to him and tell him to have fun. And tell him I want the book back."

Robert Hawkins drove down the steep winding road to the guard shack and handed the slim volume through the gate to James. The book, called *Sleeping Beauty and the Firebird,* was one Jack had read to the grandchildren under the bed.

James went back to his truck, opened up the library book and found two crisp hundred-dollar bills tucked in the pocket for the library card. He sat for a moment staring at the money, then fired up his truck and drove back to the Conoco convenience store, where he bought a case of half-quart Budweisers and a fresh bottle of caffeine tablets. Then, instead of going to find a room, James drove his truck down over the curb, made a wide awkward turn across Highway 431, and headed north for another moonlight ramble on Boulder Circle.

Perhaps, roaring along in a fog of leaky truck exhaust, beer, dope, and caffeine, James was thinking about Peggy Lowe's twin sister and the job he was going to do for her. Perhaps he thought about Peggy. Whatever he had in mind on those trips to Huntsville, it was all stewing and revolving in his head. He may have had nothing in mind. He may simply have been drinking and driving his truck. But one thing is clear: The life inside the big fancy house on Boulder Circle where Peggy Lowe's twin sister lived was exerting a powerful magnetism on James.

On Sunday Betty called Peggy.

"Where is the man you sent me?"

"Mr. White? He didn't show up?"

"Yes, he showed up. Long enough to take two hundred dollars from me."

"But he never came to the meetings?"

"Oh, goddamn it, Peggy . . ."

Betty had to stop and choke back what she felt like saying, mindful of her sister's sense of propriety.

"Look, Peggy, this man is just a worthless drunk, and he's taking you and everybody else he can get to for whatever he can get."

"I know he's bad," Peggy said, "but his daughter is in my friend's class, and I wanted to help . . ."

Betty was furious. "No, no, don't tell me about how you're going to help the son of a bitch, Peggy! He's a drunk, and he has no intention of letting you help him! You are not helping his family by giving him money. You are hurting them. He's like daddy! He's a worthless piece of shit!"

"Betty, I do not like for you to talk this way."

"You wait until I get my hands on the little son of a bitch! I want my two hundred dollars back, or I am damn well going to know the reason why! I want his phone number."

"Betty, maybe if I spoke to him . . ."

"I want his phone number, goddamn it, Peggy! That fucking little bastard is going to give me that money back!"

"Oh, my goodness, Betty. You speak so . . ."

"I'm sorry, Peggy. I am just so damned mad."

"All right. Here it is."

Peggy gave her the number. "Betty, I thought that, if I . . ."

"Peggy, I just am not going to discuss this with you now. I have to hang up. I just can't talk about things like this with you. You know that. We both know that. We shouldn't try. Good-bye, honey. I'll talk to you later in the week."

Betty began immediately making what would become a long series of phone calls to James's trailer. Each time, the phone was answered by a child or by a foggy-voiced adult male who claimed not to be James, saying Mr. White was not in at the moment. Each time Betty sat with the receiver at her ear, listening to the dial tone after the person speaking had hung up, she thought about the wretch at the other end. She could see him in her mind's eye, probably passed out in a pile of dirty clothes on the floor of the trailer with naked children stepping over him in search of food. She thought about how much money he had probably already clipped Peggy and Wayne for. She thought about her father. She slammed down the phone. Her anger became quiet and steely. She knew exactly what this little man was. She knew exactly what to tell him.

The Lowe home on Logan Martin Lake was busy that week. Peggy had extended one of her invitations to a person in need. This time, rather than bringing home flea-bitten homeless people she had found in the dump, Peggy invited a colleague and her daughter to come live with her for a few weeks.

Linda Vascocu (pronounced "Vaskew" in Alabama) was a single mother—an attractive, efficient sort who taught school at both the elementary and high school levels in Vincent and also owned her own small business. She was building a new house for herself and her young daughter. The date for completion of the house kept slipping, and she had already sold her own home. She had to move out just as the Talladega Stock Car Races were beginning—a world-class event in that sport—and there was not a single motel room available in the entire region.

Peggy had urged her to come stay with her family. Linda had explained she couldn't be sure when the builder would get her house ready for occupation. As usual, Peggy said it made absolutely no difference. They were used to having waifs and refugees in their home. Linda accepted, and she and her daughter moved in for what turned out to be a lengthy stay.

Linda did what she could to help with housework and cooking and even pitched in with Peggy to carry out a major cleaning and de-junking of the garage and basement. They had piled up the items that still could be used and stacked them in the garage. At some point recently, when James was after her for money, Peggy had told him he could come collect the items in the garage and possibly sell them.

On Tuesday, Stephanie became ill at school again. This time

Peggy had to leave her own class at the elementary school, go to the middle school, take Stephanie out, and get her to the doctor. The doctor still was not sure what was bothering Stephanie. She thought it could be an infection or it might simply be developmental, related to the changes taking place in a teenage body. She prescribed an antibiotic just to be on the safe side. With most of the day shot anyway, Peggy took Stephanie home.

Once at home, Stephanie felt much better. Peggy suggested that since she was experiencing a miraculous recovery, she might help her mother and Linda clean the house. Stephanie agreed and took a can of powdered cleanser with her to a bathroom to begin scrubbing.

Peggy was in the kitchen when Stephanie called to her that she thought she had breathed in some of the cleaning powder and was not feeling well as a result. Peggy sighed and called back, "Go out on the deck and get some fresh air." Peggy heard the door to the deck open and click shut.

The doorbell rang, and Linda Vascocu went to answer it. She came back a moment later with a look on her face.

"There is a Mr. White out here who says you told him he could have the things in the garage."

"The things in the garage?"

"That we stacked."

"Oh, yes." A maternal instinct was telling her to go check on Stephanie.

"I need to talk to him," she said, "but I can't do it now. Would you mind just telling him to go ahead and take the stuff?"

"Certainly."

Peggy walked over to the plate-glass window to check on Stephanie. She cried out! Stephanie was collapsed in a heap on the deck. Peggy threw the door open and rushed to her. She lifted her head, and Stephanie's eyes slowly blinked open.

"I really don't feel good," she whispered.

Peggy brought Stephanie back into the house, arranged her on the sofa, and then rushed to the phone. The doctor's nurse put the doctor on the phone immediately. The doctor listened grimly to what Peggy had to say, asked a couple of sharp questions, and then said, "All right, Peggy. I'm afraid this is quite serious. It's an allergic reaction to the shot, I'm sure, but it's a serious allergic reaction.

"I want you to call the Emergency Medical Service, tell them it's an emergency, but I want you to tell them that you are going to put Stephanie in the car and begin driving to meet the ambulance. Get her in the car right away and meet the ambulance halfway. They will call me from the ambulance, and I will handle it from there."

Linda helped Peggy get Stephanie into the car, and Peggy roared off, tires spitting gravel on the dirt driveway. Linda turned to go back into the house. From the garage, James gave her a smirking little bow.

The entire way to the hospital, Peggy bit back the fear that her daughter was going to die. She prayed to God to spare her. The EMS technicians began treating Stephanie on the way; her doctor met her at the hospital and completed the treatment; and by evening Stephanie was able to go home. Peggy, who had been composed and alert the entire time, was completely wrung out.

She called her adult son and daughter and asked them to come. The next day was Wednesday, May 20, 1992. Peggy called Betty early that morning.

"Please just come down here, Betty. I need you to be here now."

Betty had plans for the day, but she canceled them, threw some clothes in a bag, got in the BMW, and made the eighty-mile drive to Peggy's house.

She and James may have passed each other on the road. He had left the Talladega/Vincent area and was roaring north to Huntsville again in his pickup, getting stoned and ready to report for work.

When Betty had been at Peggy's house in Talladega for several hours, the telephone rang. Stephanie took the call. She said to her mother, "It's someone calling collect from Huntsville. She says his name is J.W."

Betty's ears pricked up.

Peggy took the phone from Stephanie.

"Mr. White," Peggy said, "whatever are you doing in Huntsville?"

"I come up here to do that work for your sister. I been calling her house, but they said she wasn't here."

"No, Mr. White, she's not, she's right here with me. But I don't think she wants you to do any work for her. She's very upset with you."

"With me?"

Betty couldn't stand it.

"Give me the phone. Peggy, give me the damned telephone."

"Mr. White, she wants to talk to you. Here she is."

Betty composed herself. "This is Mr. Carpenter?"

"This is James White, ma'am. I come up here to Huntsville to do that work your sister said you wanted done, but your maid or somebody said you wasn't in town. I come all the way up here."

"Where is my two hundred dollars?" Betty asked.

"Ma'am?"

"Don't *ma'am* me. I asked you a simple question. You came to Guntersville and took two hundred dollars from me . . ."

"Well, you give it to me . . ."

"I did not give it to you to go buy booze. I advanced it to you . . ."

"Well, I'm up here, ready to do the work. But if you never had no work or you changed your mind, well, then, fine. . . . "

"I had work. I had work for you. My sister gave you a map to find my house, didn't she?"

"Yes, ma'am."

"I have a note written out that's taped just inside my door, where I expected you to come in and get to work if I wasn't there. I think it's still there. So I had work for you. But the money I gave to you at Guntersville, I was advancing to you . . . do you understand an advance?"

"Yes, ma'am, I know what an advance is."

"I advanced it to you with the understanding you were going

to use it to stay in a motel and come attend and Alcoholics Anonymous meeting. . . ."

"I didn't buy no booze, ma'am."

"Well, good. Then you can give me that money back right now, I guess. You can go drop it at my house."

"Well I cain't really do that."

"No you *cain't,* can you? Because it's already gone, isn't it, Mr. Carpenter?"

"Yes, ma'am. I had expenses coming up here to do your work . . ."

"You're not going to do any work for me, you lying son of a bitch. And you're not going to do any work for my sister. You're not going to call my sister ever again, and you are going to get that two hundred dollars back to me, or you are going to go talk to the police about it."

James was standing at a pay phone in the main shopping center at the bottom of the mountain, below Betty's neighborhood. The teeth were moving behind the beard, his head was shaking, and the eyes were flickering back and forth. He was stuttering fast, licking his lips, and breathing in little gasps.

"I don't think you understand, ma'am, your sister can tell you I been having a lot of problems, my wife done lef' me for my bes' friend, and I had money problems, and she's been he'ping me with them. . . ."

"No, no, you're not having problems, Mr. Carpenter, you are a problem. You are *the* problem. I understand exactly. I understand exactly what you are. You are a worthless little shit, a drunk, a chiseler, and a con man. And I am telling you exactly what you are going to do. You are going to get that fucking money back to me, and you are going to stay the fuck away from me and my sister, or I am going to get your lying white trash ass thrown in jail."

She slammed down the phone.

James hung up the phone.

Betty spent the night in Talladega. Stephanie was better. Betty and Linda Vascocu drove to Vincent to get ice cream and rent a videotape. The next day was Thursday, May 21, 1992. That morning, early, Betty drove the eighty miles back up to Huntsville to finish her preparations for the weekend Santa Fe trip with Jack.

While Betty was driving back up to Huntsville from the Talladega/Vincent area, Janine Russell and her man friend were driving his daughter's car to Alabaster to get it fixed. She was telling him how wild James White had been all week and how he was talking about doing a murder, and he was telling her she needed to talk to the police.

Betty had more on her mind that Thursday morning than merely shopping for Santa Fe. That night she and Jack were helping throw a fund-raiser for Tim Morgan, a candidate for district attorney, at the home of another doctor.

When Betty pulled into the driveway at 2700 Boulder Circle shortly before noon, James was nearby, watching.

FOUR

HE MUST HAVE BEEN IN THE WOODS. HE COULD NOT HAVE been parked on Boulder Circle or he would have been noticed by the neighbors, who probably would have called the police. He could not have been parked lower on the mountain, on Chandler, because he would not have recognized Betty or her car when she drove by. So he had to be in the woods.

Betty's son Trey had been at home all morning studying. He had a short shift to work that afternoon in Jack's office, and then he had to go take his final examination for the semester.

When Betty had first asked if her son could come live with them and work for Jack while finishing college, Jack had responded enthusiastically. That two of his own sons had failed to complete college was a major source of disappointment. During Trey's time in the house, he and Jack had become close. Tall, handsome, with sandy hair swept back over a high forehead, Trey was more serious and thoughtful than most young men his age. He and Jack could talk.

When Betty arrived, Trey asked if he and she could go to lunch together. They often ate with Jack, either at home or at the hospital, but Jack had already called to say he would not be eating lunch that day. On this occasion, Betty really didn't have time for lunch either, but she did have one sticky task to accomplish. Trey had been behaving as if he assumed he was invited on the trip to Santa Fe. She was going to have to break it to him that he really was not invited. She and Jack needed to be alone in a new and distant place, cut off from all the habits, haunts, and obligations of their daily lives. Perhaps lunch was the way to broach it.

Betty said she was at a dead run, trying to complete some last-minute errands, but, if Trey was willing to follow her in his own car, perhaps they could eat together at the mall.

James was able to cut back through the woods and get into his pickup in time to pick them up and follow, as Betty and Trey drove down Garth Mountain to Parkway City Mall on the flats below.

Betty and Trey went into a music store in the mall, where Trey bought some CDs. Betty stopped at a women's clothing store and hurriedly purchased a casual dress. Then the two of them crossed the vast parking lot of the mall and ate lunch together at McDonald's.

James was very tired. He had not slept, having spent the previous night driving, drinking, smoking dope, and taking pills. It was probably at this point that he visited the Chick-Fil-A fast-food restaurant in the mall.

He needed to go somewhere to get some sleep. The nearest motel, straight down Memorial Parkway from the mall, was an aging Ramada Inn. The motel was undergoing extensive renovation and was home to one of the city's most popular restaurants. (By sheer coincidence, the woman who ran the motel's catering department was Julia Wilson—Jack's ex-wife.)

James chose the motel because it was the one nearest him when he got tired of stalking Betty Wilson and her son at the mall that day. He checked in at 12:47 P.M. and paid the $32.35 room rent in cash.

John Self, the night clerk, gave James White an appraising once-over and asked to see his driver's license. James gave it to him without hesitation and watched without interest while Self took it to a copying machine and made a photocopy of it, which he stapled to James's registration form. Then James went to his room.

He dozed. He drank. He made a few phone calls, including a

couple of calls to Betty Wilson's house. The machine there answered the phone, but James did not speak. On one occasion, he may have mumbled something to a housekeeper, but by then his speech was so clouded and slurred that she probably just hung up on him.

The fund-raiser for Tim Morgan went smoothly that night. Betty and Jack knew the right kind of people—people with money who had generally liberal Democratic leanings—to produce a nice fat little nest egg for the Morgan campaign.

When the crowd was buzzing with conversation and cheer, Betty took Morgan by the arm, led him to the front of her friend's living room and clinked a glass for quiet. Morgan made a brief, suitably modest speech, and soon a pile of checks was growing on the mahogany library table near the door.

After the party, the checks were counted and placed in a blue bank bag, which Betty took home with her. It was her job to make the deposit in the Morgan campaign account at the bank the next day and take the receipt to campaign headquarters.

Early that morning, Trey slipped into Jack's room and told him he was not going to Santa Fe with them. He was joining some buddies for a drive to the Florida beaches instead.

Jack and Betty ate breakfast together and then set off on their separate rounds—Jack to his office and Betty on a hectic day of errands.

Jack and Betty met again for lunch at home. Jack told Betty he had to go back to his office to tie up a few loose ends. Assuming that meant he was going to stay at the office until late evening, Betty set out to complete her errands.

At 5:00 P.M. that day, Betty remembered she hadn't taken care of the bank deposit for the Tim Morgan campaign. It was Friday, and the drive-through window at the bank would still be open. She hurried back to Boulder Circle to pick up the blue bank bag.

When she opened the front door, James was upstairs in Jack's room. He didn't remember later what he had felt at that moment because he was out of his mind on booze and drugs. But he probably felt a rush of fear and pleasure. Most burglars, after they have been caught and dried out, report that being inside a house with the owner always thrills them—fills them with a deeply sexual sense of power and tension, made more delicious by the foamy edge of adrenaline.

But as quickly as she was in, she was back out. He moved to a front window and saw her carrying the blue bank bag to her car, then disappearing quickly down the hill.

At 5:15, still at the office as Betty had assumed he would be, Jack made another phone call, this time to the home of Pam Hide. She had been outside mowing the lawn. Her short red curls were plastered to her forehead and she was still breathing hard when she picked up the phone.

Her husband sometimes did technical and electrical work for Jack Wilson's practice. He had repaired an old dental-chair base but had not yet returned it because Jack had been unable to decide whether he wanted it back.

"I've decided I'm going to give them that chair base to ship to Brazil," he said on the phone. He often donated used equipment to a group that did missionary work in Brazil.

"All right," she said. "I'll tell him."

"He can bring it back here and leave it at the office."

"Well, he'll want to do that Monday when he's off. Will anybody be there?"

"I'll tell you what, Pam; there's an office just next door to us that I happen to know will have people in it on Monday. I will leave a key with them."

According to his habit, Jack scratched a note as he spoke. "Hide. 17:15. 22 May." The rest of it was legible only to him. He hung up the phone. He stuffed the note loosely in a pants pocket. Then he left for home.

James went downstairs and looked around. He went back upstairs and pulled open some drawers. He saw nothing that interested him. He climbed the stairs again and went back into Jack's room.

He pulled open a closet door, and an array of strange garments spilled out at his feet. It was Jack Wilson's "Adventure" closet, filled with helmets, wigs, capes, and swords.

James kicked furiously at the wigs and helmets to get them off his foot.

The phone rang next to Jack's bed. The machine did not answer. The phone rang and rang.

"Shut up," James muttered, first to himself, and then again more loudly to the phone itself. When it continued to ring, he lurched over to it and used something, possibly the Sharpe knife, to hack the phone cord in half. The phone continued to ring in the other rooms.

He staggered over to a glass-front gun case. The door fell open easily. Inside was a single gun—a .38 caliber revolver in a wooden pistol box. Jack had bought it for Betty for protection. Next to it was a box of ammunition—.38 special bullets of a flat-tipped variety for target shooting, called wadcutters because of the neat round hole they make in paper targets. James took the pistol in one hand and was stuffing some of the bullets in a pocket.

He froze.

The front door was opening again.

Jack came in, closed the door, walked through the house to the stairs leading down to the basement level, and went down to Trey's room. Standing against a wall next to the closet door, Jack found one of Trey's baseball bats—a thirty-four-inch bronze-colored aluminum bat with brown wrapping on the grip and a red EASTON insignia. He carried the bat back upstairs and returned to the front hall, where Betty had left some Tim Morgan yard signs just inside the door.

James at this point was probably still inside Jack's room but may have come forward to the door in order to listen down the stairwell. He may even have walked out of the room and down the thick Persian carpet in the corridor to the head of the stairs.

Jack went out into the front yard, carrying a campaign sign

and the aluminum baseball bat. The boys in the side yard, who were just breaking up their golf practice, stopped for a moment and watched their neighbor at one of his typically clumsy exercises—trying to hammer a wood and cardboard campaign sign into the unyielding sod of his front yard with a baseball bat instead of the more conventional tool, a hammer.

Jack managed to get the sign loosely anchored in the yard but at a list. Satisfied with his handiwork, he stood up and backed off to admire it. The boys turned away from him, split up, and walked toward their homes. Jack walked back inside with the bat in his hand.

He must have laid the bat down on the floor or leaned it against the wall. He kicked off his loosely fitting shoes and nudged them together on the floor with a toe. Then he took out his wallet and put it on top of the shoes. He slipped off his watch and placed it on top of the wallet.

He heard something.

Jack Wilson must have picked up the bat at this moment. Carrying it, he climbed the stairs in his bare feet.

Either James was still in Jack's room, or he had fled from the head of the stairs to Jack's room when he realized Jack was coming up.

Jack climbed the stairs and rounded the corner of the railing at the top of the stairs. He walked down the Persian carpet and turned into Betty's room. He must have gone all the way into the room and then turned to come back out.

When he came out, James was facing him.

According to what James said later, Jack shouted or moved forward. He did something, either verbally or physically, that penetrated James's thick fog of drugs and booze and registered on his brain as a challenge.

James grabbed the bat, yanked it from Jack's hands, lifted it, and brought it down as hard and as fast as he could across the top of Jack's skull. The rigid bronze limb of the bat came down flat, slicing through six layers of scalp to white bone, splitting the skull like an eggshell along a straight line, with a fringe of tiny hairlike fractures flashing out from both sides of the main crack. A small amount of blood sprayed from the blow itself, and then a split second later the blood vessels of the scalp began pumping furiously, and a thick dark sheet of blood slid down over Jack's face like a mask.

Jack was still on his feet but stunned. He gathered himself and attempted to punch James in the face, but James, who had already recoiled, brought the bat back around, hissing through the air in a long arc. The bat smashed into the folded fist of Jack's delicate surgeon's hand, crumpling the bones like dry sticks.

James lifted the bat again.

Jack raised his right arm, the smashed hand hanging loosely at the end with a red and white bouquet of bone splinters protruding from the skin. He held his forearm in front of his face to parry the thrust. James brought the bat down with a ferocious jumping blow. The force of the bat splintered the ulna—the bone on the inside of the forearm, where the arm was turned up to protect—and sent jagged shards of bone through the flesh. The arm fell limply at Jack's side.

The bat came down again and crashed into Jack's forehead, splitting the skull in another long hairy line from front to back.

James lifted the bat again.

Jack raised his left forearm to shield himself.

James brought the bat down and shattered the left ulna.

Jack was still standing, facing James, both arms twisted and limp at his sides.

James lifted the bat again and brought it down, smashing the collarbone.

Jack slumped to his knees before James, his face supplicant. At this point, the brain swelling was already so severe that Jack may have been slipping in and out of consciousness. James lifted the bat and brought it down in a ferocious chopping blow. The bat smashed into the top center of the skull, this time sending up a syrupy splash of blood.

Now with each new blow Jack's head bobbed back, fell forward, lolled and rolled. James raised the bat and smashed the skull again on the top right side. The sheets of blood pouring from Jack's scalp coated the bat and James's hands.

James raised the bat and smashed it against the top left side of Jack's skull. Jack's right eyeball bulged partially out of its socket, held barely in place by the ocular muscles.

James raised the bat and smashed it against the top right side of the skull. The left eyeball bulged.

James lifted the bat and smashed straight down on the skull again.

James lifted the bat and smashed the skull again.

He lifted it again and chopped down into the skull yet another time.

Not even slacking his pace, James lifted the bat again and swung it down into the skull in still another crushing blow.

On his knees before James, splintered arms dangling at his sides, black with blood, Jack swayed far backward, then forward.

James changed his position, moving to a sideways batter's stance. He brought the bat around in a long, fast full swing that caught Jack in the shoulder. The blow lifted Jack's body and dumped him over sprawling sideways, twisted up on one hip on the floor.

James fell to his knees over the body. Jack's heart was still beating. James grasped Jack's throat, which was greasy with blood. He choked with both hands until he felt a small bone inside snap. Then he reached to his hip, grabbed his knife, unfolded the blade, lifted it, and stabbed the blade down savagely into Jack's chest, a few inches below the right nipple. He yanked the knife back out of Jack's chest and stabbed it down again into his upper abdomen, this time sawing a bit with the knife, tearing through the stomach and pancreas and hacking into two major veins.

Then James stopped.

Jack was not dead.

But James was done.

He lifted himself up from Jack.

With every failing beat of Jack's heart, blood bubbled up feebly from the knife holes James had made.

James ran back out through the lower level and garage door of the house, across the backyard and down through the woods, leaving a strong scent trail behind him. He drove his pickup back to Vincent, where he met his brother. At some point in the next twenty-four hours, James's clothes, which had to be soaked in Jack's blood, were buried, burned, or otherwise destroyed.

Some years earlier, in a crisis of overcrowding, the homicide section of the Huntsville Police Department had been banished to second-floor walkup quarters in an aging brick commercial building at 120 Holmes Avenue, several blocks from the building housing the rest of the department. A small sign out in front announced that the CRIMINAL INVESTIGATION DIVISION was a tenant of the building. In the dimly lighted hallways upstairs, cardboard file boxes were piled on bouncy wooden floors. The floors were bare in patches and covered elsewhere with an unpredictable patchwork of musty shag carpeting. Some of the doors had buzzer locks and peepholes, but burly men in boxy suits with big guns under their arms moved about casually, sometimes using file boxes to wedge a door open for air. The effect of the sign out front and the building itself and the offices with the doors propped open was so informal and down-at-the-heels that the whole place looked less like a police department than like the set for a black-and-white 1940s private eye movie.

Mickey Lee Brantley's entire life had been a dogged pursuit of the path that led straight here. He left high school and joined the Marines in 1972, served two four-year terms, came home to Alabama, and went to work for the Huntsville Police Department. Short, ruddy-faced, burly with close-cropped hair and small steely eyes, fourteen years out of the Marines, he still looked like a marine sergeant who had grown a small fastidiously trimmed mustache while on leave. He was a man of deep feelings about the way the world should be—a Pentecostal minister in his spare time, married to a pretty woman with long, very curly red hair, father of two small children. Like many police officers, he was drawn to police work as a ministry. He was as tough as nails. He had seen it all. But he was not cynical. He had come to these seedy little offices on Holmes Avenue because he intended to help set things right. Whatever it took.

He was working an afternoon shift. The streets outside were dark. He sat at a battered metal desk trying to butt his way through a small hill of paperwork, when he got the call. It was 10:06 P.M., May 22, 1991. The call was a code 1077—deceased person on scene. The first 911 call had been logged at 9:30 P.M. The address was 2700 Boulder Circle. Even as he walked down the creaking staircase to go to his car, his mind was beginning to make the calculation. Boulder Circle. A rich part of town.

He pulled up at the scene at 10:23. Neighbors in nightclothes stood staring from lighted porches. Blue-and-white beacons looped around lazily from the tops of police cars parked out in front of a large brick house at the very top of the street. All of the lights inside the house were blazing white. Flashes of white light snapping across one of the upstairs windows—photographic strobes—told Brantley where the body was. Yellow crime-scene tape was stretched across the front of the house. A blue uniform was posted in the open front door. An ambulance stood at the curb. The medics were lounging against the sides of the ambulance, waiting for the body. Next door a middle-aged woman was in the arms of neighbors, wailing uncontrollably.

In the front yard, hammered into the grass at a crooked angle, was a campaign poster for Tim Morgan.

Before the current D.A. fired him, Morgan had been one of the assistant D.A.s whom many of the higher-ups in the police department liked to deal with. Smart, easygoing, a Southern gentleman with just the right touch of good old boy, at age forty-nine he was a man who knew the ropes in the Madison County Courthouse, a deal cutter, a case closer, a pragmatist. He wore a salt-and-pepper beard under a slow smile and had humorous brown eyes. Tim Morgan was thought of by most people as a good man who knew how it was. Not really Mickey Brantley's cup of tea.

The current D.A., Mo Brooks, wasn't entirely Mickey's cup

either, but he was closer. In many ways, he defied long-held traditions. He was a Republican, a Mormon, a Duke graduate with a dual degree in economics and mathematics—a bespectacled number cruncher who seldom smiled and never regarded what happened in the criminal justice system as a game. He was hell-bent on eradicating crime, which Mickey liked. He had come into office on a promise not to plea-bargain with criminals. Nobody at the courthouse liked this—they all said he was just clogging the system with petty offenders. Brooks had been appointed by an unpopular Republican governor earlier that year to fill the unexpired term of a man who had left office to run for the Congress. As soon as Brooks arrived to take over the D.A.'s office, several of the top assistants resigned. Tim Morgan had stayed on until Brooks fired him, at which time Morgan had announced he would run to unseat Mo Brooks in November. The betting around the courthouse was that Mo Brooks, at age thirty-eight, was about to become one of the youngest shortest-term D.A.s in the county's history.

When he saw the crooked Tim Morgan sign in the crime scene yard, Mickey Brantley's mental calculation ratcheted up one more notch. Rich neighborhood. Man dead. Pro-Morgan household.

Brantley climbed out of his car cautiously, so as not to attract the attention of the media people who were beginning to arrive. He walked up slowly to the patrol sergeant who was standing out at the curb in front of the yellow tape. They barely nodded to each other.

"Would you please give me an idea what I'm fixin' to see in there," Brantley said.

The sergeant's report was brief and basic. Man dead upstairs, badly beaten, stabbed, obvious foul play. No forced entry. Some stuff ajar here and there. Television sets and videocassette players untouched, jewelry untouched, no indication simple robbery. Phone line cut, indicating attacker had been waiting. No one else in the house. Dead man the owner. Call came from his wife. She's the one bawling next door, knows nothing, came home, found the body, ran next door, 911. Nothing obvious on grounds. House and scene sealed, Crime Scene Investigator Glenn Nunnally already inside working the scene.

Brantley walked past the blue uniform standing in the doorway and stepped into the foyer of the house. Glenn Nunnally, a short, plump, mild-mannered fellow in his mid-thirties, nodded hello.

"Mick, how's it goin'?"

"Good, Glenn. How you?"

"Fine."

"What's this?" he asked, nodding down toward a pair of shoes at his feet. A watch and a wallet had been set on top of the shoes.

"Don't know yet," Nunnally said.

"Where do I want to go in here?"

"You will want to go up the stairs over there."

"Body's still here."

"Yessir."

Brantley climbed to the top of the stairs. Nunnally came up behind him to answer questions. Brantley leaned over the body. He needed only a few seconds to see what was interesting.

"B'lieve I may go speak with the wife," he said.

"Yup," Nunnally said.

Brantley walked back out the front door, crossed the yard, and stepped under the yellow tape at one end of the property. A television reporter started to move toward him, but Brantley shook his head, held up a palm, and gave the reporter a look that stopped him and his cameraperson in their tracks.

A man and woman were comforting the lady, who was still sobbing and weeping. The man stepped forward to speak to Brantley.

"I'm Don Seija. She came here and used our phone."

Brantley nodded and spoke to the crying lady.

"I'm Mickey Brantley, Criminal Investigation Division, City of Huntsville Police Department. I would like to have a few words with you if that's possible, ma'am."

It was difficult for her to stop sobbing long enough to speak.

Brantley nodded inquisitively toward the inside of the Seijas' house, and the wife of the owner urged him to come in.

Brantley said to the crying widow: "Why don't you come inside and sit down with me in here for a while, ma'am, and just help me with a few things, if you don't mind." He went in and walked to a sofa.

She took a seat across from him in the large formally furnished living room. Brantley began to take notes on a small pad. She said her name was Betty Wilson. The man on the floor was her husband, a doctor named Jack Wilson.

"Officer," she gasped, leaning forward on her chair, "is he still alive?"

"Is he still alive, ma'am?"

"Is he?"

Brantley made a small irritated smile, almost a grimace. "Well, no, ma'am. I'm sorry. He's not."

She collapsed into another fit of sobbing. The Seijas rushed to comfort her.

"Ma'am, when did you find him?"

She wiped her eyes and looked up. "I . . . I found him just before I called. I came home. It was after nine, I guess. Probably almost nine-thirty."

"Did you move him or touch him?"

"No."

"Was he alive when you found him?"

"I don't know. I think he may have been."

"Did you normally keep the house locked?"

"No, not usually, with all of us coming and going."

"What room was that he was coming out of?"

"It looked like he was in the doorway of my room."

"Your room?"

"My bedroom."

"That's not his bedroom?"

"No. His is across the hall."

"Where had you been up until then?"

"Where had I been?"

"Where had you been?"

"Well, I attended a meeting at eight P.M."

"What kind of a meeting, ma'am?"

"It was an Alcoholics Anonymous meeting."

She said the A.A. meeting had started at eight. Before that she had gone to dinner with a friend from A.A. Before that she had attended another A.A. meeting. Before that she had been at Tim Morgan campaign headquarters. Before that she had attended another A.A. meeting.

"Who else lives in the house?"

"My son Trey."

"Where is he?"

"I'm not sure. He left."

"He left, ma'am?"

"Yes."

"When?"

"Early this morning."

"Where?"

"To the beach. With some friends. I think I have . . . I think I have a number where they'll be staying in Tallahassee on the way. I'll call him."

"Yes. I need to talk to him."

"You do?"

"Mrs. Wilson, do you and the doctor have any other children?"

She provided a list of the names of the other children and where they could be reached. He asked her to provide the names of housekeepers, workmen, any other people who might be familiar with the house, and she did. She did not mention James White in her first list, but in a later conversation, she did name him, along with a few others she had failed to include in the first list. She explained that Mr. White was a carpenter who had been recommended to her by her sister, who lived in the Talladega/Vincent area eighty miles south.

On Saturday, Mickey Brantley learned that a day before the murder, the Madison County sheriff in Huntsville had passed on a tip that a rich person, possibly a doctor or a doctor's wife, was going to be killed, according to information from a rural sheriff's department in central Alabama. There was some vague information in the tip about the victim or someone near the victim having a twin sister who was involved with the threat maker somehow. Working with an associate, Detective Harry Renfroe, Brantley ran the tip back to the Shelby County Sheriff's Department, where a deputy had taken the original statement from one Janine Russell, who claimed to be a drinking companion of the man who had made the threats. When contacted by his superiors in Shelby County, the deputy said he had Janine Russell's name and phone number but did not have the name of the man she was informing on.

Brantley explained to Shelby County that a murder had in fact taken place and that it was imperative that the man who had made the threats be rounded up and questioned. At that point, however, the tip from Shelby County was only a peripheral consideration.

The murder had none of the earmarks of a burglary. It had all the earmarks of a crime of passion. Brantley and Renfroe were devoting most of their energies to an inventory of all family members and associates who might have had a reason or opportunity to kill the doctor.

The newspapers, television, and radio stations were immediately off and running with the story. It was exactly the kind of against-the-grain murder story that would catch people by surprise—a rich doctor, sort of a media personality in his own right, who had called talk shows and had been interviewed about his practical jokes, savagely murdered in the heart of a neighborhood generally considered to be a safe bastion of privilege.

Almost from the moment the first news crew arrived and saw the Tim Morgan campaign poster hammered crookedly into the yard, the story had an immediate political spin. The murdered doctor was a political supporter of the man challenging the district attorney for his job. What did it mean? How would it play?

. . .

The week before the murder, James had worked for a few days at a barbecue place in a small town near Vincent. He had failed to show up again for work during the week of booze and drugs leading up to the murder, but by Sunday morning, forty-eight hours after the killing, James had come down from his high, was halfway sobered up, and was beginning to think about keeping straight for a while. He also needed money.

He called the restaurant and pleaded with them to give him one last chance.

"I been having a lot of trouble with my ex-wife over taking care of my chid'run which is why I ain't been there, but it's all worked out now, and I sure wish y'all could find it in your heart to let me come back and work for y'all."

They agreed to give him one more chance. He was at work at the restaurant on Sunday when Shelby County deputies came in and arrested him. Janine had told them where to find him.

In the initial interrogations, James was told that Janine Russell had ratted him out, that the police knew everything, and that they had proof of what he had done. He was enraged that, as he saw it, he had been betrayed by yet another woman in his life.

Over the course of the next twenty-four hours in custody, under fairly relaxed questioning by Shelby County investigators, James continued to deny that he had murdered Jack Wilson, but he admitted that he knew Peggy Lowe, Dr. Wilson's wife's twin sister. He may have admitted that he had been inside the Wilson house, but if he did he quickly offered implausible alibis to explain why. The more he talked, the guiltier he sounded.

Mickey Brantley and Harry Renfroe were continuing to work hard on the theory that someone in the family or connected with the family had been involved in the murder. It was conjecture, but it was conjecture that made sense, supported by their long years of experience. The circumstances in the house did not fit a robbery. Even a panicked drug addict would have grabbed something from the house instead of walking away from tens of thousands of dollars' worth of easily pawned or fenced merchandise.

What they learned on Sunday, May 24, served to make them even more keen.

Harry Renfroe, Jr., a handsome swashbuckling kind of a man with thick, dark, curly hair and a roguish smile, was more a man of the world than Mickey Brantley. Still in his mid-forties, he had been on the force twenty-five years, the last twelve of which had been in homicide. If Brantley was an ideological crusader of the Mo Brooks school, Renfroe tended to be more of a pragmatist of the Tim Morgan school. But they got along well and knew how to get the work done. They agreed that they would conduct the first interview with the dead man's wife jointly, in the offices of the CID on Holmes Avenue.

By Sunday, some thirty-six hours after the body had been found, Betty Wilson seemed to have recaptured her composure. If anything, as the questioning progressed, a certain steel crept into her voice.

In questioning her about people who might have a motive to kill her husband, Renfroe asked her if she had ever had an affair or sexual liaison outside her marriage. She said calmly that she had. He asked her with whom. She said there had been several.

Brantley and Renfroe then asked her to name each of the men with whom she had had sexual intercourse while married to Dr. Wilson. She seemed willing enough to supply the names. In fact, she did not cry or even blush when they pumped her for more information. She told them about the affairs as if she were telling them about trips she had made to the grocery store.

"Did your husband also have affairs?" they asked.

"No, I don't think so. I'm sure not."

Where did she meet the men? they wondered.

She met most of them at A.A. meetings, she said.

How long ago had she stopped drinking?

It had been almost six years.

Did she do drugs?

She had, but not for six years.

Why did she keep having the affairs, even after she quit drinking?

"My husband was impotent."

In winding up the interview, Harry Renfroe said, "Now, Mrs. Wilson, if you remember any names of men you had sex with that may have slipped your mind here today, or anything else you think of that might help us solve the murder of your husband, you be sure and give us a call, y'hear?"

The conviction that there was a personal, inside connection to this killing grew stronger at CID headquarters in the old brick commercial building on Holmes Avenue. All signs pointed to it.

Jack Wilson's murder was a crazy murder. He had been hammered into wreckage, choked and stabbed. It was the kind of corpse in which experienced homicide detectives recognize something terrible—a thing polite society does not want to know about.

The joy of killing.

Jack Wilson's killing was an ecstatic murder. That kind of murder doesn't always have a personal connection. It can happen that some kid in black clothes with tattoos on his forehead wanders in for no reason and then goes over the top. But more often than not the emotion and passion that go into this kind of killing have a hard-wired connection somewhere in the life of the house. This body looked like that kind of connection. There were hatred and sex in the way Jack Wilson was killed.

His wife was a toughie. A rich bitch toughie. With a sex thing. She looked two homicide cops in the eye and told them about all the men she had had intercourse with, and when they asked her why, she said her husband was impotent, as if she were telling them what she cooked the poor bastard for breakfast on Saturdays. She was sexually eccentric.

The close ties between Jack and Betty Wilson and district attorney candidate Tim Morgan meant that the case might have some kind of political ramifications, especially if one or both of the candidates decided to make an issue of it. Political ramifications could work either way for the cops on the case—make it high profile, or make it trouble.

All of that aside, the simple physical facts of the case—no forced entry, no theft, the savagery of the attack—meant that it was natural and smart for the Huntsville homicide cops at least to give the Betty Wilson connection a good run while the case was still warm.

By Tuesday, May 26, Brantley and Renfroe had begun to put some more detailed pieces in place. According to the Shelby County tipster, the man the Shelby County sheriff had in his jail, one James Dennison White, had said he was involved somehow with the twin sister. By now, Brantley and Renfroe knew that Betty Wilson had a twin sister named Peggy Lowe, who lived in Talladega, a few miles from Vincent.

The man down in Vincent was admitting or halfway admitting that he had made trips to Betty Wilson's house in Huntsville and that he had talked on the telephone many times to Peggy Lowe. Betty Wilson, meanwhile, had told police that one of the people who might have had access to the house was a carpenter from Vincent. He had been in town the day before the murder, while she was not in town. She said she had fired him before he ever came to the house.

It was already clear that the man in jail in Shelby County was going to turn out to have a long criminal record. Shelby County said he had the look and speech and attitude of a lifelong scum-rat. He was too good to ignore.

By noon Tuesday, Mickey Brantley was in Shelby County, closeted in an interrogation room with James White.

None of what White had said to Shelby County had been taped, and there were no notes, which was just as well. Everything he had said so far had been jumbled and confused, clouded by booze and drugs. It would be necessary to get it all down properly and in the right order and form.

Brantley began by saying he knew that White was in a bad situation at the moment, and he wanted White to know he was not unsympathetic with his plight.

"I had a lot of trouble lately," White said. "I had family problems, beginning with my wife, and then we had trouble over the kids. And now Janine Russell is telling stories on me. The story of it is, women is the whole reason I am where I am right now."

"Well, I know women can get a man into serious trouble, James," Brantley said. "But you need to tell me the whole story. How did you know Peggy Lowe, and how did you know Betty Wilson?"

At this point, three full days into sobriety, James was beginning to emerge from the pall of booze and drugs. He nattered and stammered as he spoke to Brantley, but he listened very closely to what Brantley had to say. James was beginning to come into focus.

James was home at last. He was a lifelong prisoner. The only order he had ever known in his entire life was the order of jails, prisons, mental hospitals, the army and the army stockade. In this world—his world—he knew his way around.

Brantley explained that James was looking at the death penalty. Or something less than that. James didn't need Brantley to draw a picture. James began immediately sounding the waters for a deal.

"I might know some things. I might not. But I got a family, too, you know. I ain't just shit, just like a dog or something. I have kids I have to think about. I might be able to hep with some things, but I have to be took care of, too, you know. I don't know if I should trust you or not."

James said that he could talk only if Brantley would agree to turn off his tape recorder. Later, if they came to some sort of an accommodation with each other, Brantley could turn it back on.

Brantley agreed.

James said that he could not talk unless Brantley agreed not to take notes. Brantley said he had to take some notes, but he would agree not to take notes word for word at first, just jotting down general things to jog his memory, until they had come to an understanding.

James agreed.

So now they were doing business.

This kind of business, this brand of negotiation, this was James business. This was his true trade in his real marketplace, cutting deals with authority figures who had caught him red-handed at something. It was the one position in life where James Dennison White could honestly claim experience and expertise.

If there was any one principle that seemed to hold true consistently in these affairs, it was that the authorities were almost never very interested in James himself. James, after all, was just James. The only thing a law officer accomplished by collaring him yet another time was to take up valuable jail space.

The only way for James himself to become interesting was to offer the authority figures someone bigger and more important than himself. The trick was to listen very hard and figure out what or whom they were looking for.

These were things James always had understood. Sitting on a junked-out car seat on the front porch of the abandoned house next to his trailer, drinking with his buddies at the top of the hill in Vincent, James knew that the people down below on the parking lot of the First Baptist Church looked down on him. But he also looked down on them.

He made more money than most of them. He was more free. More wild. And they were always so easy to con, these townspeople. Just set them off against each other.

James was willing to start with little things and work his way up patiently, but Brantley was impatient. Not very far into the interview, he made his leap of faith. He pressed hard for a full confession by telling James that there was a lady up in Huntsville who was telling the police that James had been up there the day of the murder.

The precise chemistry of the first Mickey Brantley interview with James White cannot now be known because James did not make a full, formal taped confession until five days after the first interview. In the interval, the tape recorder appears to have been turned off and on at key moments.

Mickey Brantley was not necessarily shutting the tape recorder off and on in order to prevent people later on from knowing what James really said during those long difficult conversations. James himself was insisting that the tape recorder be turned off at certain points, while he gathered his thoughts and sounded Brantley out. In order to keep James talking, Brantley had to accommodate him to some degree.

In fact, given the outcome of the process, it may even be unfair to view Brantley as having been the dominant participant during these interrogations. It is just as reasonable to interpret it all as chemistry between an honest, well-intentioned police officer who was not Sherlock Holmes and a very clever, very dishonest, manipulative little psychopath, who was actually running the show.

According to Brantley's rough notes—some of which he claimed later in court to have lost—James began by providing details of what he said was a murder-for-hire plot, in which the twins had contracted with him to kill Jack Wilson.

It seems implausible that he could have continued denying to Brantley that he had killed Jack Wilson while providing Brantley with a gradually growing stream of corroborating detail. Since there are no tapes, however, and only rough notes—and only some of those—there is no way for anyone to know exactly what went on between the two men during those crucially important first few days when they were feeling each other out and working toward a deal.

Somewhere along the line, long before the tape recorder came on for the first time, James White figured out that the police were very interested in the bitch, Betty Wilson, and her sister, Mizrus Peggy Lowe.

If he was to implicate them somehow, there were logical questions that would have to be answered in order to make James's story work. How would he ever have met Betty Wilson in the first place? What would his motive have been? What would her motive have been? How would a wretch like James White ever have worked his way into the confidences of a rich lady like Betty Wilson? When and where would they have met, and did they ever transact the kind of hand-to-hand, eyeball-to-eyeball business with each other that would make Betty Wilson prosecutable as a co-conspirator under Alabama law?

In the notes Mickey Brantley produced in court and in his court testimony, James's story in the first few days of interviews was this: James White told Mickey Brantley he had been having an affair with Peggy Lowe. He said they had never actually had sexual intercourse, but there had been moments, both at the school and at her home when her husband was away, when she had not been able to resist a few "stolen kisses" with James.

It seems impossible that Brantley could have looked at James's snaggled brown teeth and matted beard and not shuddered at the thought of someone stealing even a single kiss from him. But the story was in its early stages. There would be plenty of time to iron out the details. And Mickey Brantley didn't know Peggy Lowe. She could be anybody. In his life, he had seen everything.

James said he had been in Huntsville on Friday morning to do the job. He said he had experienced a crisis of conscience and had begun driving back to Vincent in the early morning, but he had started drinking and taking pills on the way. When he got high, his resolve returned to him, and he turned around and returned to Huntsville.

At some time between 2:00 and 3:00 P.M., he said, he met Betty Wilson at the Parkway City Mall for instructions. Then he went to the Wilson house. At first he said he did not remember killing Dr. Wilson and thought Dr. Wilson was still alive when he fled the house. He said he fled on foot through the woods and walked back to Parkway City Mall, where his truck was parked. He drove immediately back to Vincent and then went out socializing with his brother and a friend his brother had met in a school he was attending.

He said he had been wearing blue jeans and some kind of a T-shirt.

As soon as the first interview in the Shelby County jail was completed, Brantley was allowed to rearrest White under the jurisdiction of the Huntsville Police Department and remove him from the jail.

He drove White from the jail to Vincent, where they visited the rusty little trailer next to the tumbledown house at the top of the hill above Peggy Lowe's church. They searched together through White's clothing for the garments he had worn at the murder scene.

Already, on the first day of their acquaintance and barely three days after the murder, Mickey Lee Brantley and James Dennison White were a team.

They were unable to find any of the clothes he said he had worn that day except for a pair of shoes, which Brantley put in the car. James led Brantley over to the broken porch at the front of the little house next to the trailer. He pried up a floorboard and nodded. Brantley reached in and pulled out a hard object, wrapped in a rag, which his hand recognized at first touch as a handgun.

"That's the gun they give me to do it with," James said.

Betty Wilson, Peggy Lowe, and all of their family and friends attended a memorial service for Jack Wilson Tuesday morning. The brutality of his death and the inexplicable nature of it made it impossible for people to find words. Even the poor comfort people manage to summon for each other at most funerals was beyond their reach that day. There was only bewilderment and crushing grief.

After the service, a middle-aged man came up to Betty and said, "Mrs. Wilson, do you remember me? I'm Ross Melvin."

Betty had started taking tranquilizers early that morning and was a little fogged, but she did manage to remember who Ross Melvin was—the accountant for Jack's practice and for her and Jack personally. She and Jack had had lunch with him once.

"Of course, Ross. Thank you so much for coming."

"As a friend, I just want you to know I am available to help you at this time."

"I appreciate that, Ross."

"See if you can get a copy of the will, Betty, and then call me or just come by the office. I want to do whatever I can."

"I will."

Betty was distracted. Something was chewing at her—something much closer and meaner than grief. As soon as she got back to GeDelle Cagle's house on Mira Vista, she called and left word at CID that she wanted to talk to Mickey Brantley.

It was going to be a sticky business for the police, continuing to talk to Betty Wilson without reading her her rights. As soon as she was officially a suspect, she would have to be Mirandized, at which point she would probably get a lawyer and stop talking. At this point, the police could argue that she was not a real suspect.

But if there was much more evidence against her, they were going to have to advise her she was a suspect and read her her rights. Otherwise, they might jeopardize the case.

At 8:00 P.M. on the day of the funeral, after conferring with Brantley, Harry Renfroe drove to Betty Wilson's sister's house in Huntsville, where Betty Wilson was staying. He took her back to the CID.

He sat across a desk from her and stared quizzically. At this point in the day, exhausted and overtranquilized, she was barely able to hold herself awake.

"You called," he said at last.

"I remembered something," she said, "I thought I should tell you."

He stared.

"There was another man I didn't tell you about. But I know you will find out anyway, so I thought I should."

Renfroe stared.

"His name is Errol Fitzpatrick. He works for the city. He's fairly high up, I think."

"Errol Fitzpatrick who works for the city of Huntsville?"

"Yes."

"The head of risk management?"

"I think so."

There was a long silence.

"You had an affair with Errol Fitzpatrick?"

"Yes."

"What do you mean, you had an affair?

"An affair."

"You mean you had sex with him?"

"Yes."

He stared at her. "He's married, isn't he?"

"Yes."

"Where?"

"Where?"

"Where did you do it?"

"Oh, in . . . several places. Hotels, motels."

"His house?"

"No."

"Has he ever been inside your house?"

"Yes."

"Did you ever . . . ? Did you ever have sex with him in your own house?"

"Yes."

Renfroe began reading her her rights.

FIVE

"WHY ARE YOU DOING THIS?" BETTY ASKED WHEN RENFROE had finished advising her of her rights.

"O.K., I'll tell you why, Betty. We have investigators right now in South Alabama interviewing James Dennison White. And he says he was paid by you to kill your husband."

Betty went pale, and her voice began to shake. "What are you talking about?"

"I'm talking about James Dennison White."

"I don't know what you mean."

"Oh, you don't? You don't know James Dennison White?"

"I don't, uh . . ."

"This guy lives in Vincent, Alabama. He says he knows your sister Peggy."

"Oh, you mean Mr. Carpenter. He's the man who was working for my sister Peggy. I had hired him, too, to come build an island in my kitchen and fix some screen doors."

"So you have met him?"

"No. No, I never did. He never showed up. He made some excuse why he never showed up. I had left a note for him in the kitchen to start on the work if I wasn't there . . ."

"You were going to allow a total stranger into your home?"

"Well, no. I mean, I guess so. But he never came. I fired him. My sister thought he was a good man."

"Did you pay him to kill your husband?"

Betty gasped.

"No," she said in a tiny voice. "No, I did not."

"Did you ever pay him for anything?"

"No, he never showed up."

Renfroe continued to ask questions for an hour. At times during the interrogation, Betty fell asleep and dreamed.

Renfroe had to shout at her to wake her up.

Renfroe learned that Betty's twin sister, Peggy Lowe, had come to town for the memorial service and was also staying with their older sister, GeDelle Cagle, on Mira Vista Street. At 9:00 P.M., Renfroe sent another investigator to Mira Vista to pick up Peggy. The investigator brought her back to the CID offices, put her in a room, and told her a man would be coming in after a while to talk to her.

A while later Harry Renfroe came into the room. Without introducing himself, he pulled a chair up right in front of Peggy's chair so that he was sitting with his face a few inches from her face.

"Miz Lowe, tell me about James Dennison White."

She found herself peering into Renfroe's grinning mouth. She had never heard James's middle name before and was flustered. "I'm sorry. About whom?"

"Oh, come on!" he snapped angrily. "You know exactly who I'm talkin' about, Miz Lowe. James White! The man you hired to kill Jack!"

"What?"

Renfroe began reading Peggy her rights in a flat mechanical doomsaying voice.

"What are you doing?" she asked. "What is this all about? I came up here to attend my brother-in-law's funeral today. What are you accusing me of?"

Renfroe said: "We have investigators right now talking to James Dennison White, and he has made a full confession to the fact that you and your sister paid him to murder your sister's husband."

Peggy blinked at him in silence.

"Well?" he said.

"Do you mean Mr. White said something about us?"

"So now you do know him. You changed your mind about that, eh?"

"I have never heard him called—whatever that was you called him. He has always just been Mr. White to me. But yes, if you mean Mr. White from Vincent. I met him at my school. He did some carpentry work for me there. His daughter is in my friend's classroom."

"So how well do you say you know him? Tell me about it."

"We have talked."

"You talked? How much?"

"Oh, many times. He has been having a lot of problems in his family and problems with a divorce."

"Where'd you talk?"

"We talked at the school, and on the telephone. He called me just lots of times, thousands of times it seems like, to talk about his problems. He did some work for us at the house, and he talked to me there."

"So you . . . what? You *consoled* him."

"Mr. Renfroe, I believe I do not like the sound of that word, as you say it. I tried to help him."

"How long would your conversations last, when you were trying to *help* him?"

"Sometimes not long. Sometimes quite long."

"I see. What about the last few days before Dr. Wilson's murder. What have you been up to?"

Peggy gave him a detailed accounting of her time, the hours she worked and the hours she was at home for the week before Jack's death, including the day Stephanie was ill and had to go to the hospital, all of the errands and other missions away from home she could remember. He took careful notes. By the time they were done, the entire conversation had consumed three hours. Toward the end, Peggy was exhausted and failing.

"When was the last time you saw James?"

"I don't . . . I think it was last Tuesday. I was cleaning out my basement and garage with Linda Vascocu. She's staying with us. And James came by to pick up some things I said he could have."

"What did you say he could have?"

"Just old things. Rummage."

"Is that all you said he could have?"

"Yes."

"You understand that James is down in Shelby County right now spilling his guts out to our investigator. And there is something else I think you ought to know. Your sister Betty is in the next room and has just finished making a full confession to the crime."

"Oh, I don't . . . no, I don't think so. I don't believe you. That is just not true."

"So, according to you, has your sister ever even met James face-to-face? What's your version of that?"

"No, I don't think they have. A long time ago, several weeks now, I gave James Betty's phone number. She's having her kitchen remodeled, and I thought she might be able to give him some work, but it didn't work out. He never showed up, and she was angry."

"Right. You know what we're going to do, here, Miz Lowe? I think we're going to hook you up to a little lie detector and find out just how much of this is a lie and how much isn't."

"Good, please, I wish you would. You will find out that I am telling the truth. I can't imagine what Mr. White has told you, but if he's really saying that we had something to do with Jack's death, it's just not true. I loved Jack, and Betty loved Jack. We are grieving terribly for his death. I wish you would let me see Mr. White face-to-face. I just do not believe that Mr. White would say something like that to my face."

"Right. You want to see James. Peggy, tell me, what about you and James?"

"I'm sorry?"

"What about it? Did you ever . . . you know? James is talking to us about it."

"I don't know what you are asking me."

"Are you having an affair with James White?"

Peggy stopped and caught her breath.

"Are you?" he asked.

"I can't imagine why you would ask me that. What do you mean?"

Renfroe's face moved in even closer to her own. She noticed that his lower teeth were crooked.

"Sex. Are you having sex with him, Peggy? Have you ever had sex with him?"

"Mr. Renfroe, I don't believe I like the sound of what you are saying or implying."

"I'm sorry. I'm just doing my job."

"I don't believe I will have anything more to say to you. At all."

"Oh, you won't? I see. Well, allow me to drive you two ladies home then, by all means."

He took them back to GeDelle Cagle's house and dropped them off. It was past midnight. Their sister and brother-in-law had already gone to bed. Betty and Peggy were still standing alone in the darkened den of the house, whispering to each other in fast, intense bursts as they remembered pieces and patches of what had been happening to them both that evening, when car lights appeared in the driveway. It was Renfroe, bounding out of the car and about to beat on the front door. Peggy rushed forward and yanked the door open to keep him from making a racket.

"Get out here!" he shouted. "We're not done with you."

He ordered them back into the unmarked police car and drove them back to the CID. Betty was ordered upstairs, where another investigator put her back in an interrogation room. Renfroe told Peggy to stay in the car.

"Looks like you're gonna get your wish, Peggy."

"What wish?"

"You said you wanted to see James. I think we're going to be able to arrange that. One of our investigators is driving back in with him right now, so we'll just go see if we can have a little meeting with the two of you."

"Good," she said. "I think this is a good idea."

He drove her to the darkened parking lot of a convenience store on the edge of the city. They sat in the car while he talked.

"He's told us everything, Peggy. About the affair and you all sending him up here to Huntsville to kill Jack."

She sat in the back of the car and said nothing.

Finally after an hour, he said, "Well, it looks like it's not going to come off."

He turned to the backseat and stuck a long finger in her face: "You and your sister are not to breathe one word to anyone of what has been discussed here tonight. Do you understand me, Miz Lowe?"

"Yes, sir."

He took her back to Mira Vista, where Betty was waiting.

The next morning the phone rang early at the Cagle home. The twins were still asleep. Their brother-in-law, Euel Dean Cagle, answered. A handsome craggy-faced man with short-cropped sandy hair, he bore a striking resemblance to the late film star Spencer Tracy, including a frankness of speech that was sometimes mistaken for severity. On the phone was an Alcoholics Anonymous friend of Betty.

"They're not up yet," he said. "I think they were up all hours, working with the police."

The friend on the phone asked Euel if he had seen the morning papers. He had not. As soon as he hung up, he went out on the walk in front and retrieved the *Huntsville Times*. He opened the newspaper outside and read it, then rushed into the house.

"Willya look at this?" he said excitedly to his wife. "They caught the guy that killed Jack already."

He went to the bedroom in the back of the house where the twins were sleeping and rapped on the door. "Hey, you two, wake up! We got big news out here."

There was no answer. Euel pushed the door open anyway and walked into the room. The women were asleep on either side of him in twin beds. He reached down and shook Betty gently.

"Betty, they have caught the man who killed your husband!"

Betty sat up. She stared at him wordlessly for a moment, orienting herself. She took the newspaper from him and read the headline and the top of the story. Peggy came over, sat on the bed, and read over Betty's shoulder.

Betty said, "Excuse me, Euel." She rose and signaled for Peggy to come with her. The two women went into a small bathroom off the hallway at the back of the house and closed the door.

Euel stood in the hall for a while. He could hear them whispering on the other side of the door, but he couldn't make out what they were saying. Their voices were low and unemotional. GeDelle came up behind him.

"Where are they, Euel?"

He nodded toward the bathroom. "In there."

"Well, what did Betty say?"

He turned to his wife with his bushy eyebrows raised high. "Not one word. Neither one of 'em. They just went in there with the paper and started whisperin' to each other."

When they had held these intense little bathroom conferences as small children, it had been Peggy who tended to dominate, urging Betty to do whatever was necessary to keep their father quiet. But on this occasion, it was different. Betty sat on the edge of the tub, reading every word in the story intently.

Peggy was whispering about the need to tell the truth, to explain to people what really happened, to try to talk to Mr. White and figure out whatever it was he had in his mind. Could he have killed Jack? Why? Why would he do such a thing?

"Peggy, be quiet," Betty whispered. "We are in a very dangerous situation here. This is going to be a big deal. It will be political and everything else. We have got to get a lawyer."

"Lawyer?"

"And we have got to have money."

"You have money."

"Maybe yes, maybe no. It won't be long before it's all tied up. I have a friend, Gene Montgomery, who has helped me with some business things in the past. We need to get out of here.

They may come for us right away, before we can get things arranged."

"Come for us?"

"Come on. We're getting out of here. I'm going to go call Gene."

The instant James White's arrest hit the Huntsville newspapers and television stations, the political side of the story began lurching to life. District Attorney Mo Brooks was everywhere, congratulating the police for their swift action. His opponent, Tim Morgan, was on every reporter's phone list for a quote, too, because by now it was known that the victim was not merely his political supporter but also a social friend and his personal ophthalmologist. Once the story reached that level—and did almost immediately after James was arrested—then backing down or admitting to mistakes was going to be especially expensive for any of the authorities involved.

Betty and Peggy drove straight to Gene Montgomery's house. Betty made contact with Charlie Hooper, a lawyer who had helped her on business matters. Hooper was a civil lawyer, not a criminal lawyer, but he was a former assistant district attorney and he knew his way around the courthouse. He told her she had been exactly right about one thing: She needed to move immediately to shelter some money or she wasn't going to be able to hire anybody any good to help save her from whatever was ahead.

She would need time to get things arranged. It was decided that Betty and Peggy would spend the night at Gene Montgomery's house, in order to avoid more midnight summonses to the CID and to maintain some freedom of movement.

Betty went to see Ross Melvin. She didn't mention any of the police business to him. She had forgotten to get a copy of the will.

"I can't do a lot until you bring me the will, Betty," he said. "You also need to establish a new bank account."

"Why is that, Ross?"

"You need to set up a bank account for the estate. It's very important from here on out not to mingle predeath money with postmortem funds and activities. It all needs to be kept separate. By the way, what is going to happen with Jack's practice? Are there partners, or has any arrangement been made for someone else to step in?"

"I don't think so. I don't think there are any partners. Jack just did it all himself. You know, Ross, as we talked about at lunch that day, he never borrowed any money, and he just built it up himself a piece at a time."

"Yes, well, there are good things and bad things about that. The good thing is, you probably aren't going to have any unpleasant surprises, such as finding out that the practice owes a lot of money. The bad thing is that there is no mechanism in place, I would be willing to bet, for a transition."

"What does that mean?"

"It means, I'm afraid, that you are going to have to deal with selling the practice yourself pretty quickly. I know this is a terrible time for you, Betty, and I wish you didn't have to think about these things now. But you have had experience yourself in the health care business, and you know that the most important and valuable asset here is the ongoing practice itself and the goodwill of the patients."

With Gene Montgomery's help, Betty dragged herself through the day, retrieving the will and taking it back to Ross Melvin, going to the bank and arranging the new accounts. Peggy's husband, Wayne, had already returned home with Stephanie. He went back to school and work in Vincent, having no idea what his wife and her sister were going through with the police. Betty had told Gene Montgomery most of what had gone on the night before with the police, but Peggy, remembering Harry Renfroe's admonition, had been afraid to breathe a word of it.

On that same day, Mickey Brantley and James Dennison White also were hard at work. There were some major credibility problems with White's story, to say the least. Even getting a judge to sign a warrant for the twins' arrest, let alone convincing the D.A. to prosecute them, was going to be impossible unless James could figure things out a little better.

By now, according to the rough notes Brantley made, James was saying that Betty Wilson had paid him a large amount of money to kill her husband. He had mentioned various sums, from $20,000 to $5,000. But if James received that kind of money shortly before the murder, he would have to prove it. In fact, under Alabama law, nothing he said—not one word—could be used in court unless it could be independently corroborated, that is, proved to be true by someone else or some fact other than James's word. Because he was going to admit that he was a co-conspirator, his word was worthless, according to the law, unless what he said was provable some other way.

When James paid the bills he had to pay—to the utility companies in order to get them to restore service, for example—he always paid on the basis of last-ditch, bitter necessity. On those occasions, he managed to come up with a wad of cash, either from a trove he had saved from an earlier score or from new business in the drug, asphalt, or fake-injury departments. Typically, James took his fresh wad of money around and settled the score with all of his most demanding creditors on the same day.

As it happened, James had paid off roughly $2,500 in bills one day not too long before Jack Wilson was killed. No one may ever know where that money really came from. But James, who had his antennae sensitively tuned to Mickey Brantley's every question and utterance, quickly offered the suggestion it had come from the twins.

The story as it emerged in the notes was this: James had originally told the twins he could hire someone else to commit the murder for $20,000. Betty Wilson, being cheap, had said the price was too high. Therefore, James had come in with a lower bid of $5,000. The twins had agreed, but Betty had said she would only pay half in advance, half on completion. Shortly before the killing, she had paid him $2,500.

Early in the course of the day's interrogation, Brantley had asked White how Betty Wilson had paid him the money. He said she had dumped the $2,500 on the side of the road and then told him where to go get it.

"It was on the side of the road, going toward Talladega, Alabama," he said.

Something in the course of the conversation—still not tape recorded—persuaded James that this story, Betty Wilson tossing $2,500 in cash on the side of the road and then hoping it would still be there when James came to retrieve it, was not going to fly.

There is no way of knowing whether another problem with the story was discussed, or hinted at, or alluded to, or suggested in any way by Brantley. But the fact was, money tossed on the side of the road and later picked up by James would not have provided a tight enough link, for purposes of a trial, to tie Betty to the payoff. In order for the conspiracy to work in a jury's mind, the handoff of money needed to be much more direct and personal.

By the end of the day, James had experienced one of the first of what would prove to be, in the coming weeks and months, a remarkable series of sudden memory corrections—the opposite of memory lapses. In this case, James remembered that he had been wrong a few hours earlier about picking the money up on the side of the road. When he stopped and thought about it, he realized that he had actually driven to Betty Wilson's house, where she had handed him the $2,500 in person. He kept changing his story.

In the course of asking him about the money, Brantley asked James if he had ever received any money directly from Betty Wilson. James remembered that he had and that the money, a sum of $200, had been passed to him in a library book at Guntersville State Lodge. Police investigators were immediately dispatched to Vincent, where they searched James's pickup truck and found the very book he had described—a library book that would turn out to have been borrowed in the name of Betty Wilson.

It was an important breakthrough—a material link between James and Betty Wilson. Brantley was delighted.

To the eyes of skeptics later, this process, by which Mickey Brantley encouraged James to experience sudden new memory corrections, would look very suspicious. But Brantley would claim—with some justification—that all crooks lie, that no one ever offers the full and complete truth in the first go-around, and that a good police interrogator's job is to lead and coax and push an accused down the long sinuous path that will lead ultimately to the truth. Along that path, the bad guy will always tell many lies. The trick is always to sort the wheat from the chaff. In Mickey Brantley's heart of hearts, he may well have believed the twins were guilty. Once believing, he was the kind of man who would have continued to believe.

Certainly there was never any evidence presented in the trial or anywhere else to indicate that the process, for Brantley, was anything but his own bumpy, relentless pursuit of the truth. And Mickey Brantley, by reputation and according to his own record as a police officer, was an honest man.

The process gave James lots and lots of elbow room, many opportunities to watch Brantley's face, to listen intently to his questions, read the signs and read them again in order to figure out just which truth would fetch the highest price in a plea bargain. There is no indication, in Brantley's notes or in his testimony, that Brantley ever found anything suspicious in the remarkably pliant workings of James's memory.

The structure of the relationship put James in a no-lose situation. If he lied, and if the lie didn't work, he could lie again until it did work. When he finally did hit the right note, he would be judged to be telling the truth.

James continued to be coy about his own real role in the crime. He said he had never intended to kill Dr. Wilson and had only been playing along with the bloodthirsty sisters. He said that after getting their money, he had stalled them by saying he had paid the money to the person he had subcontracted to do the killing, and that he didn't know why the man wasn't going forward.

"I said I carried the man the money. I said he's supposed to be going in, looking, check things out and check the situation out and stuff like this. Just trying to let it ride, let it ride. Been trying to get away with it. And I guess you could say I was trying to scam them for the money to get my bills caught up more or less."

This aspect of his story was going to take work, too. Tying the twins to the murder was not his only job. He had to take some share of the rap himself, and there was a major problem if he thought he was going to be able to waltz off scot-free. Then again, the less premeditation he showed in his own behavior, the more culpability could be assigned to the twins. It was all going to have to be worked out and fine-tuned between the two men.

The rest of his story that day was a welter of contradictions. He said he had received the $2,500 a few days before the killing. His story to the twins was that someone else was going to carry out the hit. But a short time later he nevertheless had to go to Guntersville State Lodge to get $200 in expense money from Betty Wilson so that he could drive to Huntsville himself to case the job.

His story mutated during the day in ways that tended to tie Betty Wilson much more directly into the murder itself. Now, instead of driving himself to the house to kill the doctor, he remembered suddenly that she had driven him there herself. He said he had gone along with that suggestion, still not intending to hurt anyone, because he thought he might be able to rob Mrs. Wilson's home, instead of killing her husband for her.

"And I seen an opportunity, because Mizrus Lowe told me that they was usually cash money in the house and stuff like this, and I seen the opportunity to maybe go in and get the money and stuff and just leave."

James White said that he had fled on foot through the woods. "I just left walking. All I knew is I wanted to get away."

There was still the problem of how James Dennison White could ever have become the confidant and criminal protégé of the twins in the first place. He said during this interrogation that he and Peggy Lowe had managed to steal a few kisses but had never had intercourse and had never really had much time to sit down and get to know one another. The impression was of fairly casual, insouciant embraces, of the sort one sees on television in fragrance commercials. This aspect of the story would need work.

He clearly stumbled on a key question—when, where, and how he had met Betty Wilson for the first time. In one part of the interrogation, he said that Betty and Peggy had called him to a secret meeting atop an isolated dam at one end of Logan Martin Lake on the previous Tuesday, in order to pass him the pistol he was to use to kill Jack.

By this time, the Huntsville police already had run a check on the pistol James had produced from beneath a floorboard on the porch of his ruined house. The gun was registered to Betty Wilson. The size of the gun and the ammunition in it would indicate it was the gun missing from the open pistol case in the cabinet in Jack Wilson's bedroom. The assumption, then, would be that Betty Wilson had supplied James with a gun registered in her own name with which to murder her own husband, who had been murdered, in fact, with a baseball bat instead.

It would do for now.

James also had to explain how and when Betty Wilson had met him and picked him up in order to transport him to her house to kill her husband. James said that he had called her from a pay phone at Parkway City Mall on the day of the murder and had told her he needed a ride to her house. She had agreed right away, he said, showing up in her big BMW around 2:30 P.M. to give him a lift. He said this meeting was the first time she and he had ever laid eyes on each other.

Perhaps sensing that things were a bit ragged at this point, he tossed in a bonus. He was sure he would have touched the door handles of her BMW, he said, leaving some good fingerprints.

Of course, the BMW already had been scoured for prints and had produced nothing—not a print, not a hair, not a fiber, not a clot of soil or rag of paper that would in any way indicate James Dennison White had ever been near it. But that was a matter that could be managed later.

So here it was: He had met Betty for the first time when he went to her house to collect the hit money. He had met Betty for the first time when she had come to Logan Martin dam to hand him her own gun to kill her husband with. He had met Betty for the first time when she had come to Parkway City Mall to give him a lift up to her house to commit the murder.

It was good enough.

That afternoon Brantley showed up at Gene Montgomery's house. Apparently he had visited Betty's bank, and someone there had told him where to find the twins. Since the twins had not been arrested, Brantley needed Betty's permission to get copies of her bank records. She asked Brantley to wait while she called Charlie Hooper. Fearing the bank would freeze the accounts soon, Hooper told her to stall Brantley until she had completed the arrangements her accountant had told her to make. Brantley was angry when he left Montgomery's house.

Peggy was beginning to collapse into panic. Betty, who had shaken off the last effects of her tranquilizers, said: "We don't have time for that, Peggy. I have got to get some of this crap done." The twins left the house with Montgomery to complete the banking arrangements.

Late that afternoon they were returning to the house and had stopped at a traffic light a block away when they saw a television news truck stopped at a traffic light facing them. Bold lettering on the side said, CHANNEL 31 HUNTSVILLE EYEWITNESS NEWS. The driver was leaning out his window scanning house addresses. Seated across from the driver was a big, handsome, dark-haired man they all recognized instantly as Cliff Hill, a hard-hitting investigative reporter for Channel 31.

Peggy sucked in her breath.

Gene Montgomery kept driving, pulled his car to the back of his house, and let them into the house by the driveway door to the kitchen.

"We have no clean clothes," Peggy said.

Montgomery brought them clothes of his own—a shirt and pajama bottoms for Betty, khaki shorts and a shirt for Peggy. Peggy threw their own clothes into the washing machine.

Half an hour later, as they were sitting down to eat, a loud thumping knock came at the front door.

"The television people," Montgomery said. "What nerve."

He and Betty went to the front of the house. He waved her back. Peggy stood in the hallway, watching and wringing her hands. Montgomery went forward and peeked through curtains at the front of the house.

The thumping continued, louder.

"This is not the television station," Montgomery whispered hoarsely. "This is the police."

Betty raced to the back of the house, shoving Peggy out of her way. She grabbed the kitchen telephone and called Charlie Hooper. He was out. Another lawyer listened while Betty told him, between gasps, what was going on.

The lawyer said: "If they have come to arrest you, Mrs. Wilson, there is nothing you can do. You should just open the door."

At that moment, the telephone operator broke in on the line.

"I have an emergency call for you," she said.

Betty handed the phone to Montgomery. She and Peggy stood inches away from him, watching his face while he talked.

"Listen," he said, "this is a private line, and you have no right to interrupt people's private conversations."

There was a long silence. Montgomery turned to them, cupped the phone, and whispered, "She says there's a Mr. Renfroe on the line who wants to talk to me."

He turned back to the phone. "You are where, sir? On my porch?" He listened a while longer. "And if I refuse? Oh. I see. Well, no, that won't be necessary. It's a very expensive door, by the way. I'll be right there."

He hung up the phone and said, "We have got to go open that door right now."

Betty, still in Montgomery's pajama bottoms and shirt, and Peggy, in his shirt and khaki shorts, followed him to the door.

Montgomery had barely turned the lock and was fumbling with the knob when Mickey Brantley and Harry Renfroe pushed the door open brusquely, swept Montgomery out of the way, and went straight to the women. Renfroe grabbed Betty's arm at the wrist, and her watch fell to the floor. She looked down at it, but Renfroe said, "You're not going to need that where you're going."

Brantley grabbed Peggy by the wrist and told her to turn around to be handcuffed.

"May I put on a pair of shoes?" she asked. "I'm afraid I'm going to be cold."

"No," Brantley said. "You're under arrest now. Just get out there and get in the car."

Brantley and Renfroe delivered the two women to be processed at the Huntsville Police Department. Shuffling down long corridors, barefooted and in what appeared to be rags, with their hair uncombed and their faces streaked, they both fit in perfectly with the hookers, public drunks, brawlers, and petty thieves coming through the system with them that afternoon. They were photographed and fingerprinted, then given physical exams by matrons looking for hidden weapons, drugs, and sexually transmitted diseases.

They finished with Peggy first and put her in a large holding cell with several dozen other female prisoners. She clung to the bars at the front of the cell, staring at the backs of the guards as they walked away, afraid to turn and confront the women behind her. When a guard brought Betty and put her in the cell, too, the twins rushed together and hugged each other, sobbing. Their fellow prisoners hooted and catcalled, taking them for lesbians.

Just as they were beginning to realize they were the center of attention, the guards came back, removed them from the cell, handcuffed them again, and then transported them to the county jail, where they went through the entire process again—fingerprints, photos, physical exams—and then were placed in another holding cell. At some point along the line, they were issued jail clothing. They spent the night on adjoining bunks.

For a while they whispered. Betty told Peggy that the policemen questioning her had suggested that Peggy had had a sexual affair with the man who did the killing. Peggy described James White to Betty in detail—the rotten brown teeth, dirty beard, greasy cap, and ever-shifting downcast eyes. Both women were exhausted and fell asleep soon.

At this point, the story James White was telling the police was hanging by one thin thread. He had told conflicting accounts of how, where, when, and why he first met Betty Wilson, but he did say that, one way or another, he had met her. His meeting her, dealing with her, and engaging in some sort of transaction related to the murder was vital.

It was already clear, in the actions of the police, in the questions they were asking James and the papers they were beginning to prepare, that Betty was the number-one target. She was the one whose life a jury could vote to take. Peggy was baggage. She was a necessary link in order to tie James to Betty, but she was also one who would be hard to convict, unless between now and a trial the police could come up with something unexpected on her.

Betty was the centerpiece. The witch.

But James had to know Betty. The authorities would have to be able to show the jury a mental picture of Betty giving money to James, or of Betty physically aiding and abetting James in the murder, or better yet—both. One way or another, James absolutely had to know who Betty Wilson was.

He did know Peggy. Peggy had admitted as much. That was no problem. But Betty had claimed in all of her interrogations so far that she had never met James White. It was the one clearly defined place where Betty Wilson, whether she realized it or not, had stuck her toe in the sand and drawn a line for Brantley and Renfroe to cross.

White said he knew her. She said he did not. If she was right, there was no case.

There was a traditional, simple, time-honored way of testing whether James Dennison White had ever seen Betty Wilson before in his life. It was a practice as old as Justice itself, used in every two-bit robbery and assault case that came down the pike, familiar to anyone who had ever watched a TV cop show. The lineup.

Put Betty in a line of other prisoners. Put James out front

where he could see the line. Say, "James, which one is Betty Wilson?"

James claimed he could pick Betty out of a lineup, but he was foggy about when and where he had met her. In fact, he had never met her, but he could pick her out of a lineup because he had stalked her in the days before the murder.

The fact that James had failed to come up with a believable story about actually meeting Betty put the police in a tricky position. What if his whole story was bullshit? What if he had been telling them what they wanted to hear?

By the time the twins were waking up to a jail breakfast of clotted oatmeal and Kool-Aid in paper cups, the social and political reality around them had already changed radically. Since six o'clock the night before, Betty Wilson and Peggy Lowe had been all over the local and state news, on television and radio stations and in all the major papers in Alabama. By midmorning of the day they awoke in jail, the phones in the district attorney's office were ringing off the wall. Calls were coming from the major television networks, the national wire services, the national news magazines, the tabloid TV shows and newspapers in New York, Washington, and Los Angeles.

From the instant the story first broke, it was irresistible to editors. From their point of view, it had all the elements: two rich ladies, some kind of involvement in promiscuous sex, a brutal contract killing, and from the very beginning, the sexiest and most fascinating aspect of all the story's attractions:

Twins.

Twinhood was mentioned at the top of every story, as if that fact alone were the eeriest and most titillating of all the lurid information now leaking out of the Huntsville Police Department. Before Betty Wilson and Peggy Lowe ever left the holding cell that morning, they were already and for all time dubbed "The Alabama Twins."

The stakes on the table in any sort of lineup were major, indeed. With what felt like the entire world watching, it was going to be a bloody day for the careers of the law enforcement officials involved if James pointed to the wrong lady and said, "There she is! I'd rec'onize her anywheres."

Conceivably the D.A. could still wriggle out of it. Given his political distance from the local law enforcement good-old-boy network, he could tell the reporters, "This is what I mean about incompetence in the police department." He could be expected to say as much.

For the police? For Renfroe and for Brantley? What if their guy pointed to the wrong lady and they then had to go out front and tell the cameras, "We're sorry we arrested the widow of the brutally murdered doctor and her sister who lives eighty miles away and happened to be in town for the funeral, but it appears the lifelong scum-rat we trusted to tell us this story has actually never met Betty Wilson"?

What then?

Renfroe and Brantley would be history. It was that simple. They were both serious cops with long careers and good records. Mickey Brantley and his wife were just on the verge of committing to a builder for a new house. Life had to go on. If they put Betty Wilson in a lineup and asked James to point her out, then everything—everything—would hang on the tip of James Dennison White's finger.

So they didn't do it.

Instead, when Betty and Peggy were chained together to be brought from the jail to the courthouse for their arraignment, they were chained also to James Dennison White. The lawyers for Betty and Peggy later would call it a startling breach of investigative procedure. Normally, they said, every attempt should have been made to keep James from ever catching a glimpse of Betty Wilson until a lineup had been accomplished. In this case, the lawyers said, the authorities had gone out of their way to make sure nothing was left to chance.

Renfroe and Brantley could claim, of course, that they had nothing to do with transporting the prisoners to the courthouse for the arraignment. But in fact the sheriff's deputies who did move them had been given careful instructions to listen for and record any exchanges that took place between them.

Peggy gasped when she was chained to White. She said to Betty under her breath, "That's Mr. White."

White turned away and then looked back, turned away and looked back several times, muttering under his breath. The cap was gone, but the matted beard, shifting eyes, and terrible teeth were all the same.

Betty gaped and then asked Peggy in a horrified whisper, "Is that the man who killed Jack?"

The deputies recorded that Betty Wilson made remarks while they were chained together reflecting that she recognized James Dennison White. A lineup would be inappropriate and unnecessary.

At a preliminary hearing that morning, the twins learned that police were seeking a charge against them of capital murder, punishable by the death penalty. The matter would be taken to a grand jury, which would decide whether or not the allegations of the police warranted formal charges. Meanwhile, the twins would remain in the Madison County jail.

Now the pressure on Brantley and Renfroe was enormous. Mo Brooks, the prosecutor, was making it obvious to them that he was not going to sign on for this cruise unless Brantley and Renfroe could deliver James Dennison White wrapped up in a very tidy bundle, everything nailed down, no surprises, no loose ends.

The problem was James. The soberer he became, the craftier. Now he was starting to mutter and natter about wanting a written contract to guarantee that he would get off relatively lightly if he gave the state what it needed to win a death penalty for Betty Wilson. It seemed, at first glance, like an absurd demand. Under normal circumstances, written contracts are almost never used in plea-bargain agreements in Alabama.

Written contracts are required in plea-bargain agreements in the federal courts, so that everybody will have a record of who promised what to whom. But because Alabama law doesn't require a written contract, the prosecution almost never agrees to provide one. Most jurors dislike plea-bargain agreements, espe cially when they are made in exchange for the testimony of one bad guy against another. Seeing the agreement laid out on paper and in black and white makes it look to the jurors as if the state is in bed with the bad guys, which it usually is, of necessity and to a limited extent. If it weren't for plea bargains, the justice system probably would come to a grinding halt. But if an Alabama district attorney can possibly avoid it, he won't put his or her agreement on paper and give the defense lawyers another red flag to wave at the jury.

In this case, there was an added factor—and a potent one politically—in that Mo Brooks, the stern young Mormon D.A. who had been appointed to his job, was preparing to run for reelection by campaigning against plea bargains. For months he had been striving to paint himself to voters as an outsider who was fighting to bring an end to the cozy, ill-smelling practice of cops, prosecutors, and crooks cooking up little deals among themselves. He was, according to his own style, Mr. No Bargains. Viewed from that perspective, he seemed like the last D.A. in Alabama who would ever give James White a written contract.

But other aspects of the case seemed to be drawing Mr. Brooks's special and pointed attention. The fact that Betty Wilson had been a supporter of Tim Morgan, his opponent, was getting a lot of mention in the press accounts. One news reporter even found out that Betty had been so pleased with some favor Tim Morgan had done her in the past that she bought him a pigskin briefcase, which he seemed to be carrying with him on the campaign trail.

Brooks was granting interviews about the case with everybody who asked, from the local media to the tabloid shows. In some of his remarks, the idea seemed to be forming already that a vote for Tim Morgan would be a vote to let the witch, Betty Wilson, escape the electric chair.

Unlikely as it might have seemed at first, perhaps there was the slimmest chance, after all, that James might get the contract he sought. It just depended on how badly Mo Brooks wanted his testimony, and how crafty James could be about holding out.

The case, which had been a joint venture by Renfroe and Brantley at the outset, was sliding more and more into Mickey Brantley's lap with each advancing hour. He was becoming the man in the department who said it could be done. The bottom line, however, was that James's story was going to have to be nailed down the right way.

Five days after the murder itself and after hours of unrecorded interrogation, it was time to turn on the tape recorder. While Betty Wilson and Peggy Lowe were being issued their jail clothes and assigned separate cells in the Madison County jail, Mickey Brantley was closeted with James, trying again in another grueling day of interrogation to get a straight story out of him, this time for the record.

For hours, Brantley asked questions and challenged James on some of his assertions. As the day wore on, James experienced many more of his sudden memory corrections, several of them apropos of nothing, if the tape is to be believed.

He remembered that the insouciant embraces and "stolen kisses" he and Peggy Lowe had exchanged had happened not at the school, where it would seem someone might have noticed them, but at Peggy's secluded home on Logan Martin Lake, when there was no one else around.

He remembered that he had misremembered the part about picking the money up on the side of the road, and he had also misremembered the part about picking the money up at Betty Wilson's house. This time, he suddenly remembered that he had picked the money up from Peggy Lowe at her house.

His sudden clarity on this point had the very happy effect, for Brantley, of forging the first hard conspiratorial link between Peggy and the plot. Up until this point, Peggy could have argued in court that she had simply been swept off her feet by James and might, indeed, have steered him toward her sister, but she had no real role in the murder plot itself. Now that James had suddenly remembered getting the payoff money from her hands at her house, she was in it up to her neck.

James told Brantley that he had begun trying to avoid Peggy after collecting the first $2,500 from her. "I felt like I had pulled a pretty good scam, myself, by taking the money to get my bills and stuff caught up and doing some things I wanted to do with my children."

James told Brantley that Peggy Lowe had begun embarrassing him by following him all over town, in part out of lovesickness but also because she was impatient to get her sister's husband murdered. She cornered him at a service station, he said, and told him shrewishly that he was either going to get the job done or she would have the money back from him.

Soon after, James said, Betty Wilson herself called him. He told Betty, he said, that the $2,500 had not been quite enough to get the job done and that he needed an additional $200. She immediately agreed and invented a scheme by which he was to come to Guntersville State Lodge to pick up the money. She would hide it in the backseat of her BMW in a book about ballet.

James said he drove to Guntersville and worked the exchange with the book in the backseat of the BMW, successfully collected the $200 bonus money, and drove to Huntsville to check out the job. At this point in James's narrative, he apparently had forgotten about the existence of the subcontractor who was ostensibly going to carry out the killing. But that was a detail that could be ironed out in subsequent interrogations.

James said Betty had told him the best place to kill her husband would be in or near his office building—the busy Whitesport Center where Jack maintained twenty-five hundred square feet of office space. James said he drove to Huntsville with the $200 in his pocket and observed the Whitesport Center site.

When he got back home to Vincent, he said he called Betty and reported back to her that he had found several large apartment buildings and a hospital near her husband's office building. On hearing his report, he said, Betty agreed that Whitesport Center might not make a good location after all. He said she suggested James kill her husband at the Wilson home on Boulder Circle instead. He said she gave him precise directions to the house.

James said he then drove back to Huntsville to kill Dr. Wilson. When he arrived at the house, however, he discovered a pickup truck parked in the driveway. Figuring it meant someone else was in the house, he turned away and returned to Vincent. It turned out that it was Betty's son Trey's truck and that she did not want her son murdered.

In all of James's wandering accounts and Brantley's questions, there were certain high points and milestones that had to be visited and revisited until they were taken care of. James was sticking to the self-serving aspects of his original story. But physical evidence had already been gathered and would have to be explained.

James kept saying that he had not entered the house with the intention of killing anyone. That assertion conflicted starkly with his story that he had driven to Huntsville several times for the express purpose of killing Dr. Wilson, at the urging of the twins.

If a jury believed James was just a dumb, drunk, drug-addled burglar who went over the top when he confronted the homeowner, the jury would have an excuse not to convict the twins. There was the matter of the gun under the floorboards, for example. If James had simply picked up the gun out of the pistol box in Dr. Wilson's room and then held on to it after the crime, that would tend to show he was only a petty burglar, hoping to pawn the gun later for a few bucks.

If on the other hand the gun was part of the murder plot, it might work just the other way—to help send the twins to their deaths.

In this day of taped interrogation, James remembered that Peggy had called him in Vincent one day to ask what he was going to do. In spite of the fact he had already gone to Huntsville to case the job several times and had made at least one mission to do the actual killing, aborted at the last minute when he saw Trey's truck, James told Brantley he realized for the first time when Peggy called him that day that he was going to need a weapon.

He said he told Peggy he needed a gun. She readily agreed to provide him with one, suggesting that her sister would be helpful in this matter.

James described to Brantley the delivery of the weapon in a clandestine meeting on Logan Martin dam.

"This past Tuesday was two weeks ago. Mizrus Wilson and Mizrus Lowe brought me a thirty-eight Special Smith and Wesson to Logan Martin dam."

Some days after the gun was delivered, James said he received a call from one of the twins telling him they wanted him to come back up to Huntsville and try again. It was on this subsequent trip, he suddenly remembered, that he had given the twins his expert opinion that shooting the doctor at his busy office was too risky. Depressed and riven by conscience, he said, he had turned his truck around and begun driving back toward Vincent.

On the way, however, James said he had started drinking. The drink, sadly, emboldened him. He said he returned to Boulder Circle in the afternoon and entered the house. He was unarmed, he said, when he went in.

"I don't think I was really gon' kill the man, because I carried no weapons, and I think mainly what I was gon' do is just get in the lady's house and ram'le around and see if I could find some money or something or another and leave anyway. And basically that's what I was doing."

James was hewing to a clever and interesting line—he was willing to provide whatever information was needed to show the cunning premeditation of his co-conspirators. But he was unwilling to give Brantley a confession in which he said he himself had carried out a premeditated plot of murder. He insisted that he himself had only intended to pull off a scam. Only the twins were guilty of premeditated murder.

In fact, he suddenly remembered in this interview that he had not actually escaped on foot through the woods, as he had remembered in earlier versions. Now that he thought about it, Betty Wilson had returned to the house just after the murder to give him a lift. She had instructed him to lie down on the backseat. He even remembered a colorful detail. He remembered that she had covered him with a pink plastic clothing bag from a fancy dress shop. Amazingly enough, the police had found just such a bag in the backseat of her car when they searched it right after the murder.

There were hitches in all this. By now, the crime scene people had been all over the car with every kind of instrument and search device and had found not one hair, drop of blood, or scintilla of other evidence, however minute, to show that James White, presumably drenched in blood from the ball-bat murder of his victim a few moments earlier, had been lying on the backseat underneath a pink plastic dress bag.

James said he and Betty had managed to chat while she drove him from the death scene to his pickup truck a few blocks away, she in the front seat, he in the back beneath the pink bag. She had assured him that if he should be captured, she would see to it that his four children were cared for in perpetuity. She had asked him how much money he would need personally while in prison, and he had told her two hundred dollars a month would be adequate. She had said such an amount would be no problem.

He told several different stories about Betty giving him small amounts of money. Most of the stories were mutually contradictory. He did experience, however, another sudden recapturing of memory which was oddly in line with the stories that had been in that morning's newspaper about the Wilsons' planned trip to Santa Fe, mentioning Jack Wilson's ill health and including a photograph of Jack Wilson peering owlishly from behind his thick glasses.

James remembered suddenly that Betty had insisted she needed to have Jack killed that very weekend because of a trip Jack had arranged for them in Santa Fe. She had told James that the thought of being stuck in a hotel room for a week with her husband was unbearable and that she needed him done in right away.

"All I was told was Mr. Wilson had one or two diseases. He was a dying man, and he was going blind. He couldn't hardly see, and he was just dealing Betty Wilson misery, and she wanted to get rid of him. Instead of leaving him, she just wanted to get rid of him."

There were some glaring inconsistencies that still had to be repaired. Brantley asked James why he had said at first that he had escaped on foot through the woods, only to say now that Betty had returned to the house to give him a lift. James said he had done it that way because he had "saved" the part about the ride as a surprise.

Eager to make things smooth between himself and Brantley, James threw in another fact. He said he once had bought a "pink ice" ring for Peggy Lowe to express his love for her.

Brantley asked him what had happened to the clothes he had worn during the murder. James said he had worn them back to Vincent and then had washed them. Of course, simple laundering would not have removed all signs of blood. Brantley asked James if there had been blood on the clothes. No, James assured him, he had managed to carry out the entire ball-bat murder without getting a drop on him.

The taped "confession" left so many holes and contained so many contradictory statements that the process would have to be taken up again and again over the next three weeks before the state could come to a deal with James White.

In the interviews that followed the first taped statement, however, there was one major difference. At the end of the statement James gave Brantley on May 28, James and Brantley agreed that perhaps James needed to get a lawyer.

He got a good one.

Under normal circumstances, Roy Miller was the kind of lawyer who could have two or three trials going on more or less simultaneously and never miss a beat. In his early forties, wiry, with wavy salt-and-pepper hair above a crafty face, he was the Jack-Be-Nimble of the Madison County Courthouse. His offices were in the basement of a handsome brick neo-colonial office building just across the street from the courthouse. In the early evening when judges and lawyers gathered at their favored watering holes near the courthouse square in Huntsville to trade the day's war stories over a warm nip of bourbon, faces lighted up and smiles broadened if Roy Miller entered the room. A former D.A., child of the Alabama soil, and a quick-witted barrister with the best of them, Roy Miller was as much at home in the Madison County Courthouse square as a tick on a dog.

Assigned by the court to represent James, he was the perfect choice to make things happen. Roy Miller was way too smart to allow things to fall through the cracks—the sort of things that might scotch a deal and ruin a case later. He would give James White honest and able representation. And he would know exactly how, when, where, and why to make a deal.

James was still insisting that he wanted a written contract. If Roy Miller could actually bring things along to that point and get him what he wanted, it would be the sort of minor miracle that can lift a lawyer's reputation on the street by several notches. At the very least, Mr. Miller would be able to serve as a proper channel of information back and forth between the police and his client.

Betty and Peggy remained in jail. Until the preliminary hearing, at which time the police would present James's statement in full and formal charges would be lodged, no bond would be set.

In the meantime, a strange process was taking place in the media coverage. Everyone involved in the case in any official way, however peripheral, had an interest in seeing that the newspaper and television reporters got every bit of dirt on the twins that could possibly be dished.

At first the police were trying to overcome a level of skepticism among Huntsville people who had known the Wilsons and found the allegations against Betty unbelievable. One of the first pieces of privileged information to fly out the door was Betty's confession of an interracial love affair with a high Huntsville city official. Within a short time, Errol Fitzpatrick's name was being given in the stories. In an even shorter time after that, Fitzpatrick had left his job with the city of Huntsville.

Leaking word of the affair worked the charm, however. As

soon as that fact was generally known, a good many people who had known Betty Wilson started lining up to talk to reporters about what a bad lady she had always been and how they had always known as much. As it turned out, there was no shortage of juicy anecdotes from Betty's drinking days.

The district attorney's race, just then beginning to heat up, proved to be an even more important source of anti-Betty feeling than the police. Speaking before a political audience, Mo Brooks said, "I can't help noticing that Betty Wilson was out campaigning for Tim Morgan the day her husband was murdered."

In order to defuse the suggestion he might be soft on Betty Wilson, Tim Morgan came down on her much harder even than Brooks. During a campaign debate with Brooks, Morgan said he was ready to see all three of the conspirators—James, Peggy, and Betty, the lot of them—go to the electric chair.

In the meantime, a steady flow of information was moving back and forth between the police and James White. Mickey Brantley was out doing exactly the kind of footwork he needed to do as a detective, going from store to store at the Parkway City Mall, for example, to check out Betty's story about where she had been that afternoon.

At virtually every place she had mentioned in her first interviews with the police, there were cash-register tapes—with dates, times, and amounts entered automatically by computer—to verify the purchases she said she had made and the times she had given.

Curiously, as Brantley began gathering the corroborative evidence, James White began remembering several of the same details with astonishing clarity. There were tapes to prove, for example, that Betty had bought a pair of flowered tennis shoes from a store called Yielding's in the Parkway City Mall at 2:11 P.M.. Through his new lawyer, James White sent word to Brantley that he needed to see him again. He had been up all night, he said, trying to remember more details of the day before the murder. Finally at dawn a single image had penetrated the fog of drugs, booze, and lack of sleep that had enshrouded him on that terrible day. As he lay on his bunk in the jail early that morning, he said, a vision came to him of Mizrus Betty Wilson bending down beside her BMW on the parking lot at Parkway City Mall, taking off her shoes and proudly slipping her delicate little feet into a brand-new pair of tennis shoes.

Flowered tennis shoes, he believed.

From here on out, everything Betty had told the police in her first statements would become corroborating evidence, bolstering James's accusations against her, if it so happened that James suddenly remembered the same things.

For James, it was all a zero-sum game, with freedom and life itself as the eventual prizes if he won and the electric chair if he lost. If he provided the police with the right statement, and if the police were able to corroborate the statement with the right independently gathered evidence, then James might still save his life. Even if he had to accept life in prison without parole, he would at least live. But if he failed to give the police what they needed to convict the twins—or if the police were unable to corroborate what he gave them—then James was looking at a visit to Old Sparky.

SIX

IN THE DAYS AND WEEKS FOLLOWING HIS TAPED CONFESSion, as Mickey Brantley trod the shopping mall in tireless pursuit of corroboration, James Dennison White kept right on tirelessly and suddenly remembering things that fit the evidence Brantley was gathering. The mystery of how James did it—whether it was sheer coincidence that he was able to come up with these details or whether he cleverly fathomed the facts from the questions he was being asked—is a truth that probably will never be recovered from the universe of forgotten moments, untape-recorded conversations, and the tragically misplaced notes of Mickey Brantley.

James suddenly remembered staying at the Ramada Inn the night before the murder. He suddenly remembered that Betty had met him at a fast-food restaurant at the Parkway City Mall, Chick-Fil-A, and had passed him one hundred dollars in a used food sack to pay for his stay at the motel. He remembered wearing the ski mask that police had found in the Wilson home. He suddenly remembered that while he was lying on the backseat of Betty Wilson's car with the pink clothing bag over him, he had noticed a light-blue bank bag on the front seat.

There were still some things that needed to be remembered. It was extremely vexing that absolutely no physical evidence had been turned up to put James in Betty Wilson's car. It would have been nice for him just to remember what had happened to the clothes he was wearing when he killed Jack Wilson.

The ultimately nice thing for James to have remembered would have been the murder itself. In his statements so far, he had been willing to remember everything right up to the murder, sometimes in astonishing detail, as in the matter of the flowered tennis shoes. He had been willing to remember everything right after the murder, such as the light-blue bank bag on the front seat of Betty's car. But he continued to refuse to remember the murder itself. And he continued to insist that he wanted a written contract with the authorities, guaranteeing him a light sentence in exchange for putting the twins in the chair.

Some of the search for corroboration was producing troublesome results. A police dog-handler had taken a scent-searching dog named Zeke to 2700 Boulder a short time after the murder. The dog was given an article of James White's clothing and instructed to search the area. The dog picked up a scent near the back of the house and then made a beeline straight down the path through the woods where James had said in all of his early statements that he had escaped on foot after the killing.

The trouble for Brantley was that James no longer remembered running away on foot. Therefore, if Zeke the dog sniffed out a strong trail James had left through the woods, then Zeke was confirming the early version, which did not implicate Betty, and he was contradicting the suddenly remembered new version, which did implicate her in great detail.

The behavior of the dog would have to be explained in court. There was always the danger, as the investigation continued, that other troubling evidence might show up, conflicting with the state's case.

In the first week of June, Mo Brooks and Mickey Brantley had to appear in court to present the charges of the grand jury and to deal with the request of the twins that bail be set for them. The hearing was before Judge Thomas Younger in Madison County Circuit Court.

Tall and courtly, with a very dry sense of humor and an occasionally bad temper, Judge Thomas Younger was beside himself when Mo Brooks arrived at the courthouse that morning and reported to the judge's chambers. The building was hostage to an encircling armada of television-dish trucks. The halls were crawling with reporters and camera crews. The judge had just finished chasing off a crew from the syndicated tabloid television show *Hard Copy.*

When Brooks tried to say that he was as appalled as Judge Younger by the fevered behavior of the press, the judge acidly remarked that he certainly had been seeing Mr. Brooks's face on a lot of the offending tabloid news programs lately.

Betty and Peggy had added a criminal defense lawyer to their team—Marc Sandlin, forty-one, who had been district attorney in adjoining Limestone County for five years, had been in private practice in Huntsville since 1980, and was every bit as much a fixture in the Madison County Courthouse as James White's lawyer, Roy Miller.

The twins brought an interesting team to court with them. Charlie Hooper, the civil lawyer, who was square-built and glowering, was the one who looked like a courthouse bulldog, which he was not. Sandlin, who was tall, bearded, and restrained, looked more like a young law professor, which he was not. Both of them were as taken aback and aghast at the media crush in the courthouse that morning as the judge and the D.A.

The hearing began awkwardly, with the judge warning the media in the back of the room several times that he would tolerate no foolishness. He listened to the charges—capital murder for both women, no mention of charges against James White. Then he turned to the matter of bail for the women.

Mo Brooks argued that there was strong evidence to suggest the sisters were guilty and that Betty, given her "life-style," would surely use her wealth to flee the country if she were allowed out of jail. To buttress his case, he put Mickey Brantley on the stand and then played selections from James White's taped confession.

When the tape recorder came on and a weak tinny version of James's voice began resonating through the courtroom, recounting a long weird tale of sex and intrigue, the only other sound in the crowded room was the furious scratching of reporters' ballpoint pens on notebooks.

On the tape, James told how he had met Mizrus Lowe at the school and how "I told her I had feelings for her, and she come back and said she had feelings for me, too." He said he then sent her a letter confessing his love. They "stole kisses" but never consummated their sexual relationship with an act of intercourse, he said.

"Mizrus Lowe tol' me she had a sister who had problems to be resolved. We talked about the lady's problems and her misery. I was trying to get her affection and love, so I told her I would talk to some people.

"I was put in a position to prove myself. I found out her sister wanted her husband put away."

He described how the sisters had kept pushing him, how they had called him to a clandestine meeting on Logan Martin dam and handed him a .38 caliber pistol "to commit the crime."

He told of the visit to the Guntersville Lodge to pick up $200 in expense money for a reconnoitering trip to Huntsville. In a significant departure from his earlier statements to Brantley—presumably the result of another sudden remembering—he said that he had picked up the $2,500 down payment for the murder the day before the crime was committed, after the visit to Guntersville, and not on one of the earlier dates he had suggested in his earlier statements. This fact, remembered just in time for the hearing, cleared up the mystery of why he would have needed $200 in expense money so soon after receiving $2,500 in murder money.

James told how Betty Wilson had picked him up at Parkway City Mall in her BMW and had told him to crouch on the front floorboard, between the seat and the dash, while she drove him up Garth Mountain to Boulder Circle. As they drove, he said, she instructed him what to say if someone caught him in the house.

"I was to say I was there measuring doors."

This detail, remembered just in time for the hearing, cleared up the matter of the "Mr. Carpenter" note Betty had left posted in her kitchen. Clearly the note was part of Betty Wilson's cover story, in case James got caught.

On the drive to the house, James said, Betty Wilson gave him instructions for how to carry out the crime. "She told me to knock drawers and make it look like a burglary."

She took him into the house through the garage door, told him where to find the doctor's bedroom, and then departed.

"I waited and waited . . . and the phone kept ringing and ringing and ringing. I got scared and nervous and was fixing to leave. I didn't hear him come in as I was starting to leave."

Finally in this statement James did what he had been unwilling to do before—he admitted he had killed Jack Wilson. But his treatment of the murder itself was still self-serving—more a case of self-defense than homicide, as he told it.

"We were face-to-face. He grabbed me and was hollering. I freaked. We rassled. I reached and grabbed something and hit him until he turned me loose."

At the time of the hearing, Hooper and Sandlin did not yet have in hand the detailed autopsy findings. They were unable to challenge James on his assertion that he had merely defended himself against Jack Wilson's attack by pointing out that he had smashed Jack Wilson's skull nine times with a baseball bat, crushed his right hand, shattered both ulnas, splintered his collarbone, choked him until he broke the hyoid bone in his throat, then stabbed him twice, sawing and twisting the blade on the second stab.

Charlie Hooper did, however, catch one glaring inconsistency that somehow had been allowed to remain in James's otherwise carefully organized taped confession. At one point on the tape, James described how he had fled from the house on foot through the woods after the murder. At another later point, he told the story of Betty Wilson returning to the house to give him another lift in the BMW after the killing.

Hooper turned to Mickey Brantley and said, "Are you aware of any other inconsistency in the statements this man has made to you or any other authorities since his arrest?"

Brantley looked thoughtful for a moment, then said, "I believe he said at one point that he wore gloves when he went inside the house, and then he said later he might not have done that after all."

Judge Younger accepted capital murder charges against both twins, set Peggy's bail at $150,000, and ruled that Betty would not be allowed to leave jail on bond at any amount. Since the twins had not been charged with conspiracy, they had an absolute right under Alabama law to be tried separately, and their lawyers insisted they exercise that right. The general view is that it's much harder for the state to make a case of individual guilt than to paint with a broad brush and make a case of shared guilt. From the moment the bond hearing ended, then, the twins and their fates were severed. They went their separate ways to judgment.

In the corridor after the hearing, reporters mobbed Mo Brooks.

"Did you offer James White a deal?" one shouted.

"What did White get out of this?" another asked.

Mo Brooks held up a hand for quiet and shook his head solemnly. "We offered Mr. White no guarantees, but we told him there was always the possibility of lesser pleas."

"But isn't your case totally dependent on this man?" a reporter asked.

Brooks said, "The strongest evidence in this case is the logic of it. Why in the world would a Shelby County man come to Huntsville, pick out this house, take nothing from it, and kill a doctor of his prominence if someone else wasn't guiding him? There is no other explanation for what he did, other than the payoff.

"Look," Brooks said, holding one long finger up to the cameras. "One. Betty Wilson believed she was the sole beneficiary of Jack Wilson's will." He held up a second finger. "Two. She had affairs."

He paused dramatically.

"You put that together . . . and you have a motive."

He shut his hand in a fist over his head.

. . .

By then the prosecution already knew one thing about Jack, Betty, and money that Mo Brooks was failing to mention in his hallway indictment of Betty. For weeks before his death, Jack Wilson had been attempting to complete the paperwork on a new life-insurance policy that would have paid Betty a million dollars on his death. All it needed to be complete were her Social Security number and signature.

She had been too busy to attend to it. After his death police found the policy in a pile of things on the night stand next to Betty Wilson's bed, with yellow "sticky" notes on it to show her where to sign and enter her Social Security number. A curious oversight, for a grasping murderess.

But it was a time of media wars, and neither side was going to say things to the press that would do anything but bolster its own case.

Clearly, in that war, Mo Brooks was winning. The stories on television that evening and the headlines in the Alabama newspapers the next day were crooning with sex and the spice of dark scandal among the rich and the haughty. In the days and weeks that followed, newspapers and magazines all over the country raced to Huntsville for a sip from this delicious spring.

The *Huntsville Times* ran WHITE'S CONFESSION: HE KILLED FOR LOVE, then followed it a week later with Betty and Peggy's high school yearbook portraits on page 1 below a headline that said: BETTY WILSON SET OUT EARLY TO BE "SOMEBODY" (Came from "Poor" Family).

People magazine said, WIDOW'S WORK? AN ALABAMA KILLER CLAIMS TWIN SISTERS HIRED HIM FOR MURDER.

The Washington Times: DOUBLE TROUBLE FOR TWINS. ALABAMA SISTERS LINKED TO KILLING.

The New York Times: OF MAGNOLIAS, PASSION AND A MURDER.

The case was sweeping ahead powerfully, and still there was no formal deal with James, and the difficulty of coming to a deal grew greater each time Mo Brooks went before the cameras and said that James would receive no special treatment.

By mid-June Mo Brooks needed things nailed down. Word went out to Roy Miller that it was showtime. At 2:40 P.M. on June 15, 1992, James Dennison White and his attorney sat down at a long table in the grand jury room of the Madison County Courthouse. A moment later they were joined by Mo Brooks, a few of his staff, Mickey Brantley, a Huntsville police officer named Bill Payne, and a deputy sheriff who acted as guard over James.

It was an exquisite moment for Roy Miller. Both sides had big guns. Mo Brooks could get up from the long table, turn his back on James White, and let him go to his death. Or he could allow him to continue living. It was all in the stroke of a pen.

But James Dennison White had a big gun to fire, too. Without him, there was virtually no case against the twins.

While Brooks had been putting a brave face on it in public, he knew all too well that the passage of time was doing nothing for this case. There was still not a shred of physical evidence to tie the twins to Jack Wilson's murder. Weeks of ferocious searching by the police had failed to turn up a single bank record, a single handwritten note, a single letter, a single witness, a single tape recording, a single serial number on a bill, a single shred of evidence of any kind whatsoever—except for the word of James Dennison White—that would incriminate either woman in any way. The longer the search for physical evidence went on, the more it turned up things like Zeke, the damned dog. The only thing going for the state at the moment was the fever pitch of public opinion, whipped up by the media.

That could play two ways. It could help Brooks, or it could destroy him. James Dennison White might be smart, but he might be crazy, too. If for some loony reason he decided he didn't want to play, then Mo Brooks, who was facing an election only a few months down the road, would have to go before the press and tell them he was turning loose the witch, Betty Wilson, and her conspiring twin sister, Peggy Lowe.

Tim Morgan had already said he would like to see the lot of them fry. If Mo Brooks allowed the twins to slip through his fingers, Tim Morgan would have a field day, and everybody in the grand jury room that day knew it.

Both sides had big guns. Neither side could walk away.

The first order of business was the matter of what James was going to have to do for the state. According to notes kept by the district attorney's staff, James was told he would get a deal only if the evidence he provided resulted in the conviction of both twins. He was told that he had to tell the truth. He was told that the evidence he provided would have to be corroborated. He was told that he would lose the deal if during the trial—as, for example, when the defense was cross-examining him—he backed off from any of the evidence he had given the state before the trial.

With its own gun pointed at James, in other words, the state was saying: "You have to put both twins in the chair, and you have to stick to your story once you get into court, no matter what."

Then Roy Miller inquired what the state was prepared to do for his client.

Mo Brooks said he would allow James to plead to capital murder with a sentence of life in prison without parole.

The notes don't indicate what happened after Brooks made that offer. But where the notes take up again, they show that James's team had acquired a new ally in Mickey Brantley. Apparently working to keep the deal together, Brantley argued that James should be allowed to plead to a charge of simple murder, as opposed to capital murder. Under Alabama law and parole regulations, such a plea probably would allow James to leave prison within seven years or less.

This was no mere "walk." Given the especially heinous nature of the killing and the fact that he did it for money, James's crime fit all the criteria for which the capital murder statute was written. By any reading of the law, his penalty, if he was found guilty, should have been death. Life in prison without parole would have been a walk. Brantley was arguing for a waltz.

But Brooks, in spite of all the tough public speeches he had been making about not giving James White a soft deal, eventually came around. James would be allowed to plead to simple murder, even though it meant he might spend less time in prison for Jack Wilson's killing than some people serve for repeated burglary.

It was good. But it was not enough. James still wanted it in writing.

At some point a typewriter was sent for. When the door to the grand jury room finally opened at the end of the day and James White emerged with his smiling attorney, they had in their possession a copy of a neatly typed contract, signed by Mo Brooks, promising James White a better deal than he could ever have dreamed of. With a price. It was up to him and him alone to put Betty Wilson and Peggy Lowe in the electric chair.

In the course of later court proceedings, lawyers for the twins repeatedly told jurors they could not remember ever having seen another instance, in their own personal legal experience or in the lawbooks, when an Alabama district attorney had signed his name to a written contract like the one James White got. In addition to the fact that it was a written contract, the lawyers hammered away at the process that had produced it and at what the contract actually said. It was, the defense lawyers argued, an agreement by which James White promised to stick to whatever lies the state wanted him to tell. Again and again, the lawyers challenged the state to produce another case in which a similar agreement had been struck.

The state responded each time that the contract required James to tell the truth, not to lie, and that there was nothing sinister or illegal about the fact the agreement was in written form. But the state never did come up with a similar contract.

It was not unusual for the state to make a deal with an accused person in exchange for that person's cooperation in making a case against someone else. That practice is not only commonplace; most people familiar with the daily workings of the criminal justice system believe the system would grind to a halt if such deals were not made. It is in the nature of crime—especially conspiratorial crime—that only the conspirators know the full story of what happened. In order to crack the ring and get inside, police and prosecutors have to cut deals, however distasteful the process may be.

Nor is there any evidence that in making their deal with James White officials were deliberately taking part in a conspiracy of their own to defeat the truth. Cops and prosecutors are like surgeons, firefighters, soldiers, nurses, clergy. Every day they come to crossroads where they have only their own best estimate to tell them which path is the right one. It is in the nature of what they do that the decisions they make will involve life and death. They have to decide. They cannot always be right.

What was intriguing about the James Dennison White deal was the written contract. He had insisted on it from the beginning. It was a very unusual practice, exposing Mo Brooks to personal political peril and opening the state up to attack and ridicule later during the trials. But James got his way. What the existence of a written contract showed was the degree to which James White was in the driver's seat.

From that point forward, James was the most important member of the legal team. As a lifelong denizen of jails and mental institutions, he knew exactly what this meant in terms of what he could demand, and he began making his demands right away.

In return for his continuing cooperation with the police and the prosecution, James was made a trusty at the Madison County jail. As such, he had a fairly free run of the facility, including the law library and even, at times, the offices of jail officials. He was able to make calls not merely to members of his family in Vincent but to people all over the country.

Security was more lax for James than for any other prisoner in the jail. Chief Deputy Charlie Norment knew he didn't have to worry about James.

James had a deal going. He was happy. In jail, he was a prodigal son who had returned home. James wasn't going to do anything to rock his own boat at this point.

In the weeks following the decision, Peggy and Wayne Lowe's friends in Talladega and Vincent, many of them members of their church, went to a bail bondsman as a group and pledged their homes to raise the bond for Peggy. Peggy was freed on bond and went home.

Betty was removed from the group cell she had occupied before the hearing and placed in a tiny windowless slit of a cell, barely ten feet by three, on an upper floor in a darkened corner of the jail. It was a space normally used for solitary confinement. She was not allowed out of the cell to exercise or to visit the library. The only people allowed to visit her were her lawyers.

She could not meet the lawyers in the prisoners' conference room—they had to come sit on the steel bunk that occupied 75 percent of her floor space and talk to her there. The front of the cell was open so that she could be observed by guards and by passing prisoners at all times, waking and sleeping, eating and using the toilet. On occasion she saw James White pass by, always chipper and sassy, and on occasion he looked in at her and gave her a tiny smirking shrug.

For the most part she kept her composure. If anything, her tough streak was emerging. On a rare occasion when a legal conference allowed her to talk to Peggy, she said, "Don't worry about me, Sister. I can take care of myself. These guys are all just little shitasses when you come right down to it. They don't even know what they're doing or why."

But in those first weeks of imprisonment she was occasionally overwhelmed and made the mistake of showing it.

One night, after a guard had insisted on humiliating her by staring at her while she used the toilet, Betty said, "I don't really understand. I don't know what would make you want to be so mean to me."

The guard came up to the bars of her cell, clutched them with both hands, and hissed, "Any rich bitch that would fuck a nigger deserves to die."

Not long after the hearing in which Betty's bond was denied, Charlie Hooper brought her the news that her case was going to be tried separately from Peggy's and that she would go first.

They sat on the steel bunk with a deputy standing not ten feet away, watching and listening.

"I'm with my client here, I would like some privacy," Hooper said.

The deputy shrugged and turned his face away from them but did not move off.

"What does it mean?" Betty asked in a whisper.

"It means they think they have the better shot with you. The media hasn't been able to get any dirt on Peggy."

"There isn't any."

Hooper gave her a long look.

"Oh, I know," she laughed. "There's plenty on me. I'm sure I could tell them some things they haven't even found out yet."

"Please don't."

He told her he had heard a rumor about one woman, a doctor's wife and former friend of Betty's. The woman's husband had committed suicide. Supposedly she was prepared to come to court and swear that soon after her husband's death, Betty had come to her and asked if she had actually killed her husband. Worse, according to the rumor, the woman was going to say Betty had asked her if she could give her any pointers on how to do it.

"Oh, it's Brenda," Betty said. "Brenda Cerha. Right?"

"I don't know."

"Well, it is. I can explain all that. She had two husbands who killed themselves. One hanged himself in a motel closet in some kind of kinky sex thing. The second one blew his brains out while he was in bed with her. They were drug addicts. He was an anesthesiologist."

"Did you . . . ?"

"Ask her that? No, of course not."

"Why would she say you did?"

"She hates me. She really hates me. She was in the hospital drying out from drugs. I took care of her little girl."

"And?"

"I took the little girl to an A.A. meeting with me."

"And?"

"I told the little girl her mother was a drug addict."

"Why?"

"Charlie . . . it's hard to explain to someone who hasn't been there. Children notice something is wrong when their father blows his brains out and their mother is walking into walls all day. They need to know what it is. It's cruel not to tell them."

Charlie Hooper let out a long sigh. "This business about the drugs and so on is going to be very rough."

"Well, I'm dried out, Charlie; I'm successfully recovering . . ."

"I know that, Betty, and you know it, but that's not how all this is going to be painted to a jury. And then your affairs. Mo Brooks is already calling you a world-famous slut."

They sat shoulder to shoulder on the bunk, both staring glumly at the floor.

She shrugged. "I'm not world-famous."

They both chuckled.

"You are now," he said.

He looked up and smiled, but the smile faded.

"What is it?" she asked. "There's something else, right?"

"It's not good."

Tears began to gather at the corners of her eyes. "What is it, Charlie?"

"Sandlin and I are going to have a full-time job representing you. Peggy will need her own counsel. But even at that, I've told you you're going to need a lot more than just us to represent you. I'm not even a criminal lawyer. Marc is very good, but he and I are both worried about this witness."

"You mean James White?"

"Yes."

"He doesn't seem like much to me. His story is so full of holes . . ."

"The point is, Betty, he's got the state of Alabama on his side. They're back there propping him up, telling him what to do. In fact, right now James Dennison White *is* the state of Alabama. And that's a whole lot to fight."

"You're fine by me so far, Charlie. So is Marc. I trust both of you to do what has to be done."

"Yeah, listen, Betty, you need somebody big, and it's not going to be cheap."

"I have money."

He paused.

"Don't I?" she asked.

The estate included $3.8 million in stocks and bonds, another $1.2 million in IRA savings, $700,000 worth of real estate investments not including Boulder Circle. With the house, a small insurance policy, and their cash accounts thrown in, the Wilsons were worth $6.3 million. Of that amount, only $2.7 million had been held solely in Jack's name. The rest of it—$3.6 million—was held jointly, which should have meant that Betty had instant access to it, even before the will was probated. It was her money.

But things were happening. It may all have begun with the media hype. Within days after the *New York Times* and the *People* magazine articles were published, Hollywood producers had begun calling members of the Wilson family, trying to buy exclusive rights to the twins' story for a movie-of-the-week. As always in such cases, the bidding was intense and competitive, with various producers trying to block up story rights in order to get the edge on other producers.

In most such cases, one producer emerges with the best package, including exclusive story rights, a great proposal showing how he or she will treat the story, perhaps even the name of a star who has expressed interest in playing the lead role, and the names of some investors who are willing to throw in the seed money. That producer, then, is the one who is able to go to a television network and secure a commitment that if the movie comes out as promised, the network will buy it and put it on the air.

In this case—as in most cases—some of the producers vying for the story rights told various members of the family that if they did not grant them their rights, the producers would go to other parts of the family. At the same time, of course, Mickey Brantley was interviewing family members and, in so doing, was explaining to them his theory of how Betty had brought about Jack's brutal murder.

Dr. Jack Wilson and Betty Wilson at Snowmass, 1985

Peggy Lowe with her mother, Nell Woods, in 1994

2700 Boulder Circle, Huntsville, Alabama, the scene of the murder

James White's house overlooking Vincent, Alabama

Betty Wilson runs the gantlet, flanked by photographers and journalists, on her way to another day in court.

Peggy Lowe testifies at her twin's trial.

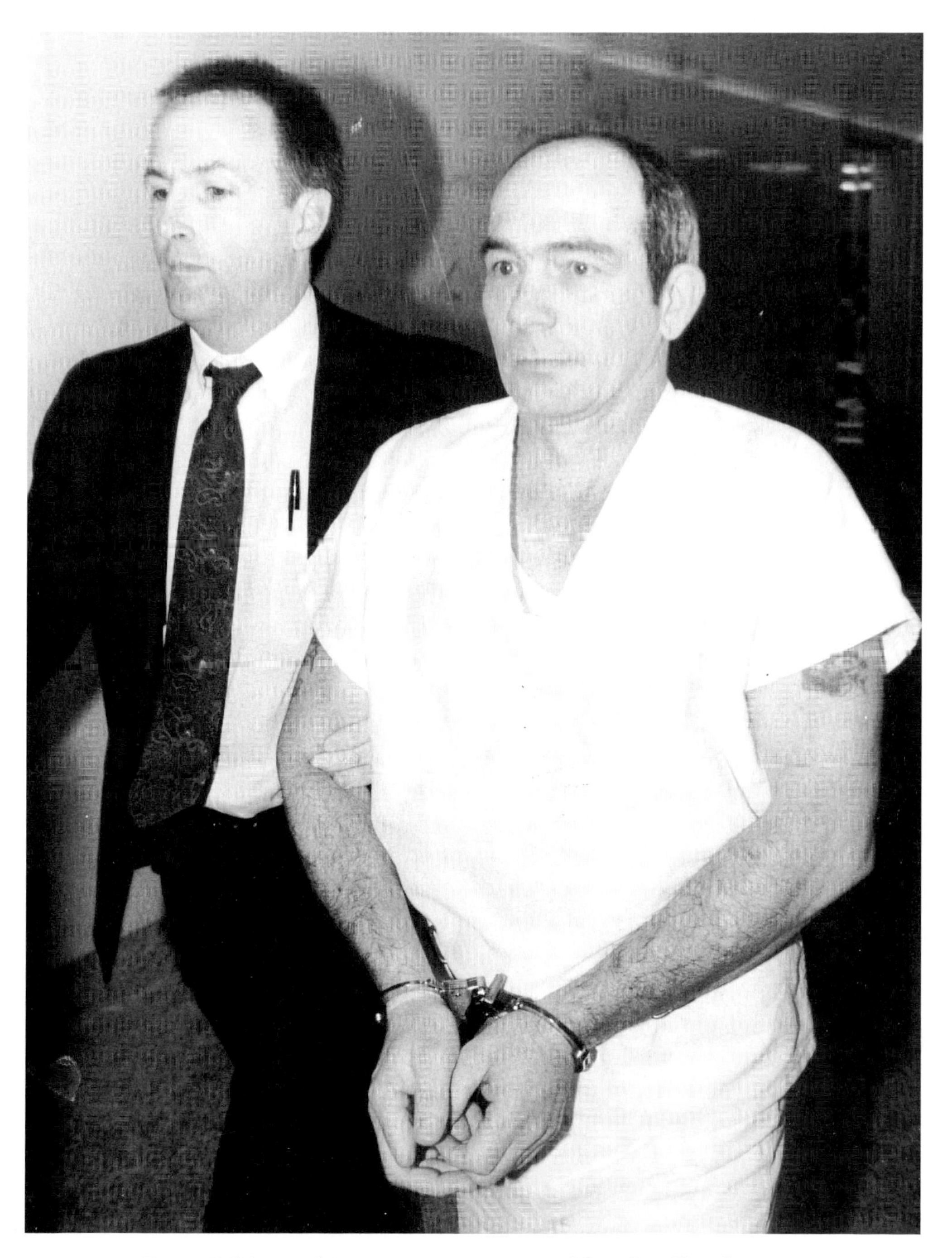

James White, on his way to court, escorted by Sheriff Ted Sexton

Jimmy Fry, moments before he suddenly smashed the bat on the podium to show the jury how James White used it to crush Jack Wilson's skull

From left: Deputy Wayne Johnson; Bobby Lee Cook, seated on rail; Jimmy Fry

From left: Betty Wilson's son Dink; her mother, Nell; and her sister GeDelle—on hearing the verdict in Tuscaloosa

Betty's own sons by her first husband—Bo, Dink, and Trey—had been told by Hooper that they would hurt their mother if they got involved in a movie deal or any other venture in which they would appear to be profiting from Jack's murder. But Hooper didn't need to tell them—they weren't interested in talking to the Hollywood people.

Jack's sons—Scott, Perry, and Stephen—were in a different position. They never had been close to Betty. Fairly soon after the murder, they had come to believe that Brantley's version was the truth. They had even hired a prominent local attorney, Joe Ritch, to "assist the prosecution"—an old Southern tradition in which people who can afford to do so help stack the deck against a purported wrongdoer by paying a private lawyer to "help" the D.A. As often as not, the private lawyer's job is to remind the D.A. that people are looking over his shoulder and that it will be known if he does a poor or a lazy job. Ritch, a civil attorney, also was charged with looking after Jack's sons' financial interests.

In his last will, Jack had provided for Scott and Stephen, but only in the same proportion as he had provided for Betty's sons, and all of their interests were subordinate to Betty's. Jack had specifically cut Perry out of his will because of the problems he and Perry had suffered over money and other matters in the past.

Quickly after Jack's murder, someone explained to Jack's sons that neither Betty nor her heirs could share a penny of their father's estate if she was found guilty of a role in his murder. On the other hand, if she did have access to his estate, a hefty slice of the money might be spent on her legal defense. Then, if she prevailed, she might decide later to leave an even larger share to her own sons than Jack had contemplated.

Believing, as they did, that Betty was a conspirator in their father's death, it was understandable that Jack's sons would seek to block her from getting any of his money. Hiring Ritch was part of a general legal strategy to do just that.

Joe Ritch, then, was in an interesting position. It was his job to protect the assets of the estate from Betty, for the benefit of his clients, Jack's three sons. It was also his job to help the prosecution nail Betty for the murder, which would have the effect of protecting the money from her.

And he did more. Since Jack's boys were siding with the prosecution and saw themselves as victims of the plot, it would do them no harm to associate themselves with a movie deal. One of the first things Joe Ritch did for them, in fact, was help negotiate the terms by which they gave their story rights to producer Larry Thompson, who was able to get a commitment for his movie from CBS television.

Because there were other producers in town, vowing that they would go to other family members for story rights if Jack's boys didn't cooperate, it made sense for Ritch to make the best deal he could, as quickly as he could.

The twins' story seemed to have an unusual appeal for Hollywood. Normally, once one producer has landed a network commitment, the others step aside. The usual outcome—unless it's a case like that of Amy Fisher, the "Long Island Lolita" who shot her lover's wife in the face, a story that attracted a truly phenomenal amount of national media attention—is that there will be only one network movie. Whoever lands a network deal takes the whole cake, and the others go look somewhere else.

In this case, however, a second producer had announced to the media that he had secured a commitment from ABC for a movie about the twins, with no story rights at all, based simply on the news accounts, court records, and other public-domain sources. If both movies wound up being made, there would be two Alabama twins network television movies.

No one can know now how great an effect the bidding war by the movie producers had on the early formation of opposing camps among the members of Jack and Betty's extended family. But another of the first legal moves by the anti-Betty faction was a lawsuit, joined by the bank that managed the estate, suing Betty and Peggy for any money they might make from a movie deal. It was an empty gesture, since neither Betty nor Peggy nor any of their family members nor any of the lawyers connected with Betty and Peggy would even return phone calls from the television producers who were hounding them.

But somewhere in that crazy swirl of events, people in the family got the idea that someone else was going to get rich from Jack's murder. The envy and anxiety engendered by that thought were enough to drive a wedge between the opposing camps quickly and permanently.

Unable to quell the storm by any action of their own, Betty and Peggy's lawyers stood by helplessly and watched while Joe Ritch and lawyers for the bank moved swiftly to lock up every penny Betty might ever be able to lay a hand on. None of it—even the part that was Betty's already—could be touched by anyone until the legal maelstrom was resolved, which meant the money would be locked away for years and years.

What Charlie Hooper had come to tell Betty that day in jail was that there was no money—not a cent—with which to mount a legal defense. He might conceivably persuade the court to pay him for his own services, since Betty did have a right to a court-appointed attorney. But Hooper, who had given up the rest of his practice and had been working tirelessly, night and day, on her case, was convinced she needed a bigger gun for trial. And this would have to be someone who was so big that he or she could afford to work for nothing, with a promise that, someday when the estate was freed from all the lawsuits buzzing around it, there might be some money left over to pay him or her.

"What are the chances of finding someone like that?" she asked.

He shrugged. "You have only one thing to offer," he said. "You are getting one hell of a lot of press. Now if we can just find somebody who's willing to work for publicity, we'll be home free."

"It's serious, isn't it, Charlie?"

"Yes, Betty. It's a capital case. If we lose . . ."

"If we lose, what?"

"You understand that you could go to the electric chair."

Her face fell. She did know it, somewhere in the back of her mind. It was not a surprise. But no one had said it out loud to her before.

SEVEN

JAMES WHITE WAS STILL REMEMBERING.

A short time after his confession was played in court, James remembered why he had not taken the gun with him to the murder. He said he had decided not to use a gun, because he had become shellshocked in Vietnam and was afraid of guns. Apparently he had forgotten he was shellshocked when he had asked the twins for a gun in the first place.

The media accounts so far had all been decidedly anti-Betty, lingering pointedly on her "liking for men," as one story put it. The only area that could be interpreted as favoring the twins was the matter of physical evidence. Late in the game, some reporters were waking up to the fact that not one bit of evidence had been gathered to support any of James White's claims.

In a press conference outside the courthouse, a reporter had asked Mo Brooks what had happened to the clothes the killer was wearing. Physical evidence was becoming the one area where the media seemed skeptical of the official story.

At the end of July, James White summoned Mickey Brantley to the small office James used occasionally in the Madison County jail and told him that he had suddenly remembered exactly what clothes he had been wearing the day of the murder and what he had done with them afterward. He said he had been wearing a pair of blue jeans with gold braid on the back and down the sides and had also been wearing a plaid shirt.

He said that after the murder, he had placed these items of clothing in a white plastic bag. He said that he also had placed in the bag the murder weapon he had taken with him that day to do the job—a three-foot length of quarter-inch-diameter hemp rope. He remembered for the first time that he had planned on garroting the doctor.

But the better part of his sudden remembrance was this: He remembered that he had placed this bag under a rock in a certain place in Betty Wilson's backyard.

In the feverish media and legal circus that exploded around this disclosure—lights, cameras, midnight searches, wild courtroom scenes, angry shouting, press conferences—no one thought to ask just what it was that James Dennison White had worn home, then, if he had taken off all his clothes and buried them under a rock in Betty Wilson's backyard. So frenetic was the mood at the time, no one even noticed that James White by his own account at this point had been carried away from the murder scene lying on the backseat of Betty Wilson's BMW beneath a pink plastic garment bag, buck naked. And then got out of her car and into his pickup truck on the parking lot of the mall at 6:40 P.M. and drove halfway across the state of Alabama.

The evening after the disclosure, Mickey Brantley and a full detail of Huntsville police officers appeared at the scene, accompanied by the entire media flotilla of dish trucks, vans, and rental cars that had taken up the story as a full-time occupation. In a few solemnly terse words, Brantley conceded that a major, perhaps even conclusive, turn in the case was just about to occur. With that he strode out into the yard, more or less directly to a large flat rock at the downhill side of the property below the swimming pool. Lifting the rock carefully with a stick, he unearthed the bag.

It was black, not white. But the pants James White had described were neatly folded inside. With them, also folded, were a plaid shirt and a length of hemp cord. In spite of a number of rainstorms that had swept the area since the murder, the clothing appeared remarkably clean, almost as if freshly laundered. Certainly there was no sign of blood anywhere on any of the clothes.

None of the gang of reporters covering the unearthing of the murder clothes that day questioned Brantley about the curiously tidy appearance of the garments. Some of the same reporters had covered the Zeke-the-dog chapter, but no one asked how it was Zeke had overlooked the blue jeans with gold braid and the plaid shirt lying partially exposed to the air beneath a round river rock at the edge of the property.

It was Mickey Brantley's day. Now they had everything. They had James White's story. They had corroborating evidence from the cash registers at the mall. They had motive (she thought she was his sole beneficiary, and she had affairs). And now they had physical evidence—the entire outfit the murderer had worn that day, found hidden under a rock a few yards from the murder scene itself.

Peggy Lowe had not heard a word of good news in a long time. The fear and weight of the criminal investigation was making it difficult for her to go through the motions of life. Her friends, fellow church members, and the people at her school were doing what they could. School officials in Vincent told her they could not allow her to continue working in the classroom with children, but they did find a job for her in the district headquarters office, described vaguely to reporters as a "consultancy." Creating a new, somewhat iffy position for Peggy, in order to protect her paycheck, was a risky and very expensive move for a tiny school district that could not afford to pay for new shelves in its teachers' classrooms. But there was a heartsick sense in the district offices that somehow all of this had befallen Peggy Lowe and her sister because of Peggy's job at the school—meeting James White there and hiring him to do work in her classroom and so on. The district wanted to do what it could to help.

Never for an instant did any of the people in Vincent who knew Peggy Lowe believe that she was guilty of anything.

But the news from Huntsville had continued to get worse and

worse. Peggy and Wayne were dumbfounded when Jack's sons aligned themselves with Mo Brooks. Then, when the opposition managed to freeze all Betty's money so that she could not afford to hire an expensive legal team, Wayne and Peggy began to get genuinely frightened.

For so long the entire saga had seemed like a strange nightmare that had drifted into their waking world, like weather from another dimension. They kept believing in their hearts that it would all dissipate; the sun would come out and everyone would see suddenly what a terrible mistake had been made.

Marc Sandlin, who was still communicating with Peggy while she looked for her own lawyer, had counseled her against that kind of optimism. "This is going to be a tough fight," he said. "All the way."

A friend who had experience in big-city politics told her the same thing: "The truth doesn't matter now, Peggy. People have taken public positions, and now they are invested in them. From here on out it's a game to see who wins, and people will do whatever they have to do to avoid losing. It's too high-profile. No one can afford to back off anything, even an inch, even if they discover in their heart of hearts they've made a mistake. Whoever loses loses everything."

Betty and Peggy had worried when their lawyers told them they were going to ask the court to move the trial out of Huntsville to a place where the publicity had been less intense.

"I guess they feel the deck is already stacked against you in Huntsville," Peggy told Betty on the phone.

"Maybe," she said. "I'm not too sure how well a lot of my life is going to go down in Boondocks, Alabama, though."

"I think we have to trust them on this, Betty."

Betty's concern was heightened in October when the court announced it was granting the request of the defense for a change of venue and had decided to take the trial to Tuscaloosa in west-central Alabama. A trial date was set for late February 1993.

"Tuscaloosa," Betty kept muttering to herself. "Seems to me I have spent a lot of time trying to stay away from places like Tuscaloosa."

Peggy's heart quickened when Sandlin called, telling her he finally had a bit of good news to relate.

"Very good news," he said.

"What?"

"Guess who has agreed to come on the team and help defend Betty?"

"Who, Marc?"

"Does the name 'Matlock' mean anything to you?"

Her mind whirled. Everything had been so surreal. "Do you mean Andy Griffith?"

In a sense, he did. Somehow, whenever a reporter wrote a profile of Georgia defense lawyer Bobby Lee Cook, the "Matlock" business was at the top of the story. Cook himself always modestly suggested he had no real idea if he was truly the model for the character portrayed by actor Andy Griffith in a popular television serial of that name. He allowed that there might be strong similarities between himself and the television character.

Like Matlock, Bobby Lee Cook was famous. Like Matlock, he was rich. Like Matlock, he maintained his home and offices in a small town in Georgia—Summerville, a picturesque community of five thousand some sixty five miles northwest of Atlanta in the heart of the Chattahoochee National Forest—even though his business took him all over the world.

He was very smart and could reel off Shakespeare like a trained actor, but he also had an aw-shucks country-boy persona that he could whip out and wield like a trusty pocket knife on suitable occasions. According to his own publicity, he almost always got his clients off: He claimed that of the three hundred murderers he had defended, only "10 percent" had served time.

Bobby Lee Cook was not surprised, he told reporters, that so many reporters, sleuths that they were, had discovered the similarities between himself and Matlock. It was unlikely the producers of the TV show ever would admit he had served as their inspiration, he told reporters, because "they would probably have to pay me royalties if it was based on me."

A wire-service story that made the rounds of the Alabama newspapers shortly after the announcement painted Cook as "drawing on a bent pipe," listening intently to a potential client's tale of woe "from behind gold-rimmed, half-moon spectacles," his face "ruddy with pink splotches" at age sixty four, "his chin framed with a bristly white goatee . . . his tea-dark hair, straggly and over-the-collar long . . . parted in the middle—an elegant, grizzled look that belongs in a daguerreotype."

The story said: "Often considered the model for TV's 'Matlock,' the pricey Atlanta lawyer played by Andy Griffith, Mr. Cook first gained public attention during a notorious 1975 murder case. In a stunning reversal of a trial-court verdict, he showed that witness testimony used to convict seven men for the murder of Cobb County pathologists Warren and Rosina Matthews had been 'programmed' through pretrial hypnosis."

Later in the story, the writer described Bobby Lee Cook's lifestyle, when he was not in Summerville playing the good old boy next door:

"At his retreat on Georgia's posh Sea Island, Mr. Cook is sipping a cool glass of Chardonnay beside a blue pool adance in midday light. The Cooks own another, larger retreat in the north Alabama mountains. A life spent in mortal legal combat has its rewards."

Another newspaper story suggested accurately that Cook probably had been added to the team with the specific task of taking on James Dennison White, the twins' one and only accuser. "Like a high school bully," the writer said, "Mr. Cook can take a witness's phrase, an inconsistency, even his appearance, and turn it into the rhetorical equivalent of a tire iron."

Mo Brooks countered the news that Cook was joining the opposing team with some mildly disparaging semi-off-the-record remarks to the regular courthouse press in Huntsville, but it was clear that Brooks had been knocked off his pace. He had hoped the moves to lock up all of Betty's assets and cash would scare off any really formidable contenders.

One aspect of Bobby Lee Cook's reputation—seldom mentioned in his own carefully orchestrated publicity but well known among lawyers in the South—was his aversion to donating his services to rich people. He did his share of pro bono work for the poor in the part of Georgia where he lived, but he didn't work for people with money unless they were prepared to slide a nice slice of that money over to his side of the table. He would not have taken on a role in the Betty Wilson defense unless he was confident they would be able to get her off and thereby free up her money.

One part of the media hype on Cook was believed by Brooks and his staff to be true: He did have, they understood, an uncanny ability to take a witness apart. He did it swiftly and efficiently, as if prying open a cheap watch. It was something in his style of float and sting. Cook could modulate from the role of wise old country colonel to big city smart aleck before a witness had time to focus. His style was especially devastating with witnesses like James White, who were put together with spit and baling wire in the first place.

Everyone on both sides of the trial understood that James was going to have to go into court and be someone very unlike his normal self. For one thing, he would have to be sober. He would have to be cleaned up physically. Somehow James White would have to become a sympathetic figure. It would be all right for him to be pathetic, but he could not come across, even for an instant, as vicious, loony, or scary in any way. He would have to be in complete control of himself.

Bobby Lee Cook treated witnesses like James White as if they were marionettes. Behind the scenes, the state was pulling the wires, making its witness say what it wanted him to say, making him smile, frown, and cry on cue. If Bobby Lee Cook could snip the right wire, the puppet would begin to speak for itself. And once that happened with James White, everyone agreed, Betty Wilson would be home free.

There was no telling where the wire might be. Cook would be armed with every shred of history on James White that could possibly be gathered. He would know all about James being diagnosed as a delusional schizophrenic, his reputation for lying and scamming, the incestuous abuse of his own child. But those might not even be the strings he would go for. By the time James got to trial, after all, he would already have been supplied with carefully rehearsed pat answers to all of those challenges: "I was drunk, I don't remember, I say it didn't happen that way, I have found the Lord since then."

But Cook didn't always confine himself to predictable attacks. One incident illustrated how well Cook could work the needle. In a case in Georgia he had been up against a state witness who had been groomed and rehearsed like a prize show dog. Normally an out-of-control psycho-thug like James, this witness had been dried out and tuned up. As it would be with James, the trick in this trial was to get the witness to show his fangs in front of the jury. But no matter what Cook did to try to break through the man's defenses, the witness stayed calm, cool, and collected.

Then, during a break, Cook saw the man conferring with the prosecutor in the hallway. Sticking out from the pants cuffs of the man's new pinstripe suit (a gift of the government) was a pair of particularly country-looking alligator cowboy boots, with ugly stainless-steel plates over the toes.

Cook circled the man several times, looking a little closer at the boots each time, until he had effectively stolen the man's attention from the prosecutor and attracted the attention of everyone else in the corridor.

"Well, looky here, will you?" Cook began slowly. "Will you look at those boots? Got the man a nice new pinstripe suit, and they forgot to take off his shitkickers."

When people in the crowd laughed, the witness turned beet red and muttered a curse through his teeth. His government handler shooed him into the witness room and went to work immediately trying to smooth him out for the remaining portion of Cook's cross-examination.

But it was a lost cause. Cook had known precisely where to probe and how deep in order to pierce the inflamed center of the man's class-bound Southern macho pride. When the trial reconvened, Bobby Lee Cook needed only to walk up into the man's face and smirk, and the man exploded in a hissing, seething, frenzied rage. In those few seconds, the witness went from being invulnerable to being completely worthless.

The better Brooks and the police got to know James, the more they realized that he was a two-edged sword. Sober, he was much cleverer and more resilient than they might have imagined he would be. But he was also prideful. The con-man side of him emerged, in which it was always very important for James to feel that he was winning something in each exchange. The one thing that would set him off would be the feeling that someone else had bested him in a public duel.

Clever and resolved as he might seem at present, James nevertheless was a prime candidate for being bested. There was a lot of target there for Bobby Lee Cook's needle. James spoke in a nervous stutter that got worse when he was under pressure. With his face twisting away and downward and his eyes flickering back and forth, James tended to reek of guilt and inferiority.

And then there was the extremely difficult matter of the nature of the accusation. The story was that James killed Jack Wilson for love. For the love of Peggy.

Peggy Lowe was two things. No matter how hard the police dug, they could not find anything to show she was other than a completely virtuous person. She was also another thing—a very beautiful woman, in a very Southern, proper, mature-former-prom-queen sort of a way.

In order to believe James's story, the jury was going to have to look at him—a scary-looking little bald man with shifty eyes and very bad teeth—and then imagine Peggy Lowe smooching him. That was what James would have to carry off in order to keep his end of his bargain with the state.

His ego would be at stake. Bobby Lee Cook would know it. And Bobby Lee Cook would come to town with his whip cracking. Therefore, there was a great deal of work to be done with, for, and on James Dennison White. As a witness, James was still in embryonic form. As it turned out, the state had nine months to get him ready for trial.

. . .

By the time the indictments were all in hand, the lawyers hired, and the process of preparation under way, the case had become more or less the personal responsibility of Mickey Brantley. In the months that followed, Brantley worked tirelessly to gather corroborative evidence, continuing to confer with James both in person and through his lawyer, Roy Miller. During this period, Brantley was under intense public and political scrutiny.

James himself was coming along quite nicely. On a steady diet of prison food and exercise, he was putting on weight and getting some color in his cheeks. His eyes were brighter, and his manner more confident and alert. The good news for the state was that beneath the layers of booze and bad living, James White was turning out to be a fairly bright fellow.

Even better news: He could take the needle. When they jabbed at him, picked at him, poked fun at him to see how he would react, James understood what to do. He put his ears back, bit his lips, and stared at them cool and smooth. He knew. If he acted like an asshole, the jury would kiss him off. If the jury kissed him off and the twins didn't go down, he would. It was worth a little self-control.

While James was roaming the jail, wearing fresh whites every day and making calls from a borrowed office, Betty Wilson spent every day and every night huddled like a rabbit in a tiny windowless solitary-confinement cell. Her jailers watched her eagerly. Two months into her confinement, rumors began coming from the jail that Betty Wilson was cracking up.

Across the street from the Madison County Courthouse in one of the neo-Colonial office buildings favored by the criminal bar, a lawyer close to the case leaned across his desk and told a visiting writer: "They say she's pretty well out of her head. I understand it's not a pretty picture."

Perhaps the jailers simply misunderstood what they were looking at. In many ways, after all, Betty had never been a pretty picture. She called them shitheads, assholes, and motherfuckers every chance she got. She screamed at them, laughed at them, even threw things at them infrequently. But on the rare occasions when she was able to talk to Peggy, her voice was hard as steel.

"Me? Nuts? They wish. That's what those bastards are hoping for. You know me, honey, I've always been a little off-center. But I'll see them all rot in Hell before I let them get to me. I'll show them what to do with their nuts."

"Betty, please."

"Sorry."

In the nine months before the trial, the political landscape around the case underwent further important changes. As the district attorney's race drew down toward its final weeks, Mo Brooks stepped up his assertions that a vote for Tim Morgan was a vote to let Betty Wilson out of jail. Finally, sensing that the issue might really hurt him, Morgan called a press conference to announce that when elected, the first thing he would do would be to recuse himself from the Jack Wilson murder case on the grounds of a personal connection with the accused.

He had already said he wanted to see Betty and her sister fry. Now he was promising the voters he would take himself out of the case, just in case they didn't believe him.

Insiders said it would be a close race. Mo Brooks was hell on law-and-order issues, but this was still Alabama, and Brooks suffered three significant disabilities. He was a Republican; he was a Mormon; and he wore wire-rim glasses. Tim Morgan, on the other hand, was a Democrat, a gentleman, and a good old boy; he was handsome and had just the merest glint of rascality in his eyes when he smiled.

Morgan won. True to his word, he announced immediately he would not take part in the prosecution of the Alabama twins, which threw the question of who would do the prosecuting into the lap of the attorney general of the state of Alabama.

In Alabama there is a complicated relationship between local district attorneys and the state's attorney general. The attorney general enjoys a certain amount of legal superintendency over local prosecutors, but local prosecutors are elected on their own hook, from their own constituencies, with their own independent political clout in their own home counties. Legally the attorney general can assign a case to a local prosecutor, but obviously it won't do much good to assign a case to someone who isn't going to pursue it vigorously. Normally the A.G. asks local prosecutors whether they will agree to take on a case.

In the case of the Alabama twins, several local prosecutors were actively courting the attorney general, trying to get him to offer them the case. Very few cases came down the pike that attracted the kind of national publicity the twins case was drawing. It was a chance for someone to make a major career move. But Attorney General Jimmy Evans took two long months after Morgan's election in November to decide whom to favor.

Barely two months before the trial, Evans gave the case to Jimmy Fry, district attorney in Limestone County, which adjoins Madison County and Huntsville. He was an interesting choice.

At age forty, Jimmy Fry was an up-and-comer in Alabama politics—a good-looking man with the right social graces and political connections for the cities but with other qualities that would help make him appealing to the rural folk as well. For one thing he had acquired early in life a staunch, bandy-legged girth, which people in the rural South still tend to take for a sign of substance in a man.

He was a natural for Tuscaloosa. In that kind of setting, small-town Alabama, one chunk of a man like Jimmy Fry, standing before the jury with his blue blazer flapping at the sides of a huge white stomach like the wings of a well-fed jaybird, would be worth ten skinny Tim Morgans slinking around the courtroom in Italian suits.

The only problem was that he was getting this case extremely late in the day. With only two months left before trial, he would have to take the entire case—the investigation and all of the legal work leading up to it—as a package deal from the authorities in Huntsville.

Normally, a heads-up district attorney can do a great deal along the way to shape an investigation. In fact, district attorneys and police detectives often serve as a kind of check-and-balance on each other. If the D.A. wants to go soft on a case because the accused is a political ally, the police can always start leaking the evidence to the press. If the police have been too ambitious and have ignored evidence that might prove the innocence of the accused, the D.A. can always tell them he wants them to go back and ask new questions, poke under new rocks, or interview new witnesses.

But the twins case had been lost in a curious limbo for several months by the time Jimmy Fry got it. Mo Brooks had pushed hard on the Huntsville police to get the case going and get it in order, but then Mo Brooks had been defeated at the polls. Tim Morgan had recused himself, and then the Alabama attorney general had taken two months to decide to whom he was going to throw this particular bridal bouquet. The net effect, then, was that the case had been the sole property and responsibility all this time of one Mickey Brantley.

Largely unsupervised, going it alone with a case that more politically savvy police officials might prefer to avoid, Mickey Brantley had made the twins case his personal crusade. He was going to see it through and see it come out right. It was his brass ring. And he was a man who believed fervently in the righteousness of his own cause.

Brantley loaded boxes and boxes of evidence into a van one gray winter morning shortly before the holidays, then got in his own police car and followed the van over the county line into Athens, the seat of Limestone County. When Jimmy Fry came out and saw the boxes, he let go a long sighing exhalation. He turned to Mickey Brantley and said, "Well, Mr. Brantley, it looks like you and I are not going to have much of a Christmas this year."

"No, sir," Brantley said. "I didn't figure we would."

They were an unlikely pair in many ways—Fry, with his sly, slow, duck-hunting wit, and Brantley, with his stern, Bible-quoting, steely-eyed sobriety—but in the long late hours they spent poring over reams and reams of evidence, they formed a relationship that was good enough for the mission.

Brantley's long patient tilling of the field over the months was finally producing a harvest. The overwhelming sentiment in Huntsville by now was that Betty was guilty, and people were coming out of the woodwork with anecdotes about her past. Most were of limited significance, but some of what the volunteer witnesses had to say might be extremely useful to the prosecution.

There had been the problem from the beginning that no one other than James White had seen Betty Wilson anywhere near her home at any time close to the time of the murder. And no one had seen Betty and James together or near each other that day or at any other time in history.

After the case had been in the newspapers and on television for some months, an elementary school counselor who lived a mile from Boulder Circle came to the attention of the authorities.

A group of teachers and administrators were gathered one day in a hallway of the school where she did special counseling work, trading gossip about the Alabama twins case. Sheila Irby always did well in these exchanges because she was able to cite the fact that she had gone to high school with the twins in Gadsden.

But on this day she said more—that she had seen the man who had confessed, James White, walking near the intersection of Chandler Road and Boulder Circle on the day of the killing, and that she had also seen Betty Wilson driving erratically near that same intersection just a short time later on the same day.

It didn't seem to occur to Mrs. Irby that this was information she needed to convey to the police. But it did occur to the police officer who was present during this bull session—a public-relations officer involved in the department's youth-awareness program to combat drug abuse in the schools. When the other people had left the hallway, the officer suggested to Sheila Irby that she needed to go downtown and fill out a report.

Sheila Irby withdrew immediately, saying she was sure the police had all the information they needed. The officer pressed the matter: The police did not have any physical or eyewitness evidence to tie Betty Wilson to the scene or to James White.

Sheila Irby said no, she was not interested in getting involved. But the police officer filed a report anyway, and that report slowly wound its way through the paper chain to Mickey Brantley's desk.

Sheila Irby was an attractive blond woman in her early forties, the mother of a twenty-year-old son and two teenagers. She was the wife of a respected businessman. She was well-spoken and definitely not shy. There were, however, some issues to deal with in her tale.

First of all, she had gone an awfully long time, seeing the case on TV every night and in the newspaper every morning, without feeling that it behooved her to come forward with such an astonishing amount of extremely pertinent information. Surely a person who had seen the confessed murderer at one moment on the day of the murder and then had seen the alleged conspirator at another moment, that same fateful day, driving in an erratic manner, might have felt called upon to tell the police about it.

When she did finally talk to Mickey Brantley, it was because Brantley insisted on it. He was very serious, humorless, and not at all in a mood for small talk.

She stuck with her story, but she attempted to let out the seams a bit. She said that she did not know Betty Wilson personally but had always known what Betty Wilson looked like. Sheila Irby had graduated from Gadsden High School two years after Betty Wilson. She had been aware of Betty and Peggy since the days when they had been Wormy Wood's daughters from the wrong side of the tracks.

She drove up and down Chandler Road all the time, she said, taking her son and daughter back and forth to school and to soccer games, baseball games—the usual run of kids' activities. She probably had seen Betty Wilson hundreds of times on Chandler.

On the day of the murder, she estimated she had driven up and down Chandler seven times between 5:00 and 7:00 P.M. The best she could tell Brantley, even when he pressed, was that she had seen Betty sometime between those hours.

She said she definitely had seen Mr. White, because the girls she was carpooling to a baseball game had noticed a "funny-looking little man who didn't belong" in the neighborhood, and one girl had even said, "Oh, yuck! Look at him!"

She was sure that she remembered Betty driving toward her home in a reckless manner on that day and not some other day, but she could not place the time any closer than between 5:00 and 7:00 P.M.

That was good enough. The evidence was presented to the media as an eyewitness account linking Betty Wilson with James White, even though Sheila Irby never told anyone she had actually seen the two of them together.

Brantley, meanwhile, had opened another excellent seam of information, from his point of view. Charlie Hooper went to Betty as soon as he caught wind of it.

"I'm operating on the assumption that you have been candid with me about your life, Betty," Hooper said.

"I have," she said. She peered into his eyes and then put her hand on his arm. "What is it, Charlie? Is it something bad?"

When he paused, her eyes began to well and glisten.

"Don't tell me it's something bad. I just don't know if I can take it if it's something bad today. This has been a very bad day for me already. What in the hell is it?"

"Betty, you have been sober for how long?"

"Umm, let me see. Time in here is so funny. About six years. Why?"

"And you've been sober all that time. No drinking."

"No. I mean, yes. No drinking."

"They're telling the A.A. members that you kept drinking. That you still drink."

"Who is? Bullshit! Tell me who it is, I'll kick his . . . who is? Brantley? That sawed-off little foot-washing fanatic son of a bitch!"

"It doesn't matter who. I don't know who. But they believe it. Some of them. And I'm not sure just how bad that is. I guess in A.A. they can forgive and forget a lot."

Betty rose from the bed and faced the wall at the end of the tiny cell, shaking her head. "No," she said, "it's bad. That's very bad. Very bad news you have brought me. That's the one thing they wouldn't forgive. I can't explain it. If you have to suffer through somebody's drying out, and you listen to all their speeches. Then to find out they were cheating!"

She turned back to face him. "God, some of my first speeches were awful. I was so full of shit when I started. I had a giant ego problem. A lot of drunks do. I made these terrible speeches about how my mother always loved my sister better than me."

"Yeah, I know."

"What do you mean, you know?"

"One of them was in the *Huntsville Times* the other day."

"What do you mean?"

"Somebody slipped the paper a tape of a speech you made at A.A."

"And they published it?"

"Yeah."

"An Alcoholics Anonymous member gave them a tape of a speech I made at a meeting?"

"Yes."

"And they published my speech?"

"Yes."

She stood still for a long moment, dumbfounded.

"Was it awful?" she asked.

He nodded.

She sank on the bed. Her head fell forward into her hands. "This is . . . I mean, I don't even . . . I'm not even thinking about the case now. These people . . . they are my family. My support."

"Your lovers," he said quietly.

She looked up. "That, too. Makes it a little complicated, doesn't it?"

"A little."

"Oh, man, Charlie. I'll tell you. There are more demons flying around an A.A. meeting than in *Ghost Busters.*"

"They think you kept drinking."

She shrugged and started to say something but paused. She shrugged again. "Well, then, they hate me."

"I get that impression," he said.

EIGHT

IN THE LONG MONTHS LEADING UP TO THE TRIAL, Bobby Lee Cook's impending visit to Alabama and his role in the case continued to be big news in that state, but the Alabama twins case earned barely a mention in Cook's home state of Georgia. There, people were more interested in the bigger cases keeping Cook busy that year.

There was an enormous flurry for a while when it looked as if he might win a new trial for Wayne Williams, convicted in 1982 of the Atlanta child murders. Before anyone had time to notice that he hadn't succeeded in that endeavor, Bobby Lee Cook was back in the headlines with an even bigger case—the "Iraqgate" arms-trading case. Coming into the case three weeks before his client, a former Atlanta banker, was to be sentenced, Cook dumped over the entire apple cart, moving to withdraw his client's earlier guilty plea.

He accused the federal government and the Bush administration of the "mother of all cover-ups." He told the judge that federal prosecutors were deliberately not calling key witnesses, and the judge was so impressed by Cook's argument that he threatened to call some of the witnesses on his own authority.

Cook was literally a lone knight, doing battle with powerful international banking and armaments interests, the White House, national Republican power wielders, and the media, not to mention the CIA. After a long struggle, he cut the government's case off at the knees, persuading the court to throw out the guilty plea and grant his client a full trial on the charges.

In Betty's mind, the fee of more than $100,000 that she was paying Cook for his role, and the enormous publicity the case was earning in Alabama, made the case a major event. In fact, the Betty Wilson case was a bit of business that Cook needed to fit in among other pressing matters.

One of the efficiencies Bobby Lee Cook employed, in order to maintain control over a wide-ranging practice, was the use of state-of-the-art computer-driven communications. Sandlin and Hooper spent a good deal of time cranking huge volumes of information into computers so that the information could be faxed or direct-transferred to Cook's offices in Summerville.

It's a system all successful lawyers and most successful business and professional people use today. Why spend days and a lot of money traveling, when the computer can spit out everything you need to know? Why not peruse the information on your laptop computer, sitting in your favorite wicker chair at the house on Sea Island?

The downside of doing business this way, of course, is that people don't spend much time getting to know each other in the old-fashioned eyeball-to-eyeball way that business used to be conducted. But Bobby Lee Cook was an extremely able and experienced litigator and a quick study, and this was how he could afford to take the case. Under the circumstances, there was no other way to get him.

The defense team was nervous about some of what they had seen of the prosecution's case during the process of discovery, in which the state is required to show the defense all of its evidence. The Irby evidence was troubling because it placed Betty and James near each other and near the house at about the time of the murder.

Betty insisted she had a perfectly good reason to go back to the house at 5:00 P.M.—to pick up the forgotten bank bag. But her lawyers told her to forget about it. If the state didn't know she went back then to pick up the bag, the defense team wasn't about to tell them. They would rather not have anyone know for sure that Betty had gone back to the house that afternoon for any reason.

Other aspects of the state's case seemed to play right into the defense team's hands. For example, James had said in the final version of his statement that he had met Betty Wilson and Peggy Lowe at Logan Martin dam on the afternoon of May 21, at which time they had passed him the intended murder weapon.

But several witnesses, gasoline slips, and phone records had been gathered by the defense to show that Betty Wilson was nowhere near Talladega that afternoon, having driven back north to Huntsville early that morning.

Not long before the trial was to begin, Brantley must have spotted the error, too. He had called Peggy's houseguest, Linda Vascocu, for a statement about the timing of Betty's departure. When Linda insisted Betty had left the morning of the twenty-first, not the following day, Brantley got tough with her. He was clearly frustrated. The defense lawyers were taking it as evidence that this was a serious hole in the state's case.

Perhaps it would all equal out in the end.

You can fly to the Tuscaloosa Municipal Airport and then drive across the Black Warrior River and up Lurleen B. Wallace Avenue to the Tuscaloosa County Courthouse. Or you can do what more people do and fly to Birmingham, then take the scenic route into Tuscaloosa across the University of Alabama campus on Paul W. Bryant Drive. Whichever way you come, the impression will be of a small Southern city that manages to be busy and sedate at the same time.

Tuscaloosa was founded by white pioneers in 1816 on the site of a Creek Indian settlement. It was named in admiration for Tuskaloosa, the charismatic Choctaw military leader who led an alliance of Indian tribes to defeat in battle with Hernando de Soto in 1540 in the region that is now western Alabama.

By the time of the Civil War, Tuscaloosa was a railroad city in the middle of a shimmering white sea of cotton, all cultivated by black slaves. During the war, Union troops burned the city to the ground.

The population of Tuscaloosa was about 77,000 in 1992, the population of the county twice that. Historically an agricultural and mining center, the city is now also the site of a good deal of light manufacturing. The area around the university includes an expanse of stately old residences. Out closer to the freeways south of town is a belt of the same hurriedly built, traffic-clogged, generic, franchised shopping-mall sprawl found on the edges of all American cities.

Beneath the drywall veneer of that shopping-mall sameness, however, beats a heart that is unique to the region. Tuscaloosa is very Southern, but it is not the frilly, histrionic, Tara-esque Southernness of a place like Atlanta.

Alabama novelist and playwright Dennis Covington, who covered Betty's trial for *The New York Times* and for one of the Hollywood production companies working on television movies about it, talked at lunch one day about the people of western Alabama:

"I look at the faces of this jury," he said, "and beneath the suits and ties and Sunday dresses, I see those truly Appalachian types—you know, the kind of women who, maybe a generation back, could go out and slaughter hogs all morning long, then wipe the blood and entrails off their hips with the butts of their hands and serve a perfect tea party."

The Tuscaloosa County Courthouse is a long narrow un-beautiful affair of 1950s vintage, large enough to accommodate the normal affairs of county business but totally inadequate to the task set for it on February 23, 1993, when the trial of Betty Woods Wilson finally opened. All morning long, before the courthouse had even opened for business at 8:00 A.M., cars and vans had been rolling in off the freeway and making their way up Lurleen B. Wallace Avenue to the courthouse square. Virtually all of the north Alabama and Birmingham media were represented, with their television-dish trucks, cables, and lights, but the media were actually the smaller portion of the mob.

In the months leading up to the trial, something had happened within the culture of Huntsville that had gone unrecognized by the officials and even by the reporters covering it. The Betty Wilson trial had become more than a big story. It was now an urban obsession—a legend in the birthing.

Some of the cars pulling up to the curb outside the courthouse to disgorge passengers were old and beat-up. Many of the cars were sleek, new German models. Women in designer dresses with Hollywood-perfect hair, screenwriters, elderly men in orange jumpsuits with lawnmower oil on their flanks, tough chain-smoking mamas, authors, bewildered young mothers with babes in arms, reporters, off-duty cops, University of Alabama law students—together they formed a horde in the hallway outside the second-floor courtroom where the trial was to take place. The horde was loud and pushy—not a pretty picture.

Ted Sexton, Sr., the young sheriff of Tuscaloosa County, was an easygoing type whom the locals were accustomed to seeing in blue jeans and a Polo shirt, taking in a Schwarzenegger movie at the mall with his family. When he looked down the corridor outside the courtroom that first morning, he may have wished he had Schwarzenegger there to help him.

Sexton and two deputies waded into the mob and began separating it into two rough lines against either wall.

"All those of you who have valid media credentials that you can show me, stand over here on this side," he said. "The rest of you who are just here to observe, stand over there. Any witnesses or members of the families, please identify yourselves to my deputies."

A moment later, two more deputies appeared with a rope barrier on pedestals, like the barriers at movie theaters. They arranged the barrier down the center of the corridor to separate the media from the public.

Then Sheriff Sexton went back to the judge's chambers to see Thomas N. Younger, the Huntsville judge who had brought the trial here and who was at that moment in the process of putting on his robes.

"Judge, I've got a situation out here. I have way more people . . . way more people! . . . than can ever fit in that courtroom, and I've got tons of media, plus authors and people who say they're from Hollywood and *The New York Times* and all like that, and they're all saying they have to be in there to do their work."

A cloud came over Judge Younger's face at this mention of the media—his personal nemesis since the entire Alabama twins case had begun.

"Are you asking me what to do with the media?" he said.

"Yes, sir. Do you have a policy?"

"Yes, I do.

Sexton waited.

Younger turned toward him, his eyes sparkling mischievously over a scowl.

"My policy is 'first-come, first-served.' "

The deputies went back into the corridor and attempted to retrieve the rope barrier before making a formal announcement, but the reporters and camera crews figured out immediately that their special highway into the courtroom was being erased. They surged forward toward the metal detector at the door, but the spectators on the other side of the corridor saw what was happening, and they too shoved forward to consolidate their own positions.

Two deputies manning the metal detector decided to relieve the pressure by opening the door into the courtroom to begin to process people. The alarm on the detector started going off madly as soon as the first person passed through it. Half of what people were dumping out for inspection on a folding table next to the metal detector was foreign and inscrutable to the deputies—odd-looking beepers, palmtop computers, miniature video cameras, fold-up cellular telephones, strange-looking bottles of water. While the deputies listened to explanations and argued with the bearers of the objects about whether the objects would be allowed in the courtroom, other people tried to slip past.

A deputy barely managed to nab one intruder by the sleeve, then made him dump out the contents of a canvas tote bag bearing provisions for the day. On the top of the pile was a small plastic bag containing a mound of horrid-looking oozy brown matter.

The deputy recoiled physically from the table and shouted, "Good God Almighty, what in God's good name is that?"

For an instant, the crowd fell silent as everyone stared at the business on the table.

"Figs," the man said. He turned angrily toward the mob behind him and said accusingly, "Somebody in this line squished them."

"Well, you cannot take them in that courtroom, sir," the deputy said. The deputy turned back to the crowd and began peeling off a list. "No figs! No bottled water!" (Each additional prohibition was greeted with loud groaning and bitter complaints from the corridor.) "No cameras! No tape recorders! No computers! No beepers! No newspapers!"

The other deputy, a woman, looked up from a purse she was searching and muttered, "No nothing."

By the time the deputies managed to squeeze shut the door against the gang of angry people left in the corridor, there were 120 or more onlookers jammed into a set of hard blond-wood pews intended to hold, at most, 96 people. Sandwiched between a white acrylic floor and a low ceiling of white acoustic tile, the room was claustrophobic, noisy, and foul-smelling. Media people and members of the general public sat watching each other balefully.

A deputy led the jurors in from a door at the back of the courtroom—twelve regular jurors and two alternates, twelve men and two women. Of the twelve regular jurors, three were black—a young man, an older man, and a late-middle-aged woman. The overwhelming majority of the jury, then, was made up of white men, most of whom were middle-aged to elderly and most of whom were working class, with the exception of a retired doctor, a management person from the university, and a retired businessman.

The jurors gazed around shyly as the deputy led them to the front of the room. Even though they were in the jurisdiction of the Tuscaloosa County sheriff, the jurors were in the personal care of Madison County sheriff's deputy Wayne Johnson, who had come down from Huntsville to help with the trial and to provide security for Judge Younger. A big red-haired man with a gap-toothed smile, Deputy Johnson paused and smiled at the jurors, giving them time to fumble their way into the two rows of seven swiveling easy chairs against the left wall at the front, looking forward from the back of the room.

Judge Younger tipped back in his chair—a bald pink head of a man in thick glinting glasses, perched like a great black bird high above the room behind the broad bench at the end wall. He gave Deputy Johnson, an old friend, a very slight, quick, almost undetectable little look, which meant, "Come on, Wayne, get 'em in the chute, will you?"

Deputy Johnson, still smiling, barely nodded to the judge and then said, "Let's move right along, folks."

Judge Younger was not in a trifling mood. He had told the judge whose courtroom he was borrowing that he was bound and determined to be in and out of Tuscaloosa and shut of the whole Alabama twins case in less than two weeks. As it happened, Judge Younger would be back home in about half the time. In the end, when all had been said and done, this jury would have relatively little trouble deciding what to do.

The visiting press and other writers and onlookers who were new to the case strained forward to examine all of the principals on the far side of the bar. At the left side of the room, at a long table just in front of the jury, was Jimmy Fry, alone. District Attorney Fry was well known in his own county for trying cases by himself. He believed that a table full of prosecutors gave the impression of the almighty government descending to persecute lowly citizens. He intended to look like the loneliest man in the courtroom.

He was even rounder in person than he appeared in newspaper photographs, with a face that moved from beamish to funereal at the throw of a switch. His hair was combed neatly with a boyish sweep across the brow, just graying at the temples and in the front. While the courtroom got itself in order, he rose, strode, leaned against the bar, engaged in quiet sober exchanges with Mickey Brantley, looked the crowd over.

At the right side of the room was another long table crowded with people. Charlie Hooper and Marc Sandlin were at one end and the back of the table. Sandlin looked calm and composed, nodding occasionally and smiling to acquaintances in the room. Hooper sat hunched forward with his elbows on the table, scowling like a boxer who thinks he is about to get his brains bashed in.

At the other end of the defense table was the legendary Bobby Lee Cook, who looked slight, exhausted, drawn, and pale. His normally trim gray goatee had been allowed to go to seed a bit, so that it stuck out in a bad imitation of Abraham Lincoln, and his hair, always a bit long, was shaggy and unwashed-looking where it hung over his collar.

Also at the table was an alert, handsome, sharply dressed lawyer in his mid-forties whom the visiting media had not yet met. Jack Drake was associated with the law school at the University of Alabama and was being seriously mentioned as a candidate for a major federal judgeship. Respected as both a litigator and legal scholar, Drake was on the team with one special mission—to catch every single thread and strand of the case that might be used later to build an appeal.

Squeezed between them all, with her back to the public and her profile to the jury, was Betty. She wore a smartly cut gray houndstooth suit. Her hair had been cut moderately short and colored bright black, streaked white on the sides in a showy pattern to complement the suit—the work of a hairdresser Charlie Hooper had brought down to Tuscaloosa from Huntsville. The suit, the hair, and an expert application of makeup—it was all intended to take the stench of the jailhouse off her and make her look like a respectable lady.

It didn't work. Betty Wilson had spent the better part of a year locked up in a cage smaller than those federal prisons use for punishment cells. Her only contact with sanity and the outside world had been through Charlie Hooper. Over the course of those long months, the Madison County jail had been seized by the kind of dementia that can happen only in prisons and jails. It was clear to everyone, guards and prisoners alike, that it was James Dennison White who wore the official seal of approval in the Madison County jail—the clean jacket. Betty Wilson was the white woman who had slept with African-American men in her sick husband's house—the loser. Scenting blood, guards and prisoners alike had closed in on her in a howling chorus of abuse.

As the months progressed, the heckling and harassment had grown worse and worse. When Charlie Hooper tried to force the Madison County sheriff to give him and his client some modicum of privacy, rumors and suggestions began to fly from the jail that Hooper and his client were having a jailhouse love affair. Betty's angry will to survive had kept her going, but barely. By the time she got to Tuscaloosa, every day of her ordeal was showing on her face.

In jail she had watched her arms and hands surrender to the horror that used to awaken her before Jack's death: Her body, incised and sutured from top to bottom by the plastic surgeons, had begun to lose its tone. The various reconstructions began to look less like natural beauty, more like surgery.

The expensive suit, dyed hair, and theatrical makeup made an unhappy match with her physical condition. She looked hard and showy. Much worse—the rearranged flesh of her face and heavy eye makeup, exacerbated by a constant effort to fight back tears, gave her face the appearance of a mask. The eyes were lost.

She was pale because she was terrified. She had no idea she was also terrifying. The net effect on the first day of trial was not good.

When the session began, Jimmy Fry left the rail and walked over to face the jury. He smiled easily at them and said, "How are y'all today?"

Virtually every member of the jury nodded and said something in return.

"Fine."

"Doing fine, sir."

"Hello."

When they had all responded to him, he said: "I'm Jimmy Fry, the district attorney of Limestone County, and I am going to be presenting the state's side of this case to you."

He gave the jury a brief, fairly official statement of its responsibilities, emphasizing the extreme importance of the matter that was being put to them. Then he stepped back from the jury box and shoved his hands in his pockets, as if he were standing around the parking lot in front of the only convenience store in a small town, trying to make small talk.

"There's a beautiful Latin phrase that I like—*tabula rasa*—which I believe means 'clean slate.' That's where y'all are now. This case is a clean slate as far as y'all are concerned."

He wandered away from them a little farther, stopped, and looked off wistfully, as if struck suddenly by a distant but pleasant memory.

"When I was a kid, I had one of the best baby-sitters in the world." He smiled broadly at the recollection. "It was called the Rich Theater. Cost fifteen cents to see a picture show."

A couple of the older jurors smiled, nodded, and muttered assent, as if saying amens.

"It was ten cents for popcorn and a coke."

All of the jurors nodded and smiled.

"My mother was a telephone operator across the street. I had to wait for her to get off from work. So I went to the movies prett' near ever' day after school."

An elderly woman on the jury nodded sympathetically and then scanned around the courtroom at Mr. Fry's present circumstances, as if to say, "You must have been a good boy."

"What you are about to hear right now," he said, "is called 'Previews of Coming Attractions.' I am going to give you a peek at the things that will be proved to you by the evidence and the witnesses later in this trial."

He told them about Dr. Jack Wilson—the Huntsville ophthalmologist whose patients all had adored him. He led the jurors up quickly to the moment of the murder. He told them about

James Dennison White, the wretch who had killed Dr. Wilson.

With his voice dramatically hushed, he said, "Dr. Wilson left work at four-thirty P.M. James Dennison White was waiting for him in his home. He had been there for some time. He set upon him."

Fry moved back in close to the railing separating him from the jurors. He put his hands on the rail and faced them silently for a moment. Some members of the jury drew back from him, sensing what was coming.

"When the police found Jack Wilson, his forearms had been beaten and broken. His skull had been beaten and crushed. He had been stabbed in the abdomen. He died on the second story of his own house, just outside his wife's bedroom in a pool of his own blood."

Fry was facing the jury. He explained to them that the state would present evidence to show that James White had been paid to murder Dr. Wilson by his wife, Betty, who was sitting at the defense table.

The moment he mentioned Betty, all of the jurors fixed their eyes intently on Fry, staring at him and very deliberately not looking across the room to where Betty sat. But Fry began to look, first with his eyes. Then, very slowly, he turned his face, then his head, then his entire body, drawing the eyes of the jury with him across the room, until they were all staring at Betty, who looked back at them from her eyeless mask.

"Who was Betty Wilson?" Fry asked quietly. "I will tell you."

He began to move toward her in an agonizingly slow ooze of a motion, so that each syllable of what he said brought him barely a fraction of an inch closer to her, pulling the jury along behind him.

"I will tell you. She was a vain and selfish woman. She was obsessed with her own image and appearance. With having things. A big house. Two expensive cars. Everything all of us would think of, I guess, as the good life."

He was halfway to her.

"It appeared she had everything. But . . ."

He drew close to the defense table . . .

". . . she wanted . . ."

He was almost there . . .

". . . more!"

Now he was finally in front of her, staring down into her face as if at a crawling thing.

"In fact she didn't want more," he said, his voice rising in biblical thunder. "She wanted it all! She wanted it now!"

He snapped away from her face and returned quickly to the jury, telling them things in a fast whisper, as if shocked—baffled by his own words.

"In public places, she made derogatory remarks about her husband. She rebuked her husband."

Fry homed in on the little old lady who had nodded approvingly to him over the story about the movie theater.

"She cursed him."

The lady drew herself up, holding her purse on her lap in both hands. She twisted her head on hunched shoulders.

"She humiliated him in front of clients and workers in his place of business. She told some of her closest friends that she was disgusted with Jack Wilson, and the only reason she didn't leave him was because she might lose her"—Fry paused here, to give the next word a special loathing spin—

". . . her *life-style.*

"She took money without his knowing it. She had lovers."

Fry looked away from the jury in delicacy at this moment. "She had lovers in Birmingham," he said, looking at Betty. "She had lovers in New York City. Wherever she wanted to go, she had them."

Fry went to a large blackboard at one end of the bench, seized a piece of chalk, and drew a large crude triangle.

"Ladies and gentlemen, you have a triangle. On one side is Betty Wilson. On the other side is her twin sister, Peggy Lowe. On the third side is James Dennison White. And in the center is Jack Wilson. It's just like wet hay in the barn. All the elements are together for spontaneous combustion."

Fry scanned the jury. They were all alert, listening and seemingly friendly. He had completed the easy part of his story—

making Betty out a witch. Now he would move to the hard part of the sale—painting James White as a human being.

"James White," he said slowly. "James White.

"He grew up in Sillicoga. His parents were not married. He took his daddy's name when he was fifteen years old. Later on he took his mama's name. He wasn't born with a silver spoon in his mouth.

"He joined the army when he was seventeen, in 1967 and '68. He went to Vietnam, and while he was there, he was like a lot of other young people, he got screwed up. He was sent home. He became an alcoholic and a pill popper.

"He uses drugs much of the time. From the time he got out of the army, he's been in and out of VA hospitals. He's not going to get any awards for good citizenship.

"We come to the summer of 1991. He's been married for two years. He has two children. His wife kicked him out.

"In August 1991 he began working as a maintenance person at the Vincent Elementary School in Shelby County, building shelves on a contract. While there, he struck up a friendship with Peggy Lowe, who was a schoolteacher in the Vincent Elementary School."

Jimmy Fry came back to the rail and leaned on it to speak closely to the jury, eager to help them understand this next point.

"James was awfully struck by Miz Lowe. It was the first time in his life that he saw a woman of another stature, of another class, taking time with him."

He paused to allow this point to sink in.

All of the lawyers at the defense table seemed to prick up their ears and listen intently to this part. Getting the jury to believe that Peggy Lowe could have kissed James, let alone had an affair with him, was always going to be the tricky part. Within that challenge, the most delicate aspect would be this matter of social class—an issue perhaps even dearer to the Southern heart and more intensely felt than race.

"They developed what you might call a telephone romance," Fry said. "Hours at a time—talking to each other on the telephone. In the spring of 1992 this was going on, mostly over the telephone. They told each other that they had strong feelings for each other."

He shook his head ruefully at the ways of the world. "She had old James pretty well worked up."

A couple of the men on the jury grinned appreciatively for a moment and then quickly composed themselves. The women pursed their mouths slightly.

"She began telling James how unhappy she was with her husband and how she wished he wasn't around. James, you know, being an old boy, he tried to impress her, he said, 'Well, you know, something probably could be arranged.'

"Come that spring, Peggy said to him, 'You know, my sister's awfully unhappy.' Old James, he said, 'Maybe I can talk to somebody for you about it.' She said, 'How much would this cost?' He said, 'Oh, I don't know, maybe five thousand dollars.'

"Well, come to find out, in May of 1992 James suddenly came into some money. Twenty-five hundred dollars to be exact. He took that money and paid his bills.

"Then Betty and Peggy began working on him to get something done. On May fifteenth, 1992, James rode to Huntsville and cased the job. But he needed two hundred dollars to cover his expenses. So the next night, on May sixteenth, 1992, James White drove to Guntersville State Park. There was a book, supposed to be in the backseat of Betty's BMW, a black BMW, one and a half miles from the entrance to the park entrance, with the money in it for his expenses."

Fry wandered away from the jury and stared off toward the back of the room, calling out the story as if from a dream.

"But he got there late.

"The gate was closed.

"So Mrs. Wilson sent a security guard out to her car to get the book and carry it to James. She told the guard to give the book to James . . ."

He came back toward the jury, his voice hushed and focused.

". . . and she told the guard . . . she told the guard to tell James . . . 'Tell him . . .' "

He paused and scanned the faces of the jury.

" 'Tell James *to have a good time.*' "

A younger man on the jury shook his head. One of the women put a hand to her mouth for an instant, then put it back in her lap.

"And she wanted her book back."

He put up his hands and shrugged as if to say that decent people might never be able to fully fathom such things.

The lawyers at the defense table were watchful, silent and tense.

"Next week," Fry said, "James told the ladies he didn't have a gun to do the crime with. On May twentieth, they gave him a gun out on Logan Martin dam—a lonely little place, an earthen dam of the type many of you know from out in the country."

Bobby Lee Cook sat in his chair with his back to Fry, staring at the table. It was impossible to tell whether he was listening or lost in other concerns. But the other lawyers at the table were exchanging shocked and angry looks.

Right up until the day before trial, the state's evidence had still included James's statement that the meeting on Logan Martin dam took place on the afternoon of May 21.

Now, almost casually, the date had been slipped ahead to May 20. On May 21, Betty wasn't in the Talladega/Vincent area or anywhere near the dam where James said he met her. But on May 20 she was.

The defense had been counting on this and other holes in James's story to nail him as a liar. But now the hole was fixed—the result, no doubt, of another of James's fortuitous last-minute memory corrections.

It was an unpleasant harbinger of what might lie ahead. What it meant was that James, Brantley, and Fry had corrected James's version of events in order to make it match what Peggy's houseguest, Linda Vascocu, would tell the court later on the stand.

Brantley had not been able to get Linda to change her story. So James had changed his.

How many more midfield adjustments lay ahead? How many more dates and details had James suddenly remembered differently in the last days before the trial, after the state had reviewed the statements of other witnesses and when there was no longer time to pass these new developments on to the defense?

"At six A.M. the next day," Fry continued, "James was out in front of Dr. Wilson's office with the gun. But it was a busy place, with a lot of traffic, so he decided he couldn't kill him there. He made a phone call from a pay phone. He talked to Mrs. Lowe, and he also talked to the defendant, Betty Wilson, who was in Talladega that day. And he told Mrs. Wilson, 'I need some more money.'

"She said, 'I'll be right there. I will meet you in Huntsville and bring you the money you need.' And she did. She drove straight back to Huntsville, met him at the Parkway City Mall, and gave him the money he needed.

"That night he stayed at a motel and made more phone calls. The next day, he went to the Wilson home on Boulder Circle, and he laid and waited."

Fry circled the floor in front of the jury as he spoke, laying it all out for them with hand gestures—James, crouched and waiting in the shadows, Jack Wilson coming home at the end of his day, innocent of what lay ahead for him.

"Dr. Wilson was late. Three o'clock went by. Three-thirty. Four. Finally he came home. He came up the stairs toward his wife's bedroom. James was there. They met face-to-face. There was a fray. The doctor was killed.

"James White was supposed to walk away through the backyards to get to the main thoroughfare. But he decided it was a bad idea."

Bobby Lee Cook was still staring at the backs of his hands, but Hooper, Sandlin, and Jack Drake were visibly on pins and needles. A key point was coming—the timing of James's escape. Betty's whereabouts were accounted for, almost minute-to-minute, for the entire afternoon, with a possible gap of a few minutes just at 5:00 P.M.

So now Fry had the murder done by 4:00 P.M.—a little late, according to the forensic autopsy, but just within the edge of credibility—and he had James White starting to make his escape and thinking better of it. And then what? James was already out of the house, steamed on booze and drugs, soaked in blood. What was Fry going to do with him next?

"So he went back in the house," Fry said.

Drake and Sandlin exchanged very small looks of incredulity. He went back in the house? Who could ever believe such a thing?

"He went back in the house, and he stayed there," Fry said. "Around five P.M., the defendant, Betty Wilson, returned to the house, probably unplanned. And James was still there. He was supposed to be gone.

"So he crawls under some clothes in the backseat of her car, some plastic-covered clothes on a hangar in the backseat. And she takes him to his truck.

"Two days later, the police in Shelby County talk to James. He breaks down. He tells little bits and pieces of the story. He doesn't know if he's caught or not."

Fry was almost ready to sit down. But he hovered at the rail, as if struggling to find a way to broach one last topic.

"Last summer, another district attorney in Madison County—not me, another man—gave James White a deal. He will be allowed to plead guilty to murder, not capital murder, in exchange for his cooperation here.

"That means he will face a sentence of life in prison but not life without the possibility of parole.

"I did not make that deal. But I am stuck with it. Do I like it?" He walked around for a while shaking his head vigorously no. Then he stopped and faced the jury. "I don't know. I don't know. The deal is, Mr. White has got to tell the truth. If he lies or misleads us here in this proceeding, his deal is off. He has got to tell the truth.

"What was Betty Wilson's deal? What was in it for her? I will tell you. Had she gotten away with this, her immediate share of the estate, within days of her husband's murder, would have been four million dollars. Four *million* dollars. That was Betty Wilson's deal."

Fry glanced up at the clock, as if to show that it had already been a very long day for the jury. Then he thanked them for listening and took his seat.

Judge Younger stared at the defense table, waiting for someone to rise. He and most of the insiders expected it to be Hooper, or perhaps Sandlin, since they were the ones who knew the story and had been on the case from the beginning. But it was Bobby Lee Cook who rose.

Cook was barely on his feet when a door at the judge's end of the courtroom opened and people began hurrying into a special viewing gallery across from the jury—spouses of the lawyers, court personnel, law professors, leading citizens of Tuscaloosa. They all had been waiting in the wings for the moment when the great man would speak.

Cook stood at the table, gazing around the courtroom, waiting for something. Finally the bailiff snapped to attention and whispered hoarsely to him, "The podium? Now?"

Cook nodded yes, a bit imperiously. Wayne Johnson stepped forward to help the bailiff, and together the two uniformed officers hurried to fulfill Mr. Cook's request, sliding a battered brown wooden podium into position in front of the jury box. They turned to see if he was pleased, but Cook waved at them with the backs of his fingers to signal that he wanted it moved closer to the jury.

When it was in position, Bobby Lee Cook stepped up to the podium, dropped a sheaf of papers on it, and then gripped the podium with both hands. Speaking carefully, his broad Georgia accent squeezed into a perfect enunciation of each syllable, he said, "Ladies and gentlemen of the jury, I am not going to tell you anything about my childhood or about the movies or Latin expressions. I do not feel it is necessary for me to inform this jury of its responsibility, because I feel like you already know how important a matter this is."

Suddenly he smiled at them. And they all smiled back, as if in relief.

"Ladies and gentlemen, my client has her faults. Don't we all.

She has admitted voluntarily that she has had affairs."

The elderly white woman on the jury looked a bit disappointed to hear this.

"But this is not what she is charged with in this case."

A young man squinted and looked at Cook, as if waiting to hear whether she would be charged with the affairs in another case.

"In July of 1978, she married Dr. Jack Wilson. Each had three children of their own by previous marriages.

"Betty," he said, "was an alcoholic for a number of years. She has been cold sober for the last six years. She has religiously attended and participated in Alcoholics Anonymous and other drug programs almost on a daily and nightly basis."

Several jury members turned for the first time and looked straight at Betty.

Cook told the jury about Betty's twin, Peggy, who lived in Vincent, was married to Wayne, sang in the choir, and taught school.

"Both Wayne and Peggy like to help people—homeless people, people down on their luck. This man, James White, came to them. He had a drinking problem, a drug problem. He poured a driveway for Wayne Lowe and for Wayne Lowe's mother, and he was paid for it."

Cook dropped his eyes from the jury and began reading from the sheaf of papers before him.

"In August of last year, James White went to a VA hospital with a complaint that he was having visual and auditory hallucinations."

Cook looked up at the jury. "Voices."

The jurors drew forward, intent.

"He left that hospital without proper medical treatment."

Cook swung out from behind the podium like a boxer coming out of his corner. He stalked up and down before the jury.

"The state's case . . . is predicated . . . on the believability . . . of James Dennison White.

"He was screwed up before he ever went to Vietnam!"

He stepped back behind the podium and lifted a long finger

in the air. In the long dirgelike tones of a Southern colonel, he said: "I came back from World War II to this very city, Tuscaloosa, Alabama, and I enrolled in the great university here, two months after I landed in San Francisco."

Again he left the podium, moving this time to the rail, which he gripped with two white-knuckled bony hands. Allowing his face to color as he spoke, he said, "James White was discharged for character and behavior disorders. He shirked his duties. He deserted his post."

Looking toward the older men in the jury, he said, "If everyone in our war had shirked or deserted their post, we all would be speaking either Japanese or German right now."

The older men nodded their assent submissively. The faces of the middle-aged men on the jury were blank.

Bobby Lee Cook paused, examining them.

"This man, this James Dennison White, was arrested for drug selling. He fled. He was extradited. He is a pathological liar. No businessman or person on this jury would rely on his word in making business judgments. He is not someone you would want to buy a used car from."

Cook returned to the podium and read from the papers there. "He has been diagnosed repeatedly as psychotic, paranoid, suicidal. He abuses alcohol, amphetamines, organic solvents, intravenous opiates, LSD."

He looked up. "The only time he's clean is when he's in the pen. He has sexually abused his own daughter while drunk. He has hated females since high school. He has a history of blackouts. And he has always blamed all his troubles on the government."

Cook picked up a single sheet of paper. "Now I want to read you this. This is what the doctors said about him last time he went to the VA hospital. Listen to this:

" 'Patient is likely to fantasize and daydream excessively. He may chronically misinterpret the words and actions of others.' "

Cook whittled away at the last-minute change James had made concerning the date when he and the twins supposedly had met at Logan Martin dam. By this point, all of the jurors were beginning to look a bit glazed. Except for Jimmy Fry's brief mention of it, no one had really explained to them yet where or what Logan Martin dam was, what role the gun did or did not play, what the relationship was supposed to be between James White and the accused, and except for the sketchiest of outlines, what had really happened in this case.

Cook continued to dredge through the papers in front of him, discovering other inconsistencies in White's many statements and calling them to the attention of the jurors. When an elderly man on the jury began to snore audibly, Judge Younger called a noon recess.

The sidewalks outside the courthouse were crowded with television crews stumbling over one another's cables, rushing to do stand-ups that would be shipped back via dish truck to their home stations for use on the early evening newscasts. Up and down the sidewalk, handsome young men and beautiful young women stood before cameramen repeating the same phrases over and over again:

"Famed Atlanta lawyer Bobby Lee Cook . . ."

"The famed Atlanta litigator . . ."

". . . Cook opened the Betty Wilson trial today on an aggressive note . . ."

". . . Cook dazzled the jury with his litigative prowess . . ."

". . . jurors listened spellbound as Cook angrily attacked . . ."

". . . displaying his famed courtroom prowess, Cook came out swinging . . ."

One reporter was overheard telling the viewers back home, "Limestone County District Attorney Jimmy Fry gave the jury a long official account of the facts of the case."

After lunch, Fry began putting police witnesses on the stand, beginning with the first officer called to the scene, then moving on to Officer Glenn Nunnally, who did the crime scene work. Bit by bit, a tiny piece at a time, Fry was putting the entire crime on the table for the jury to see and understand. He did it methodically and carefully, watching each juror's face to make sure no one was being left behind.

During the lunch break, someone had provided the jurors with notepads, and several of them busily scrawled notes as the witnesses provided them with details—what was found, what was not found, when the calls came in, who showed up. Nunnally told them about the gun case that was found lying open in a cabinet in Dr. Wilson's bedroom, about the type of bullets found next to the case. Some of the jurors noted each fact on their notepads.

Betty sat absolutely motionless at the defense table, staring at each witness but sometimes not hearing what they were saying. She had cried off some of the makeup during the lunch break and looked more human.

Almost everything the police witnesses were saying seemed to be precisely as she had remembered it. The facts would all seem to argue for her obvious innocence. If she had provided the killer with a gun, for example, would she have given him her own gun, registered in her own name, and then left the case and the extra bullets for it out in plain view?

Bobby Lee Cook's portrayal of White seemed damning beyond repair. The psychiatrists who had examined him over the years said not merely that he was crazy, in a general sort of way, but specifically that he was prone to fantasize and misinterpret what people said to him—exactly what must have happened when Peggy reached out to help him. He had interpreted her kindness as a sexual advance. When it didn't work out that way, and when Betty called his bluff, he plunged into the kind of violent psychopathic rage he had exhibited all his life. The footprints were all over his official medical and military record. It was so clear.

Once he was in police custody and dried out, he reverted to the other aspect of his personality, which also showed up so plainly in his record—the jailhouse sharp, the con-wise operator who knew how to slick the cops and pull the wool over the eyes of the authorities.

So Brantley wasn't that smart. Or he got hung out to dry by

a couple of politically ambitious D.A.s. They wanted to use the case for campaign fodder and didn't care especially what happened to him and his career. So maybe he did the only thing a cop can do. He took his orders and plodded ahead with them. He made it happen.

But now . . . surely now this horror would end. The terrible death of Jack. A year in a rat cage, being heckled and abused by prisoners and police officers alike. Surely now, when the good and decent people on this jury heard the facts, they would see what had happened, and it—this nightmare—would end.

Slowly, hesitantly, Betty began to turn and look toward the jurors as the afternoon wore on. A few of them glanced nervously her way but quickly averted their eyes when they met.

Her initial jittery fear of the trial itself was waning, but a far worse sensation was growing inside, like frostbite coming up from the feet. The more she looked at the jurors, busily scribbling away at their notepads and avoiding her gaze, the larger the sensation of cold and dread loomed.

They could take her life. These fourteen people in easy chairs against the wall to her left could hear all of these same facts a different way. They could misinterpret what they were being told. And they could vote to take her life.

As her initial nervousness faded, Betty began to focus much more closely on what the lawyers were saying and on the effect it seemed to be having on the faces of the jurors.

Late on the afternoon of the first day of trial, when all the jurors were beginning to sag in their chairs and some to doze, Jimmy Fry brought on Dr. Joseph Embry, the chief pathologist for the Alabama Department of Forensic Science. A small man in his early forties, his somewhat grayish face hidden behind thick glasses, Dr. Embry spoke in a soft voice that fell just between sweet and laconic. As he handled and commented on the color photographs of the body and murder scene, he often sounded like the popular American children's television character, Mr. Rogers.

"Here you see nine tears in the head, between seven eights of an inch and two inches in length," he said softly. "Most are about one and a half inches in length. There are two in the forehead alone, as you can see."

The pictures were eight-by-ten-inch glossy police photographs, made under harsh light and at close range to show all the details of the injuries. As Embry finished narrating each picture, Fry took them over to the jury box to be handed from juror to juror.

"These injuries were really all over the head," Embry said. He spoke so softly that Judge Younger had to ask him to move closer to the microphone so that the jury could hear what he was saying.

"Some, like these, went through five or six layers of scalp. A couple were more superficial. The most severe was this one in the front of the head, which caused a skull fracture in the midline of the forehead."

Fry handed the jurors a portrait, shot straight-on from a few inches away, of Jack Wilson's face on the floor, the front of his skull caved in and crimson with blood, his eyes bulging from their sockets.

The room was absolutely silent. The media and public onlookers in the back did not so much as rustle their clothing or breathe audibly. Judge Younger was watching the jury every instant, eagle-eyed for stress. The lawyers at the defense table sat and looked at each other.

Fry picked up another photograph and seemed, for an instant, to blanch. "This is . . . this is pretty rough. What is this, Dr. Embry?"

Embry took the photograph in one hand and used the other hand to adjust his glasses. "Yes," he said mildly, "this is a photograph of the skull area with the scalp peeled back in order to show the pattern of the fractures here in the bone."

Fry walked to the jury with it. "I'm sorry, ladies and gentlemen," he said quietly. "This is important evidence, and I have to ask you to look at it."

"Are you people doing all right?" Judge Younger asked from the bench.

They looked at each other and shrugged. They nodded to the judge. One or two whispered that they were all right.

Betty didn't know how to look. When Fry carried the pictures from the witness stand to the jury box, she saw them—caught glimpses, saw the red, saw Jack's dead face with the eyes knocked out of his skull, the bloody skull with the scalp peeled back like half-removed clothing. She was afraid that any emotion she showed might be interpreted by the jury as fake. She was afraid that failing to show emotion would be interpreted as callousness. She sat rigidly in her chair, looking from the witness stand to the jury, trying to push the pictures from her mind.

One of the younger men on the jury, dressed in a suit and tie, looked at the photograph of the forehead area for a moment, put it down in his lap, and then lifted it up again. Fry paused, watching him. The man passed the photograph on to the woman sitting next to him and signaled to Fry with his eyes that he was all right.

"The voice box was smashed," Embry went on. He cataloged a number of bruises on the corpse. "There were complete fractures of both arms in each forearm—that's the ulna, here, broken all the way through, and also the radius, in the mid-portion, on both arms."

Fry took the pictures of Jack's shattered arms, bone fragments spearing the flesh, and gave them to the jury.

"The phalanges here were broken. You see here, the bones in the small fingers."

"They were broken?"

"Smashed."

"And, Dr. Embry," Fry said, "do you not say in your report that Dr. Wilson's hand had something you called a 'boxer' injury of some kind?"

"Yes."

"A boxer . . . ?"

"The right hand was broken in what is called a 'boxer fashion,' which means from hitting. You see here in this picture, all of the fingers were bruised near the knuckles and there is a cut around the ring. The bones cut out through the skin when fractured."

"So the victim fought back?"

"Yes, he would appear to have."

"I see."

Fry paused. Several jurors who had been rigid in their seats heaved sighs and breathed deeply, relaxing because they thought Fry was about to conclude his examination of Dr. Embry.

But Fry walked to a long table in front of the bench where evidence had been piled. He lifted up the thirty-four-inch bronze aluminum Easton bat with which James had murdered Jack. Carrying it with his fist at the base, resting the fat part of the bat on the open palm of his other hand, he popped it gently against his palm a few times on his way back to the witness stand—the familiar, reflexive action of a man who likes the feel of a bat in his hand.

"How hard was he hit?" he asked.

Embry shrugged. "Well, there was bleeding inside the brain and other indications that would suggest a large amount of force was used."

"Could this have done it? This baseball bat?"

"Yes," Embry said.

Several of the jurors slumped in their chairs when they realized it was far from over.

Fry led Embry through a painstakingly careful description of the two stab wounds.

"The one just above the navel is U-shaped," Embry said, "and goes through the abdomen wall, through the stomach and pancreas, severing the inferior mesenteric vein and the left renal vein, stopping just in front of the aorta, about two and a half inches deep into the body."

Embry concluded by telling the jury that both the knife wounds and the baseball bat injuries would have been fatal, each without the other. It was a thorough killing.

"Thank you, Doctor." Fry nodded thank you to the jurors as well, then passed the witness.

Jack Drake rose from the defense table. He was a slender man, with sharp features and a dashing head of red hair. He had the manner and profile of a Southern William F. Buckley. He moved easily to the witness stand and said a smiling hello to Embry.

"The injuries you describe, Dr. Embry . . ." He paused and smiled at Embry again.

Embry nodded, unsmiling, waiting.

"The injuries you describe—the broken forearms, the boxer's injury to the right hand, the others—would these injuries not be consistent with a man having been surprised at home by someone, and they beat him to death?"

"Yes, they could be."

Drake nodded, as if mulling over what the doctor had said. He turned suavely toward the jury and, asking it over his shoulder to the witness behind him, he said, "Isn't it true, Dr. Embry, that contract killers normally shoot their victims?"

Speaking softly, almost sweetly, Embry said, "Not in Alabama."

Judge Younger leveled his gavel at the back of the room and warned the people back there in tones of unmistakable authority that there would be no disruptions from them from here on out or they would be removed, the lot of them. Then, before adjourning for the day, he turned to the jurors and explained what was about to happen to them.

For however long the trial would last—at least a week, possibly two, perhaps even longer—they would be the virtual prisoners of Deputy Wayne Johnson. At any time when they were not actually sitting in the jury box, Deputy Johnson would accompany them, guard them, make sure they made no unauthorized contact with any person, friend, family member—anyone who might speak to them about the case. They would be allowed to read no newspapers. They would watch no television news—in fact, they could watch television only under Deputy Johnson's watchful eye. The court would put them up in a motel. Deputy Johnson would escort them to and from meals, all at county expense.

A great deal of effort and money was being expended to make sure that whatever verdict they reached would be free from taint. The one thing that would be avoided at all costs, the judge explained, was the sort of chance or accidental encounter that might poison this elaborate and expensive process and make everybody's effort and sacrifice a waste of time.

With that, Judge Younger gaveled the day to a close. The crowd in the back rose to its feet while he departed the room. Then there was a frantic rush for the bathrooms.

Tuscaloosa offers a variety of eating places, from fast-food franchise joints on the edges of the city and around the malls to a handful of older, more distinguished establishments closer to the center of town. Many business visitors, in town for any length of time, make their first night's choice a place called The Landing—a rambling old-fashioned steak house given to overstuffed red leather upholstery, dimly lighted corner booths, well-poured bourbon, and experienced adult waiters. Under normal circumstances it is a place where business, pleasure, and discretion may be mixed in equal portions.

One of the first parties to arrive and be shown a table at The Landing on the evening of the first day of trial was headed by Jack Wilson's first wife, Julia, several of her friends who had come down from Huntsville to give support, and Gary Houck, the general manager of the Huntsville Ramada Inn, where Julia worked as a caterer and where James White had stayed the night before he murdered Jack. Houck was in town because the state had subpoenaed him to give testimony about the times when White had checked in and out and made phone calls.

Tense, after a long day jammed in the crowded courtroom or in the corridors outside, the group ordered wine and quickly dissolved into nervous laughter. The laughter stopped suddenly and they all began digging elbows into each other's ribs, however, when the entire legal team for the defense filed by their table—the august Bobby Lee Cook, Jack Drake and his stylish wife, the ever-detached and amused Marc Sandlin, and a thoroughly morose Charlie Hooper, who even stopped and glowered at the group with his hands on his hips, as if to say, "Nothing better to do with yourselves?"

Cook motioned with a flap of the hand that he wanted his waiter to find a table as far from the ugly scene as possible. There was an empty spot most of the way across the cavernous room.

The waiter took the Cook party across the room, and they were just settling in to their table when Judge Younger came in with a small group and was seated exactly midway between the defense party and the Julia Wilson party.

Everyone was taken aback when Deputy Wayne Johnson appeared, smiling broadly and leading the way for a long snaking line of jurors, several of whom bumped into tables while their eyes adjusted to the extreme darkness of the place.

Judge Younger, who from the extreme agitation on his face must have been seeing visions of a mistrial, sat bolt upright, staring at Deputy Johnson and clearing his throat loudly. Johnson smiled back affably and nodded hello. The judge nodded quickly around the room toward the offending tables. Deputy Johnson, following the judge's eyes, turned and smiled in turn to each table. Finally, when Deputy Johnson's gaze turned to a table full of reporters, a dark cloud fell over his face. He turned one last time toward the judge, whose eyeballs were bugging and whose eyebrows by now were at the very top of his forehead. Deputy Johnson whirled, caught a waiter by the sleeve, and began whispering. Even from a distance and in the darkness it was clear that the deputy was speaking with emphatic self-control. The waiter seemed ready to shrug and resist, but Deputy Johnson leaned even closer in to his ear, with his teeth bared and quivering as if to bite off the man's earlobe. The waiter drew back reflexively, appeared to shudder, then quickly nodded and led Johnson and the bemused jurors through a door into a small private dining room.

As soon as they were out of sight, Judge Younger snapped open a broad linen napkin and smiled suavely at the rest of his party.

In all the confusion and rush of preparing a case on short notice, Jimmy Fry had managed, nevertheless, to carefully orchestrate the appearance of his witnesses. Getting them to show up in the order he wanted and on time was no mean feat, given that they all had to travel and many had legitimate excuses that had to be worked around—child-care issues, medical and dental emergencies, and so on. In spite of all these difficulties, he had lined them up and arranged them with the skill of a Broadway producer.

Outside the courtroom at the beginning of the second day, the corridor was absolute madness. Realizing there were far fewer seats inside than people who wanted them, and because Judge Younger would make no special concessions for the media, all of the reporters and other writers covering the trial had come to the courthouse at 7:00 A.M., the first moment when the doors would open and an hour before the beginning of the day's deliberations.

But the general public, friends and supporters of the accused, and people who had come to town accompanying the various witnesses had seen, too, on the first day, what might be expected on the second day, and so they, too, showed up early.

The courtroom was at the far end of a long narrow corridor, and the corridor was jammed with people long before the first deputies showed up to begin manning the metal detector in front of the courtroom door. The mood of the crowd was not pleasant. People accused each other of breaking into line. One elderly woman, trying to save places in line for members of Peggy and Wayne Lowe's church in Vincent, was battered to the wall as television and print reporters rushed to seize the spots.

"I've never heard of such a thing," she sputtered, smoothing her skirt indignantly after recovering her balance, "knocking down an old lady."

Standing next to her, an enormous black-bearded cameraman, whose polo shirt barely stretched to cover a large stomach, stared off into the blue and shrugged mountainous shoulders, then turned and said softly, "I'm really sorry, ma'am, I didn't mean to bump into you, but if we don't get into that courtroom, we lose our jobs."

When the first deputy showed up, another reporter called

down the hallway: "Are you people going to let us go to the bathroom today without losing our seats?"

The deputy smirked, embarrassed, but said nothing. A moment later, Sheriff Ted Sexton appeared from a stairway door just to the right of the courtroom. He smiled genially, held his hands up for quiet, and made an announcement for the day.

"The judge has instructed me that entry into the courtroom will continue to be on a first-come, first-served basis. If you leave the courtroom for any reason, you will lose your seat and the next person in line will be admitted."

A groan went up from the crowd.

"The courtroom will be cleared and locked at the lunch break. Do not leave your possessions in the room. You may not save your seats over the lunch break. Whoever is in line when court reconvenes after lunch will be admitted on a first-come first-served basis. You may not carry or consume food or beverages of any kind in the courtroom, and you may not take newspapers, radios, cameras, recording devices, or computers into the courtroom."

By the time he finished speaking, the mood of the crowd was black, and there was loud complaining and grousing, especially from the general public. The working media people tended to be quiet and intent, their eyes fixed on the courtroom door in silent ferocity.

But inside the courtroom, where the lawyers had taken their seats, all was tensely quiet. The defense team was busily shoving file boxes here and there across the table, handing manila folders to each other.

Jimmy Fry sat alone with his hands folded over a bare table. His witnesses were lined up and ready for the morning, one sitting nervously in the witness room, trying to sip a cup of vending-machine coffee, the other still waiting in a cell upstairs, his arms and legs in shackles. Together, the two witnesses would achieve just the effect Fry wanted.

After a while, the defense lawyers could find no more files or papers to shuffle, and so they all sat back in their chairs and eyed each other nervously, knowing what was about to take place. It had not happened on the first day of trial. On the first day, because of the scheduling of things, Betty had already been in the courtroom before the corridor crowd had assembled. Today she would not be so lucky.

Outside in the corridor, where the deputies were still keeping the door sealed, the crowd had settled into a sullen murmur. All eyes were on the metal detector and the courtroom door.

A door burst open at the opposite end of the corridor. There was a gasp of surprise:

"There she is!"

"It's Betty!"

The public onlookers, who had been leaning against both walls, shuffled into the middle of the corridor to look. There was a loud rapid series of metallic clacking noises behind them as television lights snapped on and cameras began firing rapidly, and suddenly the corridor was illuminated as if with the harsh light of an explosion or fire. Caught by surprise and terrified at first, the onlookers turned around and saw a battalion of television cameras and lights pointed over their heads. The onlookers melted quickly back against the walls, clearing the way.

She came with her head bowed low, holding her shackles before her in front of her waist. At each shoulder, a deputy held her and pushed her firmly ahead into the gantlet.

People drew back as she came, staring openmouthed at the shackles and into her face.

With her face low, trying to manage the shackles, pressured by the deputies at her shoulders, she appeared to scuttle more than walk. The cameras closed in expertly as she approached, each crew pressing for its shot but allowing the next crew to come ahead in turn, each reporter trying a question, all of them knowing exactly how close to press before the deputies would become alarmed.

As Betty moved down the corridor through the wall of gaping onlookers, the cameras danced and curtseyed around her. As each new crew stepped in front of her and snapped on its lights, her face contracted and jerked backward as if struck by a bucket of cold water. At one point between the flashes, she saw faces of friends along the wall and paused instinctively to say hello, but the deputies hurried her along, so that she stumbled for a moment before regaining her balance. The 35-millimeter motor-driven cameras of the newspaper photographers whined and snapped like giant mosquitoes around her face, freezing her expression of fear and humiliation into portraits for the next day's front pages.

The courtroom doors opened and swallowed her, and then she was gone. The lights died, and when the eyes of the onlookers readjusted to the gloom, they found that most of their places in line had been taken by media people during the confusion.

The first witness was Barbara Smith. Fry led her gently through an introduction to the jury. She had worked for Jack Wilson in a number of capacities over the years in his office. She was a slight, middle-aged woman with a small voice that quavered slightly in nervousness over the public-address system. She gave the impression right away of being extremely uncomfortable with this sort of appearance but bound to do her duty, nonetheless. She started right off using phrases like, "as I told you" and "as we discussed," showing that she had gone over her testimony in some detail with Fry before appearing in court. Her entire demeanor was of a sincere, honest person who had come to court to tell the truth, however awkward.

"I worked for Dr. Wilson," she said in response to Fry's question.

"What kind of man did you find him? What was he like to work for?"

Fry turned away from her to let her formulate her answer.

"My father . . ." she stammered.

"Ma'am?"

"My father was diagnosed with cancer. Jack let me go home five and six weeks at a time to El Paso to be with him, and he always let me come back to my job."

"He never got mad?"

She shook her head no. He started to ask another question,

when she began speaking again, softly, almost as if to herself. "He never got mad . . ."

"Pardon me?"

"He never got mad at anybody. Even if somebody was mean, he would just say they had a bad day."

"I see. Well, would you say . . ."

"I loved him," she said.

Fry regarded her gingerly but said nothing. The courtroom was silent.

Turning to the jury, she said, "I loved him as a person. He was so kind. I used to sit and think that. All his patients felt that way. When I . . ."

The sentence trailed off. Fry was motionless, waiting for her to gather herself.

"A little old lady about eighty years old," she said. "There was a little old lady who just had surgery. She said, 'Dr. Wilson, can I take this patch off my eye?' He slammed his fist on the counter, and he said, 'Don't you dare! If you take that patch off your eye, you are going to drop dead!'

"Everybody busted out laughing. I had just started working there. I didn't know what to think at first."

Fry nodded, smiling at her. He said nothing, waiting again. There was rustling and coughing in the back of the room.

"I used to just sit . . ." she began. She stopped, embarrassed, eyes glistening.

"Ma'am?"

"I used to just sit and think about how much I loved him." Speaking directly to Fry as if to a friend, she said, "You can't tell people that, or they'll think you're interested in some other way."

Fry nodded his understanding. He waited another beat, then said, "What was your impression of the relationship, from what you yourself could observe, of the relationship between Dr. Wilson and his wife, Betty."

For the first time, and only for an instant, Barbara Smith turned and looked at Betty at the defense table. Betty smiled, and Barbara turned away quickly, focusing narrowly on Fry.

"I truly think he loved her," she said quietly. "He felt he could help her with all the problems she had. He was always giving her help and advice on the telephone."

She drew herself up and looked toward the back of the room. "I heard him tell somebody she had a library of self-help books. If anybody wanted to borrow them, she had them."

An audible snicker sounded in the back, fading quickly when Judge Younger shot an eagle-eyed stare at the onlookers.

Barbara Smith was excused. A few observers in the back of the room, already regretting that last cup of morning coffee, were beginning to look longingly at the exit. Jimmy Fry turned his ample girth toward them and said in a loud clear voice, "Your honor, the state calls James Dennison White."

NINE

JAMES WHITE WAS SPARED THE CRUCIFIXION ROUTE through the mob in the corridor; instead, the bailiffs slipped him neatly into the courtroom through the judge's door at one side of the bench. He wore a white jumpsuit. His face was clean-shaven, and his balding salt-and-pepper hair had been cut close to his skull. He was shackled at the wrists and ankles. A bailiff stepped forward and released him from the ankle shackles as soon as he was inside the courtroom, so that he could walk freely to the stand. The wrist shackles were left on.

James had filled out on his jail diet. He appeared to be in great weight-lifting shape. Without the long greasy hair and filthy beard, his face was round and boyish. His eyes were clear and bright. What had appeared evil in him before was now merely mischievous. He looked uncannily like the writer Hunter S. Thompson.

But the biggest surprise came when he was asked his name and opened his mouth to answer. Instead of the mouthful of unappetizing brown and yellow stumps that had been there before, two long, perfect pearly rows of teeth appeared. During the year of incarceration, while Betty was kept in a cage and prevented from exercising or even using the toilet in private, the state had been busily remaking its star witness. The authorities admitted to having helped James with a certain amount of dental repair and suggested that relatives of his probably had helped him retrieve some old bridgework that had been lying around lost for years in his trailer-house.

However it happened, the change in his appearance, from the day of his arrest to the day he appeared in court, was no casual matter. Among other things, he was now suddenly a much more kissable fellow.

A woman reporter in the back leaned to a colleague and whispered, "He's kind of cute."

When he began reciting his biography for Fry, however, the cuteness faded. His eyes flickered back and forth strangely; his tongue slipped in and out of his mouth as he spoke, and the words came stuttering out in an odd lipless garble.

He recited the dates and geographical facts of his military service—Germany in '68, a reenlistment, Chu Lai in '69—leading up to his discharge from the army in 1970. "I moved to Georgia with my mother. I went to work in a fast-food restaurant."

He pronounced it, "faist-foo raystrowun." It was the extreme dialect of rural white Alabama, and even in Tuscaloosa, people had to strain forward and listen hard to discern his words.

"I was a short-order cook. People called me 'Cookie.' "

"How'd you get that name, James?" Fry asked.

James was confused for a moment, as were some of the jurors, since it seemed obvious how he got the name: He was a short-order cook, and they called him Cookie. Then, as if remembering his place in the script, James nodded to Fry and said, "There was a German girl who kind of liked me, I guess, and she called me Cookie. The name stuck, I guess."

"Go on."

"I come back, and I was back about two years, and I got married in Lawrenceville, Georgia."

"And how long did that last?"

"That lasted about six months. I was at work, and she got caught in my car with about seven or eight guys. Then I got married a second time. I have a daughter about twenty years old from that marriage. I have no contact with her. In 1978 I got married again in Sillicoga, Alabama. I have two children from that marriage. We was married about three years. That was another problem of running around and incompatibility."

"During that time, James, is it safe to say you had some problems yourself?"

"Yessir," he said, nodding quickly, the eyes shooting back and forth, never returning Fry's gaze. "I had alcohol and drug-abuse problems."

"Where are your children from your third marriage?"

"They're with their mother in Roanoke, Alabama."

"Did you get married again?"

"Yessir, I got married another time in 1983. We had an outside marriage ceremony in Sillicoga. I had two kids in that marriage. That lasted nine years. It ended in July 1990. I found out my wife was running around on me with another man who was supposed to be my best friend. She married him. They live in a trailer park in Harpersville, Alabama."

"And James, are you testifying truthfully here today, to the best of your knowledge?"

"Yessir."

"And have you been told by the state and by the police that you must testify truthfully?"

"Yessir."

Jack Drake rose from the defense table.

"Your Honor, I'm going to object to this witness testifying as to what he was told."

"I'll rephrase it, Your Honor," Fry said quickly. "What are you supposed to do here today, James?"

"I was told I had to give colloborating evidence."

Drake objected again, this time more vehemently. "This is a legal term."

Fry jumped back in again quickly to rephrase, but no matter how Fry asked the question, James said again in a robotlike deadpan, "I was told to give collobollating evidence."

"Your Honor," Drake said, "this is ridiculous. Why can't the witness just tell us what he knows?"

Bobby Lee Cook signaled Drake, and Drake sat down. Cook leaned and whispered. Drake relented, but he looked unhappy about it. He clearly felt that Fry was getting off easy. James

White was being allowed to sing his long country-music song of woe for the jury ad nauseam, without so much as an interruption.

But James Dennison White was Bobby Lee Cook's fish to gut. This was what the great man had been brought to Tuscaloosa to do. When Fry was done leading this wretch by the nose through his canned, overrehearsed testimony, Bobby Lee would rise and shake him apart. In the meantime, Bobby Lee appeared not to want anyone else messing with his man or his moment.

Judge Younger had had enough. James's attempts at pronouncing *corroborating* were arousing titters in the gallery, which made the judge angry.

"We will recess for lunch."

The onlookers rose while the judge left the chamber, then waited for Wayne Johnson to lead the jury out, then waited again for Betty and James White to be led off in chains, Betty through the shouting mob in the hallway and James through the judge's private door. Outside the courtroom in the corridor, an explosion of light erupted when Betty appeared.

When people from the public pews at the back of the room finally burst out into the hall, thinking about bathrooms first and lunch second, they were shocked to find a long line of people halfway down the corridor—people already lined up and waiting for seats for the afternoon session. The public onlookers hurried off, hoping to grab a bite and get back in time for a seat. The reporters and writers who were there earning a living all went to the bathrooms first and then returned grimly to the corridor to get in line again.

Arrangements were made by which certain people were sent out for sandwiches and drinks and their places held. The older woman who had been shoved against a wall that morning—already back in line herself—objected that she thought holding places was supposed to be against the rules.

"Not for food," a reporter said. "That's a necessity."

Up and down the line, people were beginning to feel slightly bolder than they had that morning. Several middle-aged women who had come down together from Huntsville the day before commented on Betty's demeanor during the forensic testimony.

"Did you see her when they showed those bloody pictures? She didn't bat an eye," one woman said.

"That woman is hard," said another.

"Hard, hard, hard," another said.

From a few feet farther down the line, a friend of Peggy and Wayne Lowe said loudly to her husband, "Some people can tell whether a person's innocent or guilty just by how they look at a picture, I guess."

One of the women in the first group said, "I never said she was guilty."

The other woman turned her back abruptly.

Then the first woman added, "But she is."

Her friend laughed and said, "Guilty as sin! Both of 'em."

Reporters who had been watching the exchange lost interest. One of them looked toward the elevator and said, "I know she's never going to find a toasted tuna salad in this town."

Another reporter said, "I would never order tuna here. I think that's really a risk."

Betty sat in a tiny room with the shackles removed. Her own sons, Wayne, and Wayne and Peggy's three children sat around a small table with her, sharing a bag lunch. So far, the defense team was keeping Peggy herself at home, far from Tuscaloosa.

They ate in silence for a while.

Then Wayne said, "I didn't recognize him. They bought him new teeth."

Betty ate quietly, staring through a small window to the treetops outside. She turned and looked at the rest of them. There were tears spilling from her eyes.

"How did this happen?" she asked.

Trey dropped his sandwich and rushed to hug her.

Betty took his hand. "I'm so scared," she said. "I can't stop shivering."

In the afternoon, the courtroom was alive with anticipation. James White was just about to get to the good part. The warring factions in the back of the room traded barbs and dirty looks. Deputy Wayne Johnson waited by the door to the jury room, which was at the wall behind the public section, at the opposite end of the room from the bench. It was not his job, as a visiting deputy, to enforce order in the room. That was up to Sheriff Sexton's people, who were doing a good job so far. But as Wayne stood guarding the door to the jury room, he looked out over the noisy fractious pews full of onlookers, shook his head, and said softly, "Y'all people gonna have to quiet down. Judge Younger don't put up with nonsense."

When James came back to the stand, he took up the story exactly where he had left off, as if reading from a book. "In the spring of '91 I was living in a trailer park in Vincent. I was doing odd jobs including some jobs at Vincent Elementary School. They had a new addition built on the school, and they asked me to do some shelves and closets."

"Who asked you to, James?"

"The principal handed me some money for the work I was doing. Sometimes the teachers would pay me in cash. The principal paid with checks.

"Kelly, my daughter, she started in preschool there, and she went into the first grade in 1991. I had seen Mizrus Peggy Lowe around. I was doing some work in my daughter's teacher's room, Miz Melanie Little. Then I met Mizrus Lowe."

"Did she pay you? Peggy Lowe?"

"For my work, she said she would take me to a lake and we would have a nice dinner."

"Did you ever have occasion to talk to Peggy Lowe on the telephone?"

"Yessir I did, many, many phone calls. From my house to her house is about twenty miles. You have to cross Logan Martin dam to get there. So we talked on the phone a lot. Sometimes for hours."

"Who called who?"

"She called me."

"What would you talk about in these long phone conversations?"

"We talked about our relationships and so on. I told her how my wife had run off and left me for my best friend. She knowed the man. She said, 'Well, he's a whole lot uglier than you are.' "

"What did she tell you?"

"She said her and Wayne hadn't slept together in five years. She said she didn't want to leave him because the children would have to leave with her. They lived on Logan Martin Lake in a hundred and fifty thousand dollar home. She had three kids, but only one was at home, Stephanie. She was in Vincent High School. They had a lot of things. Mr. Lowe bought a pontoon boat."

"So Peggy Lowe showed feelings for you?"

"Yessir, she did."

"How did you respond to that?"

James turned toward the jury. His speech was slowing down and becoming more even, easier to understand.

"I considered myself a common man. I consistently told her that her children would not accept me."

"But that didn't discourage her?"

"Nossir. She told me on the phone one night, 'James, I love you.' Her troubles with her husband was going on. Wayne told her one night to put on a bikini so he could look at her, but she cringed every time he touched her.

"She said she wished something would just happen to Wayne. I jokingly said I had connections and something could be arranged.

"Then later on she said she had a friend that was in the same situation."

Fry barely lifted the fingers of one hand and James fell silent, like the woodwind section. Fry prowled up and down the jury box in silence, as if thinking deep thoughts.

With his face to the jury, his back to James, Fry called out to him: "James!"

"Yessir?"

"Why would you listen to such talk? Why would you yourself suggest that you could help with such a thing?"

James ducked his head back slightly on his shoulders, shrugged nervously, then turned his body to face the jurors. He seemed to compose himself for an important effort, then said:

"She was the type person I had dreamed of dating ever since

I was in high school, because she was a higher type society person than I was."

The jurors all gazed into his face, and for a long moment he returned their gaze, his eyes wide and wounded.

"What else did Peggy Lowe say to you?"

"She said I might go boat riding with Wayne. I said, why? She said, 'Well, boat accidents happen.' "

"Did your relationship with Peggy Lowe ever progress beyond the talking stage?"

"Yessir it did. We met at Walmart's one afternoon, and we went to a little park nearby. We sat in her car together. We kissed and hugged.

"After that she called me six, seven, eight times a week. We might talk thirty minutes, we might talk a couple hours."

He nodded toward the jurors and barely smiled. "Shorter if Stephanie or Wayne was around."

One of the male jurors smiled back reflexively, then looked up at the judge, stiffened, and composed himself soberly.

"Was there a time when these conversations got more serious?"

Without missing a beat, James said, "In March and April of 1992, these conversations got more serious. There was more pressure put on about getting rid of a person in Huntsville. I told Peggy I knowed a man, and I would talk to him. She told me to go ahead and make the connection.

"I said it would cost about twenty thousand dollars. Of course I never really talked to anyone. That was a figure out of my head. She said her sister was almost broke and couldn't pay that much. So the price agreed upon was five thousand.

"I said the man had to have some money up front. So the end or the last part of April, Miz Lowe called me. She said, 'I went to Boaz and met at my mother's house, and Betty give me twenty-five hundred dollars.' "

"And did she give this money to you?"

"Miz Lowe give me the money in a white plastic bag with a black design on it. It was three hundred dollar bills and the rest in twenties. Cash money."

"What did you do with that money?"

"I caught my bills up. My checking account was minus four hundred dollars. So I put in five hundred. I had some bad checks out, so I needed to go around and take care of those."

He carefully listed the names and addresses of the businesses where he had paid off bills. He named the exact amounts, to the penny. The jurors listened intently as James described his efforts to set his personal accounts to rights.

Then Fry asked him about the large payments he had received as workmen's compensation settlements in 1991. James said he had received $34,000 in early 1991 but that by 1992 the money was all gone.

"Where did it go?"

"Well, sir," James said, "I had all four of my kids with me at that time. My ex-wives was having a hard time. And . . ." He seemed to falter.

Fry waited patiently.

"Never in my life have I been able to carry my kids to town and say, 'Buy what you want.'" James bounced in his seat and shook his head backward. His eyes were welling with tears. "I just . . . I guess you could say . . . well, we had a very elaborate Christmas."

One woman on the jury dabbed her eyes with a handkerchief. Almost all of the jurors appeared touched, except for an elderly man who was sound asleep.

"Was there a time," Fry asked, "when your relationship progressed beyond the point of stolen kisses and heavy petting?"

"Yessir, there was."

A sudden stirring went through the back of the room, followed by dead silence. All eyes in the back were fixed intently on James. Most of the jurors were looking shyly away from him. One of the anti-Betty ladies in the back said in a hoarse whisper, "Now we're gettin' somewhere."

Judge Younger put his hand up for Fry to wait and then scoured the back with his eyes, hunting for the one to throw out. All of the people in the back returned his gaze innocently, like children in a schoolyard. With his eyes still fixed on the back of the room, Younger nodded for Fry to continue.

"Tell us about that," Fry said.

"Mizrus Lowe called me at home on May fifteenth," James said quickly, "and she said, 'I'm not going to school today, and I'm here all alone,' which I took for an invitation, so I went over to her home, and we engaged in some heavy petting."

James waited and watched Fry's face.

"Go on," Fry said. He was watching the jurors closely.

"The phone rang," James said, "and it was her daughter calling. Peggy said, 'Stephie's at school and she's not feeling right.' She said she had a headache or cramps or some such like that. So I guess I got mad, and I said, 'That's it, that's it, you just run to your daughter ever' time she whines or cries.' And she said, 'I'm not going.' "

James paused and waited for Fry's signal.

"Go on," Fry said.

"We started off downstairs, and we got going pretty good, and then we went upstairs to her bedroom, and we had sex there."

Fry turned to James. "Do you remember anything else about the incident?"

"Sir?"

"Do you remember how Mrs. Lowe appeared or what she was wearing, anything like that?"

In a quick monotone, he said, "She had on a white shorts outfit with the top tied at the waist. Her underwear was frilly and sort of a pinkish-purple color. It was a real pretty type underwear."

"Did you ever have sex with Peggy Lowe again on a subsequent occasion?"

"No, sir, that was the only time. I never did have sex with her again."

"What did you do after you had sex with her on that occasion?"

James told the story of his drive to the Guntersville State Lodge to pick up an additional two hundred dollars in expense money for the killing from Betty. He described the handoff of the money in a library book as if it were a chapter in a spy novel.

James told how he drove to Huntsville, planning on entering

the Wilson house and murdering Dr. Wilson. He explained that he found a blue pickup truck parked outside, which he deduced to mean that Mrs. Wilson's son Trey was at home, having been informed by someone earlier that her son drove such a truck. Rather than endanger the son, he decided not to carry out the crime. He returned to Vincent, he said, where he continued to drink heavily and take pills.

"Two or three days later, Mizrus Lowe got ahold of me, and she asked me, more or less, 'What the fuck was going on?' I said, 'Trey was there. Do you want both of 'em killed?' She said no, she didn't."

"So what happened subsequent to that?"

"Miz Lowe kept calling me up, saying her sister was crying, she couldn't stand to be around Jack Wilson and on like that. Peggy said if the crime didn't happen, she was going to have to pay back her sister the twenty five hundred dollars. Peggy said it had to happen before May twenty-fourth, because Betty and Jack was supposed to go to Santa Fe, and Betty could not stand the thought of having to go out there and be in the same hotel room with Jack."

"Did you have a problem with getting it done?"

"Yessir, I did, on account of I didn't have no weapon. I had a thirty-two caliber pistol that belonged to my ex-wife, but I couldn't find ammunition for it. I just never could buy ammo for it. So I told Miz Lowe I didn't have a gun. I received a phone call on May twentieth, and they told me that they had the tool and the equipment to do the job with. They asked me to meet them out on Logan Martin dam.

"There's a pulloff on the dam with eight or nine parking places. I went out there. There was nobody else there. I was drinking pretty good. I was looking for Miz Lowe's car, but this big black BMW pulled up with Mizrus Betty Wilson and Peggy Lowe in it.

"Miz Lowe got out, and she had a white sweaterlike thing in her hands. She took it to my truck and let a pistol fall out on the seat."

"What did you do with that gun?"

"I hid it in the old house next to my trailer. There's some boards missing in the porch. I put it in there."

"Did Peggy Lowe say anything to you when she gave you the gun?"

"She said, 'Be careful.' "

James explained that Peggy Lowe also told him to await a phone call. Later the same day, he received that call.

"I was told to go to his office and do it there."

"Who told you?"

"Mizrus Lowe told me."

"What did you do?"

"I drove back up to Huntsville, to 333 Whitesburg Road, which was Dr. Wilson's office. I arrived around four-thirty or five A.M. and parked out in front of the building. Then I moved over across the street to the back of a shopping center there."

"Did you have the gun?"

"No, I didn't take no gun. I guess I was going to strangle him. I had a rope in my truck."

"Why didn't you take the gun?"

"A gun makes too much racket. I'm kinda gunshy from Vietnam."

"So what did you do?"

"I waited for him to pull up. I was told he would be driving a brown Mazda. But, you know, there was already a lot of people jogging up and down in that area. People was already pulling their cars into the buildings around there."

For the first time in the proceedings so far, a few jurors sat back in their seats and allowed themselves to exchange quick, furtive looks of skepticism. In the entire progress of James's long, carefully self-controlled telling of the story, this was perhaps the most implausible moment.

He had told the jury in the first place that he possessed a gun, kept from among his ex-wife's possessions—that he knew the caliber of the gun, a .32—but that he was unable to find .32 caliber ammunition. He had demanded that the twins supply him with a gun, and they had arranged a secret meeting on top of a rural earthen dam in order to do so.

That very night, acting on their instructions and plan, he had driven to Huntsville in order to murder Jack Wilson the following morning as he pulled into the parking lot at his office building in a busy section of the city. He had not taken a gun with him—any gun—because his experiences in Vietnam had made him sensitive to the loud noises associated with gunfire.

Instead, James had parked all the way across the busy thoroughfare. He was uncertain exactly how he was going to end the doctor's life, but he may have been planning, he thought, to run to the back of his truck when he saw Dr. Wilson arrive, grab a rope, race across the street with the rope through five lanes of morning rush-hour traffic, dodge the joggers and other arriving office-workers, and strangle the doctor as he got out of his brown Mazda.

The jurors and the spectators in the back had hung on James's every word through his description of a sexual liaison with Peggy Lowe, but now this was beginning to tax credulity. Watching the faces of the jurors like a hawk, Fry must have sensed it. He kicked the testimony forward abruptly.

"Tell the jury what you did after you decided it would not be possible to carry out your plan."

James told the jury he had called Peggy Lowe from a pay phone on the front side of the shopping center, out of view of Jack Wilson's office building, and complained that there were too many people around. When he called Peggy on this Thursday morning, he was surprised to find that Betty was present also at Peggy's house. He said he spoke to both of them on the telephone, explained the problem with the joggers and the fact that other people were coming to work.

He said he told Betty Wilson that he did not have enough money to spend the night in Huntsville in order to try again at some point. He said Betty told him she would get in her car immediately and drive to Huntsville. It would take her three hours to get there. She would meet him at the Chick-Fil-A restaurant at Parkway City Mall at about noon and supply him with additional funds.

James described a rendezvous in the waiting line at the

counter at Chick-Fil-A. Pretending not to know Betty when he saw her in line, he said casually to her, "Is the food supposed to be good here?"

She said, "Yes, it is."

When they had been served, they both sat on the same bench out in the open area of the mall but were careful not to speak. As soon as Betty had finished eating her lunch, she handed James the empty bag and said, "Would you mind throwing this away for me?"

He agreed, of course. Before throwing it away, he looked inside and found a crisp new hundred-dollar bill.

Fry asked James if he remembered anything else from his visit to Chick-Fil-A on May 21, 1992. James seemed to ponder for a moment, then said he remembered he had been waited on by a Hispanic woman whose name, according to her identification tag, was Christina.

He described taking the hundred-dollar bill and going to a Kmart store nearby to buy a T-shirt, underpants, and a small traveling kit with razor and toothbrush. He paid for these objects with the hundred-dollar bill. He then went to the Ramada Inn where he paid cash to check in. He remembered being required to show his driver's license. His plan was to try again in the morning.

James called Peggy Lowe, he said, and they shared a moment of tenderness on the telephone. "She said she didn't want me to get caught, because she wanted us to have a life together."

So far, whenever James had finished delivering a portion of his speech, he had paused and waited obediently for Fry to signal him to go ahead. But at this moment, James spoke up suddenly on his own.

"I was pretty hot, and then Mizrus Wilson drove by in Trey's pickup truck and handed me a glass of water out the window."

Fry was nonplussed. "What?"

"She give me a glass of water."

"What else did you observe on the street?" Fry interrupted forcefully. "Was there anything else you saw?"

This story of the glass of water had never been mentioned

before in any of James's countless interviews with the police. This was the first time he had ever suggested anything remotely like it. It was strictly a volunteer improvisation on James's part. There was no telling how it would fit with other evidence concerning Betty's whereabouts. But more important, from the state's point of view, it was a dangerous sign that James White, who had been absolutely robotlike in his self-control so far, was beginning to become somehow untacked.

"I seen a guy who was out in his yard with a weed eater," James said. "I just took the water and then went on about my business."

Faint expressions of skepticism were beginning again to ghost across the faces of the jurors. According to James's story, Betty drew a glass of water from the tap, carried it to her son's truck, backed the truck out of the driveway with the water in her hand, drove less than a block down Boulder Circle and handed the glass out through the window of the truck to the assassin, in full view of a neighbor. Did she then wait for the assassin to finish his glass of water and take it back? Or did James spend the rest of his time there jogging around the neighborhood with an empty glass in his hand?

Fry hurried along to a detailed catalog of his activities the next morning—a visit to a Kmart store for some auto parts, which he listed in detail, a phone conversation with Betty in which he talked her out of yet another strangling attempt at the crowded office building.

By this point, the anti-Betty ladies who had gathered themselves in a knot on a couple of pews in the back of the room, were staring off archly into space. The pro-Peggy group were staring beady-eyed at the anti-Betty group, as if to say, "Listen to this nonsense, will you?"

There was no pro-Betty group.

Judge Younger adjourned for lunch.

In the hallway outside the door, the line of people waiting already reached almost to the far end of the corridor. The media people rushed directly to the end of the hall to get in line again, but they had to compete with members of the public who were just as determined not to miss the rest of White's testimony. During the hourlong lunch period, there were several shouting matches between partisans in the corridor.

When Sheriff Sexton made a rare appearance in the hall, a cranky middle-aged writer snatched at his elbow and said, "Jeez, I can't believe you people won't even let us take bathroom breaks."

"You can take a break, sir."

"Yeah, and you'll give my seat away. I've never heard of . . ."

"We're following the judge's wishes, sir."

"I'll tell you what. This is a health hazard for a man my age. I think I may just come in here tomorrow catheterized. How would that be?"

"That would be fine, sir."

After the lunch break, Fry had James pick up his story several hours after the point at which Betty, the good Samaritan, had brought him a glass of water. Now it was 2:30 P.M.. on Friday, May 22, 1992—the day Jack Wilson died. James said he had informed Betty that morning that he did not want his truck to be seen anywhere near Boulder Circle, even though he had been driving around the neighborhood for weeks, casing the job. It was a 1984 Ford F150 with chrome wheels, no wheel covers, and the left front fender painted a lighter blue than the rest of the truck—too identifiable, he said, to be used in the actual crime.

Betty had agreed immediately, he said, to come pick him up at Parkway City Mall and give him a lift to the house. At about two-thirty, she pulled up in the BMW. Before he could get in, she got out and squatted down on the tarmac to change her shoes. He noted that she was putting on a pair of canvas shoes, beaded, with a bright flowered pattern.

"She asked me if I was ready, and I said yes. I got in the front seat with her and scrunched down on the floorboard. We went to her home. It didn't take too long. She pulled into this garage-like thing. Just as we got there, she handed me another forty dollars in cash."

Fry skipped a beat. "What?"

"She give me forty dollars. I have no idea what for."

It was another ad lib that had appeared nowhere before in any of his statements. The jurors' faces were tipped down again in faint frowns. The lady drives the man to her house to kill her husband, for which she has agreed to pay him a total of $5,000, and as they arrive in the garage, she gives him $40? For what? A tip?

Fry pressed ahead quickly. "Tell us what happened when you got out of the car."

"She told me where his bedroom was. So I went on upstairs. At that point, we had not actually discussed a plan. She said he would be home in about thirty minutes, and then she left.

"I started going through some drawers to see what I could find. There was some jewelry laying around. But it looked like costume jewelry, so I did not take anything."

"Then what happened?"

"Well, then it was two and a half to three hours before he come home. I got pretty psyched. I was already taking prescribed medication plus some pills. The phone kept ringing and ringing in the house. I started getting real paranoid and scared. I prowled around upstairs some."

"Did you have a weapon?"

"I carried a rope. I don't know if I had a knife or not. The one they showed me looked like one I carried in my truck all the time.

"I looked out a window and I seen some kids playing a game. Then he come home."

Fry walked up closer to James and faced him straight-on. In a quiet voice, he said, "What happened then, James?"

The courtroom was silent. James twitched his shoulders nervously and cocked his head from side to side, the eyes flitting.

"He come on upstairs. And he grabbed me. We rassled. I grabbed some kind of an object, which I've been told it was a baseball bat, and I hit him until he turned me loose."

"Where were you at this time?"

"Upstairs."

"Then what happened?"

"Well, sir, everything's foggy after that. When I come back to realization, I was somewhere in the woods outside the house. I was told I could go down through the woods behind the house. Mizrus Wilson told me. But I squatted down behind some trees, and all's I could see was other houses and backyards and stuff. So I went back to the house.

"Just then, Mizrus Wilson pulled up. I didn't expect her. But I told her to carry me back to my truck."

"Did she ask you what had happened?"

James looked confused. He had been on the stand for several hours, all told, and during most of that time he had been perfectly composed. But now, at this point, he was beginning to go just a little fuzzy.

"I cain't remember if she asked me anything."

"Was Dr. Wilson still living when you left him?"

"I don't know if he was dead or alive."

"Did she ask?"

"I cain't remember if she asked me anything or not. I got in the car. There was some clothes in a plastic bag in the backseat. I covered up with them. The ones over my face was a pinkish color."

"Did you see anything else in the car?"

"I saw a bank bag in the car."

"Then what did you do?"

"Well, she carried me back to the mall. I went to Taco Bell and got a large Mountain Dew soda. It's right at the intersection across from the shopping center by the Winn-Dixie, where I used the phone on Thursday. I left the Taco Bell and walked through an empty field back to the Ramada Inn and got my truck. Then I went home."

(No one seemed to notice, then or later, that James's truck had been at the mall at the beginning of his story.)

"I bought some more beer and went home. Then I went to a bar with my little brother."

"Were you ever paid the rest of the money owed you?"

"Nossir. I was supposed to get the money on a table in her house. Then there was a new plan. Peggy was going to go up to Huntsville to console her sister and get ready for the funeral. She would get the money and leave it in a box in her garage at the lake. So I went there on a Sunday to get it, but the money wasn't there."

"Did anyone see you?"

"Yessir, there was some people in the house next door doing yardwork. I said, 'Tell Mr. Lowe I come back for my ladder and my paint pan and brushes because my brother was going to do a job.' "

"Were you subsequently arrested?"

"On May twenty-fourth I was contacted by the police. I was on the job at Barbecue Sixty-Six, a restaurant in Cohalla Heights. I had worked there the week before, and I called and asked them to give me another chance and let me come back to work, so they let me.

"The police asked to search my vehicle."

"James, in your interviews with the police, did you tell them the truth?"

"Nossir I did not," he said quickly. "I lied in the early interviews and fed them little bits and pieces. Finally I said I wanted to talk to an attorney."

Fry turned to the judge. "No further questions at this time, Your Honor," he said.

Fry took his seat at the table. The courtroom was still for a very long moment. No one moved.

Suddenly, remembering their instructions, the bailiffs hurried to place the podium back in front of the jury box.

Moving very slowly at first, Bobby Lee Cook rose from his chair and walked to the long table beneath the bench where the evidence had been laid.

This was the moment of truth. In James's testimony, the state had just presented the entire center of its case. In the days ahead, the state would call other witnesses to provide the supposedly corroborative evidence. If James said he went to the Kmart and bought car parts, the state would produce a Kmart clerk with a computer-generated cash register tape to show that he had gone to the Kmart and purchased the car parts he had claimed. If James said he remembered being waited on at Chick-Fil-A by a Hispanic woman named Christina, the state would produce a Chick-Fil-A manager who would testify that the restaurant did, indeed, have such a person in its employ at that time but that she had since departed, unfortunately, for her native soil in the Philippines. All of the incidental details of James's story would be buttressed by this sort of testimony.

None of the so-called corroboration would be persuasive or even pertinent if the jurors believed that James was lying. If the core of his accusation was a lie—if the twins had done nothing to encourage or abet him in the murder—then all of the other details might be only fragments of truth he had woven cleverly into a fabric of lies. In fact, those details could even have been supplied to him by the police during his many long un-tape-recorded interviews with them.

"James, there's a gal that was working at Chick-Fil-A that day who's no longer in the country, so she can't be subpoenaed, but the manager says she was a Hispanic gal and her name was Christina."

"Damn! I do remember that! Yeah, she was a Spanish lady, and her name tag said something like 'Corinna . . .' "

"Christina."

"Yeah, Christina. I remember that."

There was no physical evidence. There were no witnesses. There was only James Dennison White's accusation. If he came apart, the whole story came apart.

For this, the august and famous attorney from Summerville, Georgia, had been summoned. This was his mission: to take James White apart, seize this monster of false teeth and false words, rip him open, and show the jury the vile nest of snakes and lies inside.

But how to do it. That was the question.

If the police had gathered the facts first and allowed James to change his lies to match the facts, then it was an extremely subtle and complex process. It would be a grave tactical error for Betty's lawyers to assume this had happened as the result of anything so crude as a conspiracy. That just wasn't how this sort of thing happens in the real world.

A policeman, hung out to dry by politically ambitious superiors, desperate to get to the end of the story without being personally ruined, sitting for hours with a ferret-eyed jackanapes who has never had a principle or a scruple in his life but who is clever and knows the game from top to bottom—if it happened that way, then it was not a conspiracy but a long slow seduction.

The rascal had what the policeman needed. But the policeman had to come and get it.

The rascal, being a rascal and knowing his own game well, would be sure to leave the policeman plenty of space for face-saving. The rascal would know better than ever to say out loud what was going on all the time. Both legally and morally, the policeman would need enough room to allow him at any moment to put up his hand, stop the process, and say, "I knew exactly what was going on, and I never meant to go all the way."

At the very heart of it was a principle worth all the diamonds and gold in the world to a man like James Dennison White: If you start out with the conclusion you want to reach already in mind, you can build a case to say anything.

Anything.

You can weave a seamless, powerfully persuasive argument to show that the president is a foreign agent, the pope is a car thief, and Mother Teresa started the Chicago fire. If instead of investigating honestly and objectively, not knowing or pretending to know where the facts may lead, you decide first where you are going to wind up, then you can gather facts and wink, and nudge, and whisper, and shove, and coax, and pull until the case winds up proving whatever totally outlandish lie you want it to prove.

If you start weaving the fabric at just the right moment, if you weave it skillfully and very carefully, you can fool and make fools of all the important, powerful, proud people who will come later to pass judgment. If the lie is a good story, the media will publish it and say thank you. If the lie works the right way politically, the authorities will wave it on through.

James may well have faced a sterner test than that. Mickey Brantley may never have given him a single wink, nudge, or word of encouragement. But then, James wasn't accustomed to encouragement. As long as he could figure out where the sweet place was, he could find his way there on his own. He knew the one thing that was important: that it is possible to go before them all—the cops, the lawyers, the judges, the jurors, the reporters, and the cameras—and lie through your teeth. And win.

The only way to take apart such an intricately woven lie is to unweave it intricately. To do it, Cook would have to take the yards and yards of transcribed statements James had made to the police, find the errors, find the contradictions, find the rhythm and the tenor of the questions from the police, then show the jury how the music had been composed. That way of doing it would require charts and diagrams to help the jury see when each piece of evidence had been gathered, when precisely James was asked each question, when exactly he had changed each detail of his story to match the corroborative evidence being gathered by the police.

It would be a huge amount of connected detail for the jury to follow and keep straight. In order to attack the lie itself in a way the jury would be able to follow, the defense would have to put on a sophisticated defense that was the product of months of intense preparation.

Or there was the other way. Don't attack the lie. Go after the man. James himself. Hammer at him, scratch at him, tweak and pinch him, poke him and call him names until he comes apart on his own, blown to bits by his own madness. That way would require skill, experience, instinct, and flair . . . but no preparation.

Bobby Lee Cook looked slight, stooped, and a little decrepit as he approached the evidence table. He pawed through the things there and then found what he wanted—the ball bat. He picked it up, and when he turned with it in his hand it was as if he had been transformed. Suddenly he was powerful and intense, lighted by an inner fury. He looked at the jury, then stared down at the bat in his hand. His voice began low and soft but lifted quickly, growing louder and angrier with each syllable.

"He says he does not remember the bat.

"He says he does not remember the knife."

He went back to the evidence table, put the bat down, and picked up a knife. He carried it to the witness stand and put it down on the front ledge of the witness box, directly in front of James. As soon as he did it, the bailiffs became tensely alert. Even though James was still partially shackled, it was disquieting to see the knife inches from the hands of a confessed killer.

The jurors moved uncomfortably in their chairs. James stared out over the knife, refusing to look down at it, but the eyes were flickering wildly, and his tongue was slipping in and out nervously.

Cook turned his back on White, walked back to the defense table, and picked up a legal pad, from which he read notes.

"The witness said, 'As far as I can remember, I did not take it [the knife] with me.' "

Cook walked toward the jurors.

"He left all his personal belongings in the truck, except his keys and a bag with a rope in it. It was a white bag with handles cut in it and a black design on it, the same bag Peggy Lowe had given him the money in."

Cook moved to the podium, where he continued to read from his notes.

"He's had several aliases. Cookie. He used the name Howell, his stepdaddy's name, until he was twenty-one. His birth date was March fourth, 1951."

Cook moved back to the evidence table. "It was a white bag with handles cut in it, and a black design on it." He pawed through things piled there and extracted a plastic bag. Lifting the bag high, Cook turned and stared at the DA accusingly.

"Well, this must not be it!" he shouted triumphantly. The bag he held was a white plastic bag with a red, rather than black, design on the sides.

Back at the podium, apparently reading from one of White's statements to the police, he said, " 'I was on prescribed medication.' Lithium."

Cook gathered up an armload of paper, apparently transcriptions of White's statements, and carried the paper to the witness stand. He put all of it down in front of James White on top of the knife on the stand.

Cook started to walk away from James, then whirled and shouted at him. "How do we know when you are lying? Is it when you open your mouth?"

James stared into the beyond, his eyes sullen but fixed. He made no attempt at answering.

Leaving the stack of statements in front of James, Cook went back to the podium, where he had his own copy of the statements. He began leafing through them. "Look at this May twenty-sixth document on page twelve. You told Mr. Brantley, did you not, that you went to a location and got the money, and you would not say where you got the money."

"Yessir," James said.

"Why wouldn't you say?"

James said nothing.

"Did you want to think about it?"

James stared back levelly into Cook's eyes.

"Did you want to make up something?"

"I was trying to protect myself, sir. I didn't have no attorney."

"On May twenty-seventh," Cook said, flipping through the pages of transcript, "on page seven, if you want to refer to it, Mr. Brantley said, ' . . . and she give it to you?' You said, 'No, sir, I was told where it was at, and I picked it up.' "

"Yessir," James said.

"On the side of the road?"

"Yessir."

Cook moved in close to James, so that their faces were only

one or two feet apart. Red in the face, Cook shouted: "That was a bald-faced lie, was it not, Mr. Witness?"

Calmly, James said: "Yessir."

"And did it bother you to lie?"

"Yessir."

Cook straightened and walked toward the jury. With his back to the witness, he said, "And so when your lawyer got there, you saw the light."

Several people in the back of the room tittered.

Cook returned to the evidence table and dredged through the artifacts there. He held up the gun. "This gun certainly didn't come from Betty Wilson's house, did it?"

"Nossir."

Cook asked him if he had been charged in other crimes. James said he had. He asked him how much he had to drink on the Parkway City Mall parking lot the day he waited for Betty to come give him a ride to the house. He said he had consumed about eighteen beers.

"You said in your statement to Brantley that you had consumed one beer."

"Yessir."

"That was sort of a ballpark lie, wasn't it?"

"Yessir."

Cook stood for a long time in silence at the podium, leafing through statements.

"On May twenty-ninth, page twenty-six. Go to your record, Mr. Witness. Look at it."

"Page what, sir?"

"Twenty-six."

"Yessir."

James was unruffled, but the jurors, who were looking up from their notes and whispering to each other, were perplexed. They stared at Cook longingly, as if hoping he would now make his point.

Cook, still leafing through the statements, forged on.

"There was a mistake over whether the gun was put under the porch or in the woodpile?"

"Yessir. Mickey Brantley just got it wrong."

Cook continued leafing through the statements for a long while. The jurors wriggled uncomfortably in their chairs. Judge Younger began taking long pointed looks at the clock, which showed the afternoon growing long.

Finally, as if suddenly finding his place, Cook stiffened his back and said ostentatiously, "Statement! May twenty-ninth. 'I don't think really I was going to kill the man, because I had no weapon. I was just going to get in the house and ramble around and see if I could find some money and stuff, and basically that's what I was doing.' "

Cook stopped reading and peered at White.

White said, "Yessir."

"Statement! Also May twenty-ninth. 'My purpose in being at the house was to commit murder.' Was that a lie?"

"Nossir, it's not a lie, because I was told to make it look like a burglary."

"You didn't mean to kill him?"

"Nossir, I didn't."

"You don't know what you hit him with?"

"Nossir."

For another hour, Cook sifted through the stack of transcribed statements, which seemed to be unmarked and which he apparently had to read for himself at the podium in order to find each new point of interest. He challenged James on tiny detail after tiny detail—how many beers did he really drink that day? What did he do with the glass Betty Wilson had used to bring him water? James answered almost every question with short sentences or his robotlike "Yessir" "or Nossir."

Cook hounded him about the suicide attempts on his medical record.

"Haven't you tried twelve or fourteen times?"

"Yessir," he said.

By this point the jurors had stopped taking notes and were gazing on the process with what began to look like dismay.

James White had curled himself into a psychological ball like a wet cur, resolved to take a beating and not bite or die. The longer James survived, the more the jury seemed to pity him.

Cook picked at the transcripts, jumping from page to page, point to point, making no attempt at a coherent picture. He challenged James about when precisely he had checked into the Ramada.

When James gave his answer, Cook leaped at him, almost screaming: "You're just a big liar, aren't you?"

"Nossir. You're wanting a time for everything, and I can't tell you, because I don't carry a watch with me."

If anything, as Cook grew more manic in his attacks, James seemed to take on strength and resolve. Fry and Brantley had spent months coaching him how to stand up to the famous Mr. Cook. Now he was doing it.

Cook asked him about all of the times he had been committed to mental hospitals. He read a portion of one diagnosis in which James was described as hearing voices.

"Have you been hearing any voices in here today other than mine?" Cook asked sarcastically.

"Nossir."

Cook paused, then returned to the podium. He was reading something to himself in the records. He carried the folder back to the witness stand, still reading.

"In April of 1990, you confessed to sexually abusive behavior with your daughter."

Cook dropped the document from his face and peered out over his half-rim glasses into James's face. James stared back at him, and for the first time there was a flickering suggestion of resentment.

"I was drunk," James muttered.

Cook waited and peered at him. It had been a long afternoon, and Bobby Lee Cook looked tired, visibly weakened by the ordeal, if not drained.

James lifted his head and looked back, but now the anger was gone from his eyes.

Cook said nothing and returned to the stack of paper on the

podium. He read from James's record, pausing occasionally for James to confirm or deny.

"A charge of sodomy while incarcerated."

"Yessir."

"You wrote a letter to your stepfather's wife and said you would show her a good time because your stepfather was too old."

"Yessir."

A male juror smirked, then quickly threw his hand over his mouth.

Cook read on down through a long incredible list of mental diagnoses and clinical notes—a white-trash résumé. James said yes and no to each point as serenely as if chanting responses in church. As the catalog of his sins grew longer, the jury seemed less and less interested, let alone surprised.

Finally, as the day drew to a painful anticlimactic close, it was clear that Bobby Lee Cook was very tired and that James Dennison White was feeling the best he may ever have felt in his life.

Cook passed the witness. The judge adjourned the court. Wayne Johnson went to the front of the room to lead the jurors out of the room.

As they filed out of the jury box, several of the jurors looked over to the witness stand. Then the bailiffs came to take James to his holding cell.

When he rose in his shackles and chains, James threw his head back and stared out over the crowd of press and onlookers with pride in his eyes.

Earlier in the day his story had seemed so absurd—the loony contradictions about the gun and his corny invented lovemaking dialogue with Peggy, all of it. But the soul of a trial is contest. A trial, especially a trial in which the charges are serious and the stakes high, is every bit as much an athletic contest as a Golden Gloves boxing match or a Thai kick-boxing event.

James Dennison White had gone up against a feared gladiator, and he had bested him. In the eyes of the jurors, of the press, and of the public onlookers, James White was a much bigger man at the end of the day than he had been at the beginning.

TEN

AT A CATFISH RESTAURANT ON THE BLACK WARRIOR River that night, a group of writers and reporters argued over their drinks:

"Matlock, schmatlock," one said.

"Cook didn't even nick the guy," said another. "Betty's dead in the water."

"Bullshit," a third said. "They still have no physical evidence and no witnesses. The jury cannot convict this lady of a capital crime solely on the word of a total piece of shit like James Dennison White."

"I agree," said a fourth. "It cannot be done. It's hard enough to convict a rich white woman of murder in the South. They won't do it on the basis of a white-trash asshole. They'll walk her."

The next morning in the semidarkness of 6:30 A.M., an hour and a half before the courthouse doors would be unlocked, the line was forming on the lawn. By the time the crowd got inside the darkened building and began lining up outside the locked courtoom door in the upstairs hallway, there were already enough people to take all the seats in the courtroom, and more kept arriving every minute—entire classrooms of law students, vanloads of ladies from Huntsville, fresh teams of reporters from towns and cities even farther afield.

The mood in the hallway was uglier than ever. People shoved

and snatched at each other to protect their places in line. The anti-Betty ladies sent up a gloating chorus of exclamations over how well James Dennison White had done the day before.

"He's poor and ignorant, and he has been a bad man, but he's tellin' the truth in there about Betty!"

For the first time, the pro-Peggy people, most of them from her church in Vincent, began directly confronting the anti-Betties in the crowd.

"How could you honestly believe such lies? The man is just lying to save his own skin. He'd say anything."

The media people were more determined than ever not to be shut out of the courtroom by the swelling gang of public onlookers. Finally the deputies opened the courtroom doors and people began pouring in. A print reporter who barely made it in rushed over to an attractive young woman television reporter, already comfortably ensconced in the front pew with her notepad open.

He shouted at her, "I knew it! How'd you get in ahead of me? You were not ahead of me in line! You've got some damn deal with these deputies, and I am not going to put up with this shit!"

The bailiffs, who had been whispering to each other at the front of the room, whirled to see where the noise was coming from.

"Watch your language in here!" one of them shouted.

The television reporter whispered hoarsely to the print reporter: "I do not have a special deal, you asshole."

"Then how did you get in here ahead of me?" he whispered back angrily.

"I cut in line!"

"Oh," the print reporter said, chastened. "Sorry."

The crowd of public onlookers was more restive than ever. As the state began putting on its long parade of corroborating witnesses, the people in the back of the room started audibly cheering for their favorites and hissing and booing the ones they did not like. Sheriff Sexton's deputies, acting as bailiffs, attempted at first to deal sternly with the noise at the back but as the crowd grew more defiant, the deputies became more embarrassed and bemused.

These were Huntsville people, one deputy told a writer. People from Tuscaloosa don't act like that.

Judge Younger, for his part, interfered less and less with the process, appearing eager to move it along by whatever means necessary.

Some of the witnesses were amusing and distracting. The guards from the Guntersville Lodge were a trio of affable country boys. Their testimony about bringing the book down to James at the gate was often interrupted by laughter from the back, and even Judge Younger allowed himself a chuckle or two.

Betty watched from the defense table. As the day dragged on, she felt herself increasingly removed from the process unfolding before her. Her lawyers were squabbling badly during the evening planning sessions. After his defeat with James, Bobby Lee Cook was asserting himself more as leader of the team—a role not necessarily ceded him by Hooper, Sandlin, and Drake.

During the day, as one state witness after another appeared on the stand, Drake and Hooper seemed to be competing to show which one could be the toughest interrogator, as if demonstrating to Mr. Cook how it should be done. Betty worried that they looked as if they were browbeating innocent witnesses and that, especially when they went after female witnesses, the effect on this Tuscaloosa jury was not good.

But her lawyers had a tough job to accomplish. The right way to have killed the snake would have been for Cook to destroy the story at its source. That effort had failed. James had won that round. Now the defense team had no choice but to go after the story through the corroborative witnesses. It was a bumpy and often dangerous process for them.

Jack Drake did well with some of the state's witnesses. Jack Wilson's former bookkeeper came to the stand to tell the court that Betty Wilson had once called Jack a "son of a bitch" and that she had even "flipped him the bird."

Drake asked her, "Did you ever call your own husband a son of a bitch?"

The bookkeeper looked suddenly stricken, as if she would have given anything not to have to answer. Then, in a barely audible, piping voice, she said, "Well . . . not to his face."

If he could keep up this rhythm, he might be able to show the jury how absurd most of the witnesses' stories were—nothing more than the sort of gossip one might hear at the back of the bus on the way home from a church softball game.

But Sheila Irby was a disaster for the defense. She was the attractive blond housewife from Huntsville who had bragged in a school corridor that she had seen both James and Betty near the intersection of Boulder Circle and Chandler Road at different times on the day of the murder. From the moment Mickey Brantley had latched onto her to the day she appeared in court to testify, almost ten months later, no one had ever given her an inch of breathing space in which to reconsider her story. If anything, her long stretch in the limelight had served to stiffen her resolve. By the time she arrived in court, she was dressed to the nines and beautifully made up; her hair looked exactly like Marilyn Monroe's, and she was clearly ready to see the day through with her dignity intact.

She recited her story for Fry, throwing in many semirehearsed cocktail party punch lines about her own driving, such as "I'm known to hit parked objects," which brought laughter and applause from the back of the room.

When Drake asked her his first question, she stared at him archly without answering for a long moment and then demanded, "What is your name?"

People in the back shouted, "All right!" and "You tell him!"

Drake hammered at the holes in her story. She had not voluntarily reported these crucial sightings to the police until after the crime had been in the news for months. She claimed to be able to pinpoint times and locations when she had seen Betty, even though she had seen Betty in that part of town all the time, every day for years. She had known Betty since high school. She would have had no reason to remark on or remember a certain sighting of her at the time. It was like saying she remembered two months later that on such and such a date when she passed such and such a corner at precisely such and such a time she had seen two fast-food cups and a used Styrofoam food package protruding from the trash can at the bus stop. It was the way hindsight works, not memory.

But Drake never got past Sheila Irby's wall of one-liners. When he asked her if she remembered ever voluntarily reporting the events, she said, instead of answering, "I remember Charlie Hooper calling me and harassing me about it!"

The crowd in the back whooped and clapped.

Frustrated, stung by the jeers of the crowd, Drake grew snappish and sarcastic with the witness. "But now that you're here in front of all the media, you remember those events perfectly, don't you?"

Sheila Irby did not respond but instead drew herself up into a posture of wounded, ladylike propriety—a call to arms for any Southern audience.

"You should be ashamed of yourself!" a woman hissed in the back of the room.

"The man has no decency," a man muttered loudly.

The faces of the jurors turned back and forth from the witness stand to the back of the room as if watching a tennis match. They all looked deeply worried and perplexed by the decision they were going to have to make.

By then the jurors had figured out who all the reporters were in the room. They were the people who sat together taking notes and trading wise looks. Whenever there was a witness on the stand whose testimony was surprising or contradicted other testimony, the jurors looked at the faces on the press bench to see what they had to say. Consistently, no matter who was testifying or what was being said, the reporters made it plain, with their faces and body language, that they had heard it all before.

When the judge adjourned for lunch and Sheila Irby hit the corridor, there was a barrage of lights, action, and shouted jocular questions from the media that might normally be associated with a Hollywood premiere.

. . .

That evening when the defense team met back at the hotel, it was clear to them all that the battle was slipping from their grasp. They had failed to put a bullet in the eye of James White's story. The corroborative testimony was working against them.

Intimidated by the obstreperous anti-Betty partisans, the pro-Peggy people were staying away from the trial in droves, so that the mood in the back of the room was swinging more and more obviously against the defense. The judge seemed uninterested in controlling the problem. At one point during the previous afternoon, a state's witness had made a slip of the tongue while answering a question about the plastic bag found under a rock in Betty's yard. Before the witness could gather her thoughts, a woman in the back rose halfway to her feet and said to the witness in a hoarse stage whisper "No, no, it's white with a red design."

"Oh, yes," the witness said, "white with a red design."

It was not a significant point, except that it showed the jury that everyone in the world was pulling for the state's witnesses and hoping for a conviction.

The bitter rancor of previous evening meetings was set aside. The team obviously needed to do something dramatic to turn the tide in the courtroom or Betty Wilson was going to lose her life for a crime she had not committed.

For months before the trial, the defense team had debated putting Betty on the stand. She wanted to do it. She believed she could explain the whole thing to the jury—make them see how it had happened and, in the process, let them see that she was not the kind of person who was capable of murder.

The lawyers were less sanguine. The state's witnesses had included a parade of people who knew Betty from Alcoholics Anonymous, some of whom had been damaging in the area of Betty's character. The lawyers were afraid putting Betty on the stand might only make matters worse.

Betty's Alcoholics Anonymous chapter had been devastated by the steady stream of leaks coming from the Huntsville Police Department describing Betty's sex life. Betty and her lawyers knew the reality of A.A.—that A.A. chapters often are hotbeds of sexual intrigue and imbroglio, and how could they not be? Alcoholics Anonymous becomes more even than family for its members; it is the intimate center of their emotional universe. Among themselves and behind closed walls, there is even an earthy, bawdy tendency to laugh at mere weaknesses of the flesh, as opposed to the more deadly weakness of alcohol addiction.

But Betty and the lawyers knew there is also, among A.A. people, a morbidly sensitive, exquisitely defensive sense of their own respectability. These are, after all, people fighting to regain lost propriety. They know all too well that most people expect them to fail. Any perception that they are, indeed, beginning to backslide, in any way, wounds them to the quick.

All the front-page and 6:00 P.M. newscast stories of Betty picking up men at her A.A. meetings and taking them home to bed had been terribly painful for the members. To make things worse, someone close to the investigation was continuing to plant among the members the untrue story that Betty had continued secretly drinking while she was a member. Those two things—making the group look bad and continuing to drink secretly—were unforgivable sins.

Knowing all this, the testimony of the A.A. witnesses the state had brought to court was faintly ridiculous. Mary Ann Lau came and told the story of how she had discovered that Betty was betraying her husband with an old boyfriend in New York.

Unlike some of the other A.A. witnesses, she seemed to take no pleasure in supplying evidence against Betty. Fry had to remind her twice that she was under oath and bound by law to testify. Her reluctance, however, only made Betty look worse—a grown woman who no longer had the excuse of alcohol, who had made a game, almost a joke, of cuckolding her husband. It was not a pretty picture.

The picture got worse when Mary Ann told the story of Betty's dream, in which Jack's car had careened off a cliff, and her subsequent flip remark, "I guess I'll just have to be patient."

In several instances, however, the A.A. members had been forced to dredge deep in order to supply the state with a bad story. One member came to the stand and told how Betty had failed to attend a party commemorating the member's tenth year of sobriety. Betty had given an illness in her family as an excuse, but the implication was that Betty was a false friend.

Taken one at a time, it didn't amount to much. Betty was confident she could get on the stand and dispel the impression of herself as a wicked fire-breathing monster. But her lawyers were less certain. It was unlikely the people on the jury knew all the ins and outs of A.A. politics and personal life. They might see any split between Betty and her fellow members as evidence of Betty's perfidy, and it might get worse the more Betty tried to explain it.

The defense team had hired a couple of experts to come sit in the courtroom and watch the jurors, in order to gauge how each witness was affecting them. At this point, it still wasn't possible to tell which way the jury was leaning. Cook might not have destroyed James White, but there were obviously parts of James's story that were very difficult for the jury to swallow.

The incremental effect of the A.A. witnesses had not been good, but it was not possible yet to tell how bad it had been. The defense team had told the jury on several occasions that Betty Wilson had not led a perfect life. Most of the jurors were small-town types, and they would know all too well how a small community may close ranks against one of its own members who brings disgrace upon the group.

One fact still had not been brought to light—a point the state might be able to make if Betty herself went on the stand and had to submit to cross-examination. So far, the state had failed to make the point to the jury that some of Betty's lovers had been black.

Betty said, "How bad can that be? This is 1993."

"Who gives a shit what year it is?" a member of the team shot back. "This is Tuscaloosa."

There were still a few state witnesses scheduled to testify. The lawyers decided to wait and see what guns the state had left to fire before taking any big strategic decisions about how to shoot back.

The next day of the trial was a complete disaster. The deputies bringing Betty from her holding cell had to push and shove through the angry crowd in the corridor in order to get her into the courtroom. As she passed, a few people in the crowd hissed, "Murderer! Bitch! Slut!"

The mood in the room was no less noxious when the judge came in to take his seat. He gaveled for order and issued a mild warning about disruptions, but his voice was faint, and he appeared weary.

The day got off to a terrible start for the defense with the testimony of Betty's brother-in-law, Euel Dean Cagle. Burly, plain-spoken, enormously pained to find himself testifying against family members, Cagle was a riveting, extremely believable witness. Fry led him through the whole story of the morning when he had wakened the twins with the news that Jack's killer had been caught.

"I immediately went into the bedroom and woke them to tell them what I thought would be uplifting news for Betty. I said, 'Betty, they have found the man that killed your husband.' "

"What happened then, Mr. Cagle?"

"Betty sat up. So did Peggy. Betty put her hands in her lap. Peggy turned to the window and didn't say a word to me. Neither one of them. Betty hung her head down and looked at her hands."

"What did you do?"

"I was a little confused. I went back in my wife's bedroom and told her what had transpired. She and I went into the den. In about five minutes, Betty and Peggy went into the bathroom and stayed there for twelve or fifteen minutes. I didn't hear the shower. I didn't hear a word."

"They were in there whispering?"

"Yes, sir."

"Then what happened?"

"They came out into the den. I asked, 'Do either one of you know this Mr. White?' "

"What did they say?"

"Peggy said, 'I do. He did some work for me at the school.' I asked Betty, did she know him. And she said, 'Indirectly.' Then people started arriving at the house, and we never had a chance to talk more about it."

On cross-examination, Drake asked Cagle if he knew that Betty was "medicated" at the time. He said no.

Of course, the explanation for the twins' behavior that morning was that they already knew about White's arrest from their interrogation the night before. They had been instructed forcefully by Harry Renfroe not tell anyone about their interrogation. But Euel Dean Cagle didn't know any of that on the morning when he went to wake them, and now, a year later as he sat on the stand, he still didn't know it.

Unfortunately, no one on the defense team had put together the timing closely enough—who knew what and when—to realize what Cagle's problem had been. So no one asked him about it, and the point was not made. Instead, what the jury heard—and the jury listened intently to every word he spoke—was an honest man, speaking against his will and telling a very damning story about members of his own family.

In all the nervous stewing and hubbub both inside the courtroom and out, there was an even louder thrill of noise, lights, shouting, and excitement as the state brought in what would prove to be its biggest gun in the entire trial. Subpoenaed from his new life in California, dragged back unwilling into the worst nightmare of his adult life, former Huntsville Risk Manager Errol Fitzpatrick came down the crowded corridor.

He walked stooped forward, attempting to hold a legal pad over his face as a shield against the cameras. But the camera crews danced in and out around him, probing and falling back, washing him with light. Someone in the crowd who recognized him sang out, "Ooooo, Lover Boy!" and others laughed. Once inside the courtroom, Fitzpatrick stopped, straightened himself, glanced at the hungry mob at the back of the room, and then proceeded straight to the witness stand.

A handsome African American with light-brown skin and short hair, wearing an expensive business suit, accustomed to testifying in court in his role as a public servant, he was cool and extremely self-possessed as Fry began questioning him.

Fry, for his part, was elaborately polite.

Fitzpatrick recited his name and the fact that he had been an executive in the Huntsville city government between 1987 and 1992. The jurors seemed bored at first, probably thinking this was yet another expert witness who was going to tell them something technical about the investigation or about Jack and Betty Wilson's finances.

"Would you tell us where and when you first met Betty Wilson?" Fry asked.

A couple of the younger jurors seemed to focus.

"We met in Alcoholics Anonymous in about 1987."

Now all of the jurors were staring at Fitzpatrick.

"Would you describe your relationship?"

"We met at a meeting," he said coolly. "A friendship developed. That led to a relationship."

The faces of the few black people on the jury bore faint expressions of wry resignation, as if to say, "Oh-oh, here it comes."

The white jurors, especially the older ones, were peering straight at Errol Fitzpatrick with unblinking intensity.

"Mr. Fitzpatrick, after 1987, when did your relationship become other than a friendship?"

Fitzpatrick paused, staring at Fry.

"It did escalate to beyond the normal A.A. interaction shortly after I arrived in Huntsville."

"How soon?"

"Not too long."

"How long would that be?"

"Maybe a month."

"Did it become . . ."

Fry paused and held his hands up, as if searching for a word of delicacy. "Did it become an *intimate* relationship?"

Fitzpatrick nodded. "Sexual. Correct."

The jurors, transported beyond any self-conscious awareness of how they appeared, were following Fitzpatrick's words so intently that several of them nodded when he nodded, shrugged when he shrugged.

"Sexual intercourse?" Fry asked.

"Correct."

"Where did you first have sexual intercourse?"

"At my apartment in Huntsville."

"Whose idea was it to go there to have sexual intercourse?"

"It was my idea."

"What was the frequency of your sexual intercourse?"

Fitzpatrick stared back for a long moment, as if not quite able to believe what he was hearing, and then, apparently deciding to give the question a generous interpretation, he said, "There were intermittent gaps that lasted months at a time. We simply stopped seeing each other. We might go two to three weeks, or six months. It just happened, or it didn't happen."

"Did you ever have sexual intercourse with Mrs. Wilson anywhere other than at your apartment?"

Fitzpatrick exhaled, and several jurors exhaled with him.

"Yes," he said. "At the Radisson Hotel in Huntsville."

"And when you had sexual intercourse at the Radisson, who paid for the room?"

"I got the room."

"How long were you there?"

"At the Radisson?"

"Yes, sir."

"We were there three or four hours."

"Anywhere else?"

"In Birmingham. We went to the Holiday Inn off I-65, there at the Oxmoor Road exit, near Homewood."

"When you rented a room to have sexual intercourse with Mrs. Wilson, who typically paid for the room?"

"She did sometimes. I did sometimes. If I had a work-related effort going on and I had a room voucher, then I probably did. There were times she would pay for the room."

Thus far the faces of the jurors had been intent but not visibly judgmental. They might have been listening too hard, up to this point, to have bothered reaching conclusions. Fry surveyed them carefully to see how they were faring. Then he turned back to Errol Fitzpatrick.

"Did you ever have sexual intercourse with the defendant, sir, in the defendant's home?"

Fitzpatrick nodded slightly, with a barely perceptible shrug of resignation. He knew where this one was going. Sex with the white lady in the white man's house. Tuscaloosa, Alabama. A jury overwhelmingly dominated by working-class white Southerners.

As if trying to separate himself from what was going on in the courtroom, he answered clearly and simply, with a frigid dignity:

"Yes, I had relations with the defendant in her house. I went there one evening. Dr. Wilson was not there."

The white jurors all sat up straight and raised their eyebrows as one. Fry saw it from the corner of his eye: the arrow home.

"Did you ever go to the defendant's house during the day?"

"I went to the defendant's house during the daylight hours about five times."

"Did you have sexual intercourse?"

"No. We did not have relations then."

"Were you friends with the defendant's husband?"

"He and I were acquaintances."

An older white woman on the jury gave her head a tiny shake—the man would not deign to call Dr. Wilson a friend, just an acquaintance.

"Were you ever present in the home when Dr. Wilson was there?"

"I was a guest in their home one evening. Peggy Lowe was in town. I went by for some conversation and soft drinks. Dr. Wilson was there."

"Where did you have most of your sexual intercourse with the defendant?"

"At my apartment. We met there predominantly."

Betty slumped slightly at the table. She had been watching the jurors' faces. She knew exactly how it was going. She had grown up in Gadsden. Wormy Woods, the racist alcoholic cop, was her daddy. She knew exactly what the tiny sneers meant at the corners of the mouths of the white jurors.

One of the jurors, a woman, caught the tiny slump in Betty's shoulders. She stared at Betty for a moment with a ferocity born of racial sexual loathing.

"When was the last time you had sexual intercourse with the defendant?" Fry asked Fitzpatrick.

"It was some time in May of 1992. A week or two before Dr. Wilson's death."

Fry turned away from Fitzpatrick and did a little tour of the area in front of the jury box, walking this way and that, face low, face high, pondering the imponderables. Then, as if a question had just occurred to him out of the blue, he turned back toward Fitzpatrick.

"Did she ever say she loved you?"

Fitzpatrick was icy.

"No. She never expressed love for me. Our meetings were for sexual purposes."

"Did she ever express an interest in marrying you?"

"No. There were no marriage plans. The relationship was solely sexual."

Fry turned back toward the jury and gave a little shrug as if to say, "Well, there you have it."

He passed the witness, and Drake rose.

Drake introduced himself.

Then he said to Fitzpatrick, "Mr. Fitzpatrick, are you African-American?"

A woman on the jury smirked.

"Yes, I am," he said.

"Does it offend you that Mr. Fry brought you here all the way from California because he thinks it's important for the jury to see you are black?"

Fry leaped to his feet with surprising agility and shouted an objection, which the judge promptly granted. The jurors gazed down on Drake angrily.

Drake nodded. "Thank you, sir. No further questions."

When Fitzpatrick was excused, he tore two sheets of white paper from the legal pad he had brought in with him. Walking to the courtroom door, he lifted a sheet of paper in each palm, pressing them against both sides of his face. A white bailiff leaned forward and pulled the door open for him. Just then a blazing fury of television lights and shouted questions erupted in the hallway. With his face bent forward and leaves of paper pressed to his cheeks, the former risk manager of Huntsville, Alabama, plunged ahead into the rest of his life.

Fry immediately called Shirley Green—the housemaid who had left Betty after Betty tried to split her days with another former maid.

"I cleaned house for them for four years," she said. "I started right before Christmas in 1987, and then I stopped in November 1991, a year before Jack died."

"And what all did your duties include, Miz Green?"

"Everything. I called Parisians to come pick up her furs for her, took care of pest control and so on. I started at seven-thirty A.M. and stayed four hours. Sometimes I stayed in the afternoons. I started out working two days a week and then went to three. I cleaned the whole house."

"What did you observe with your own eyes of the relationship between the defendant and her husband?"

"Sometimes his bag would stink," she said quickly, turning toward the jury. "She hated that. It would make the house smell."

"That was what bothered her?"

"Just Jack, period, she didn't like. No matter what he did, it wasn't right."

"What did she say, when his bag was smelling?"

Shirley Green paused for a split second, then said loudly, "She called him 'Shitbag.' "

Fry waited a beat for it to sink in. Then he said, "What else did you see or observe?"

"Sometimes Jack's bag would not be real tight, and there would be things happen. One time I was told by Betty that Jack couldn't make love to her. Just couldn't do it. He got these machines or pumps and tried with that, but his bag come loose. She pushed him to the floor. He said he would never ever touch her again."

"Did she talk to you about the incident?"

"Yes, she told me all about it."

"Did you observe anything else?"

"Jack told her once he might as well kill himself, that was what she wanted anyway. And she told him she'd go get the gun for him if he wanted her to."

"Did you ever see Mr. Errol Fitzpatrick in the house?"

"At least once a week. They'd go off together. He would come to the house and ask where she was. I'd tell him, and he would go where she was. Sometimes in her bedroom, sometimes in the kitchen."

"Did you ever see them together in the bedroom?"

"I saw them in the bedroom together talking."

"What did you do while this was going on?"

"I worked elsewhere in the house. They wanted their privacy. That was just understood between us."

"Did anyone else ever come to the house to see Betty?"

"Nelson Hogg. He was a friend of Betty's. He came all the time, too. Betty took me to his place once. He had an apartment off Drake Avenue. I was to clean his apartment. She would pay me. She told me not to mention it to anybody."

"How did you get in?"

"The door was locked, but she had a key. There was no cleaning supplies there, so she went to get some."

"What did you observe there?"

"He had clothes lying around, pictures of his children and so on. I looked in the closet and saw a gown of Betty's. It was a Victoria's Secret thing, real pretty."

The defense lawyers were listening acutely. Nelson Hogg was an African-American man. They knew from their own interviews with Shirley Green that she was especially angry about having been ordered to clean his apartment. But they wondered if and how Fry would let the jury know his race.

"What else?"

"Well, when you dust, you open drawers to get to the top part so you can dust it."

"Yes?"

"I found a note."

"What kind of note? Did you read it?"

"Yes."

There was laughter in the back, and a few jurors allowed themselves smiles.

Shirley Green paused, then said: "It was from Betty."

"What did it say?"

"It said, 'Everybody needs a little love now and again, and I need you.' "

She smirked, embarrassed.

A younger woman on the jury looked at Betty with an expression that was a mixture of surprise and compassion.

Fry, with his impeccable ear for awkward moments, kicked the testimony ahead quickly with a sharp question:

"Did Betty ever tell you why she married Jack?"

Answering quickly, as if reading a line in rehearsal, she said: "She told me the first time she married for love and the second time she married for money."

Charlie Hooper took the cross-examination.

"Your husband's name is Wayne?" he asked.

"Yes."

Hooper asked her if it was true her husband had called one of the movie companies working on the case to see if he could sell his wife's story rights, saying that his wife "wanted her part of the money."

Shirley Green immediately began shaking her head no.

"I said to the guy from Hollywood, if there's any money to be made, I want Jack's children to have it. I didn't ask for any for me. I wanted it for Jack's children."

The opinion of the jury-watchers was that Errol Fitzpatrick and Shirley Green had exerted a powerful influence on the jury—all of it bad for Betty. Fitzpatrick's behavior may have been understandable in human terms. His entanglement with Betty had destroyed his marriage and derailed his career, and now he was being dragged back to Alabama and paraded before a jury in a murder trial solely to show the jury that the defendant had slept with a black man. But his frosty irritation with the process had not helped Betty. The looks on the faces of the jurors gave the strong impression they thought he was haughty and, that worst of all Southern sins, proud.

And Shirley Green they had simply believed, wholeheartedly. She was of the blood and kith of the jurors—their own folk. She had portrayed Betty as rich, spoiled, and mean.

What the lawyers shrank from telling Betty was that she was, in fact, rich, spoiled, and mean. She was many other things and much more. Her relationship with Jack had been intense, deep, and wonderful in her own view of it. The terrible problems they had suffered—his physical health, her mental health—had only made their love the more poignant.

But that was a story you probably had to be with them for. Her lawyers knew that the people on the jury were going to have a very hard time getting past the part about the black lover and the rich, spoiled, and mean.

Betty still wanted to take the stand. But there was one more major opportunity ahead for the defense. The state finally had come to its own most vulnerable moment. It was time for the testimony of Huntsville police detective Mickey Lee Brantley.

Brantley was stolid and emotionless as he took the stand—a little fireplug of a man with a burr haircut, trim mustache, and the tough eyes of a cop. He recited his biography—fourteen years on the force, married with two kids.

Fry walked him through all the details of the crime scene itself, from the initial call to his arrival at the house. It was a story the jury had heard already from several witnesses, but rehearsing it again gave Fry a chance to set Brantley up as a careful and responsible police officer, immersed in the facts of the case.

Brantley told the story of his early interrogations of Betty, in which she provided him with a minute-by-minute accounting of her whereabouts on the day of the murder—a visit to Parisians, Yielding's, other stores, a stop at the bank, the pharmacy, and so on. Then in very general terms, Brantley told about his interrogations of James White.

At this point in the trial, Betty had already lost all of the rounds—the James White testimony, the corroborating witnesses, the A.A. witnesses, Errol Fitzpatrick and Shirley Green. If there was a single window of escape left her, it was here in the matter of how and when Mickey Brantley had learned what he had learned and how, when, and if he had conveyed information to James White.

James's story in the first interrogations had been a lie—a lie anyone could see. His early stories made no sense. The facts fell all over each other in mutual contradictions. The tone of the stories was the half-silly, half-sly tone of a liar.

By the time James came to court, his stories had been tuned and tightened up until they made fairly strong sense. He had remembered his way out of all the contradictions, and he had recalled a fairly incredible catalog of tiny details—the fact, for example, that when Betty came to pick him up on the parking lot of the mall, after he had consumed eighteen beers and unknown quantities and descriptions of pills, on his way to kill a man, James Dennison White, heretofore not known for his clothes consciousness, had noticed that Betty was wearing new canvas shoes with a beaded floral pattern. And he had remembered the new shoes out of the blue, months later, like a deep-buried, painful secret of early childhood.

The key, the secret, the formula, the magic ingredient was in the timing of Brantley's investigations with Brantley's interrogations. When did he gather the cash-register tape showing Betty had purchased floral shoes, for example, and when did James experience his sudden recollection of the floral shoes? In order for the jury to see those linkages and understand how they had worked, someone would literally have to draw a picture for them: Over here we have the date and time of Detective Brantley's visit to the mall to pick up the cash-register tape; on the other side of the chart, we have the date and time of James Dennison

White's first mention of the canvas shoes in an interrogation.

From point to point, fact to fact, someone would have to draw it out simply and clearly for the jury, in order to explain and turn around the very damaging picture the state had succeeded in painting so far of James as a weak, wretched man whom the twins had exploited and who was telling the truth in this instance; of the twins as weird simply because they were twins; of Betty as a mean, rich, spoiled, race-mixing slut who had mistreated her husband and wanted him dead; of the twins as murderous witches.

It was a lot to undo.

Judge Younger adjourned for lunch. Over the lunch break, the word went out that the cross-examination of Brantley would be handled by Bobby Lee Cook. By the time the court reconvened, the room was packed. People were jammed on the pews and standing in the back. Folding chairs had been wedged into the area on the other side of the bar, all around the lawyers' tables and against the wall across from the jury.

The jurors, when they returned to their seats, were nervous and intent. All of the signals in the room—the crowding, the hushed murmur—conveyed to the jurors that something very crucial was about to unfold. The bailiffs had to go out into the hall several times to quell the angry mob outside.

Cook started in slowly on him, honing the knife.

"You interviewed Mr. White on July thirtieth, did you not?" Cook asked.

"Yes, sir, I did."

"Did you make a tape recording of that interview?"

"No, sir."

"Did you make a tape recording of your interview in jail with James White on August third?"

"No, sir."

"On May twenty-sixth, in your interview with James White, did you ask James White to give you a description of Betty Wilson?"

Brantley shrugged but did not answer, as if he could not recall.

"Here you've got a man who has accused Betty Wilson of murder," Cook said. "And you never asked him to describe the lady? Isn't that pretty poor investigative technique?"

"No, sir," Brantley said.

"Was it a mistake?"

"No, sir."

The more Cook needled and Brantley answered, the more the exchange began to look like a replay of Cook's exchanges with James White—Cook obviously digging for the hot button that would make Brantley lose his composure and say something foolish, Brantley obviously determined not to lose his composure.

"Was it a fair and responsible way to handle the investigation?"

"Yes, sir. I say it's fair."

Cook moved away from him. With his back to the witness, looking at the jury, Cook said, "You did a lineup of the employees at Taco Bell where James went to buy a glass of Mountain Dew after the murder, to see if James could recognize any of them. Not one of those people's liberty was at stake, and yet you did a lineup there. And yet you never once asked this man to even describe Betty Wilson."

Cook went to the evidence table and picked up the plastic bag that had been found under a rock in Betty's yard. He grilled Brantley about why there were no prints on the bag and why the clothes inside, after being outside for weeks in the rainy season, were freshly laundered and folded.

"How did he happen to remember where his clothes had been for over two months?"

"As far as I remember, he said he just remembered."

Cook read through a long series of Brantley's handwritten notes to himself on the margins of the investigative record. None of the notes led to any particular conclusion, one way or the other, about the investigation.

Cook dickered with Brantley over a key point that rested on three issues: 1) when James had first said he had sex with Peggy; 2) when Brantley had learned from Peggy's school that she could not have had sex with him that day but would have been at home on another date; and 3) when James had changed his story to say that he had had sex with Peggy on the day she was absent from school.

But the point was never clarified. Before the jury could even discern exactly what it was that Cook was implying, Cook whirled on Brantley, came in close to his face, and said, half shouting, "Were you instrumental or were you the guiding hand in striking a deal with this crazy cold-blooded murderer?"

"No."

"Don't you know you are the one who recommended a deal that would put this homicidal maniac back on the street in seven years, back on the streets of Vincent, of Huntsville, of Tuscaloosa!"

"No, sir."

"Certainly you would not strike a deal and supply physical evidence to corroborate this man's story and lead to the conviction of these ladies?"

"No, sir."

"Let me hand you a deal that nobody's seen yet," Cook said angrily. He pushed a sheaf of papers at Brantley, who refused to lift his hand to take them.

For the next half hour, Brantley and Cook wrangled over the meaning of the deal the state had struck with James White. Cook argued it was a contract offering White a light sentence if he thought up evidence to get the twins convicted. Brantley said it was an agreement offering White a reduced sentence for telling the truth.

For the next two hours Cook dredged through the details of the investigation, suggesting at one point that the state had concealed evidence from a confidential informant who had explained to police that James had received the money he used to pay off his bills from a source other than the twins. But the informant was never named by Cook; the evidence was never presented by Cook, either; the point was never cleared up; and the effort wound up looking like another in a long series of attempts by the defense to drag red herrings across the path.

Cook asked Brantley if anyone had ever seen Peggy Lowe kiss James White.

"No, sir."

But Cook leaped immediately from that point to the question of why Zeke, the bloodhound, had failed to find the bag of clothes under a rock. Brantley said Zeke was suffering from allergies that day.

Cook began snapping and tearing at the Sheila Irby testimony but then jumped again:

"When James supposedly had sex with Peggy, were they naked?"

"I have no idea, sir," Brantley said, rounding his shoulders in a show of proper dismay at the question.

"You didn't ask him whether they did it with their clothes on or their clothes off?"

An older woman on the jury fluttered her eyebrows nervously.

"All I know is, they had intercourse."

"Did you ask him if she had any identifying marks?"

"Yes, sir."

"Did you know that she had extensive scarring from an appendectomy and extensive scarring from a hysterectomy?"

"No, sir."

"Did you ask James White about that?"

"He couldn't remember any marks."

Cook jumped to the question of physical evidence at Boulder Avenue, pointing out that forensic-evidence technicians had gone over the BMW minutely to find hairs, tissue, any remnant or stain that would show that James had ever been in the car, but they had found not one shred of evidence.

"Was any fiber or foreign materials recovered in the BMW which tied it to the clothing, hairs, or person of James Dennison White?"

"No, sir."

By the time the day ended, several jurors were slipping in and out of slumber. But Brantley was basically unbowed. It was a ragged, stuttering end to a long confusing day—less clear and less clean than the victory James White had won over the famous lawyer. But no less a victory.

In the days ahead, the defense put on its own witnesses. A detective told the jury he had found a life-insurance policy for a million dollars on Jack's life, left incomplete because Jack had been unable to get Betty to sign it. Other witnesses told stories that tended to contradict the detailed chronology set forth by the state.

There were promising moments. David Williamson, the sports-photo salesman whom James had confronted in the lobby of the Ramada Inn, told how James had ranted, "I'm going to make that bitch pay for what she done to me. I'm going to show her what lonely is all about."

It was the first hard-hitting testimony the jury had heard which directly contradicted the chronology set forth by the state and also gave a window into what actually had been James's state of mind before committing the murder—his drunk and stoned psychotic rage against Betty. As such, it was the only glimpse the jury would ever see of the real motive—James's loony-tunes version of revenge.

But Fry was deft in his own handling of Williamson. He asked him about his business—selling sports photos in motel bars—in a manner that managed, without ever saying as much directly, to make Williamson look like a miscreant. He harped on the same flaw in Williamson's behavior that Drake had addressed with Sheila Irby—the length of time it had taken Williamson to report his confrontation with James to the authorities. But because Fry never lost his temper or appeared to abuse his witness, he was much more effective than Drake had been in making the witness look bad. In the end, Fry managed to leave the jury with two or three decent reasons why they might decide Williamson was a liar.

The trial had ground on for six very long days. When the judge adjourned at the end of the day Saturday, he announced that court would reconvene promptly at 8:00 A.M. on Monday. Most of the media people and the court watchers then left the courthouse expecting at least one more full week of trial, possibly more.

But in a long painful day of meetings at the hotel on Sunday, the defense team finally admitted that it could not afford to allow the trial to simply run on and on. As things stood, they now faced an uphill battle to save Betty's life.

Jimmy Fry's handling of David Williamson was a painful lesson in why the defense team could not rely on a strategy of small witnesses poking little holes in the state's story. Fry was too smart—too good a lawyer. No one in the courtroom suffered the misconception that the D.A. from Limestone County was a big-bellied good old boy who could be pushed around by the slicks. If anything, it was the opposite situation. If they came at him with anything less than a fatal shot, he would turn the bullet around and make them eat it.

Betty hated him.

The lawyers knew better. It wasn't that Jimmy Fry wanted to put an innocent woman in prison. He probably didn't know whether Betty was innocent or not. It wasn't his job to know. That was the jury's job. Jimmy Fry's duty was to do the best job he possibly could of presenting the state's case to the jury. It was Betty's bad luck that Jimmy Fry happened to be very good at his job.

What the defense team needed to do at this point was lower the sails, take a position, load its very best cannon with its very best ball and shoot straight amidships. It was a waste of time to keep chipping away.

There is a possibility the defense might have reconsidered and put Betty on the stand, had the lawyers known more about the true nature of her relationship with Jack. The marriage had been painted in court and in the media as the victimization of a sweet and passive man by a monster. Perhaps if the jury had heard Betty talk about why and how she and Jack came together in the first place and what they had gone through together, the ugly spell cast by the state could have been broken.

The only lawyer who knew Betty well was Charlie Hooper, and in the rarefied glare of this very high-profile trial, Hooper had been relegated to a secondary role on the team. Drake and Cook were the two who seemed to be vying for the role of team captain, and they knew Betty mainly from the information that had been sent them by modem in the weeks and months before the trial.

It was the decision of the defense team that it was too dangerous to put Betty on. That decision probably was influenced by a feeling that Betty was more or less the bitch the state had made her out to be. And in a sense, of course, she was.

The decision was made to put matters in the hands of the family hero. Peggy, the prettier twin, who had led the much more virtuous life, would take the stand on Monday and tell the jury the truth about herself, her sister, their family, and their lives. The lawyers deemed that she was the type for the job—not Betty.

The state's case required the jury to believe that both twins were equally guilty. It was not possible to call one guilty and the other not. The state's whole story would collapse. Peggy, after all, was the only link between James Dennison White and Betty. How else could Betty ever have met White? And by the state's own version of things—according to White's own testimony—the murder plot was already well under way when he finally met Betty for the first time. In fact, White said he met Betty for the first time on Logan Martin dam when she came with Peggy to bring him the gun.

The motor driving the entire conspiracy was James White's love affair with Peggy and, in particular, the single act of sexual intercourse he said she granted him in payment for his crime.

If Peggy could persuade the jury that she herself was innocent, then the jury would have to conclude that Betty was innocent, too. It was a piece of logical wiring woven deep in the state's version of things. It had to do with what may even have been the initial seed of the entire nightmare—their twinness.

Would Mickey Brantley ever have believed a word James White said, had they been sisters separated by a few years of age? Would the media ever have taken such ferocious interest, if there had been no twin angle? Was the entire accusation, in fact, rooted deep in the superstitious beliefs of people about twins—that they are somehow fundamentally unlike other people, that in their whispered confidences is a subtle and evil reworking of the mechanisms of conscience and will?

Be that as it may, it was time for the defense to try to turn the twin thing against the accusers. By putting Peggy on the stand, they felt they were giving the jury the better twin—the one who would be much harder to convict. If the jurors could not take Peggy's life from her, they would have to spare Betty, her twin.

Peggy had not visited the trial, so her appearance on Monday morning was the first occasion for the jurors to see her. She had not been allowed to visit Betty in jail. A few moments before the trial reconvened on Monday, they met and embraced tearfully in the anteroom—their first physical reunion since their arrest.

Peggy's auburn hair was softly done in a medium-length cut that set off her enormous blue eyes. She wore a black suit with a long white collar. A single strand of pearls was echoed by the pearl-white cuffs of a silk blouse. Speaking in a hushed, careful, somewhat stagy voice, as if in church, she named her children and gave their ages.

"Angie, twenty-five. Blake, twenty-three. Stephanie, who is fifteen. And I have a grandson, Cole, who is twenty months old."

She smiled sweetly.

Cook led her through the details of her working career.

"I taught kindergarten one year, and the rest of the time I have taught first grade."

Suddenly tears appeared in her eyes, and then she began to cry in small muffled sobs.

Cook was visibly taken aback.

"Are you all right, Peggy?"

"I saw my sister just briefly a moment ago for the first time since last May," she said.

Cook paused for her to compose herself.

The jury was watching her intently. Some of the jurors had

expected her to be an identical twin, so they were confused by her appearance. Others, especially the men, sharpened their focus when she cried.

"I was born in Gadsden in 1945," she said in response to a question. "I had a happy childhood. When I was in junior high school, I started realizing that we had a very atypical home. My father was an abusive alcoholic. He was physically abusive of my mother."

This was not exactly what the defense had hoped to put before the jury. If anything, tales of a dark childhood might tend to help the jury believe the twins were witches. Cook hurried her on through the history of her first marriage and her union with Wayne.

When she came to that part, Peggy fell right into the groove of her public-speaking persona—the bulletproof sweetness and the assertiveness that seems not to assert.

"We sent two kids to college. We have a good loving relationship. Our family is our life—the center of our universe."

Then Peggy launched into the story of Jack's death, how she had heard of it, what she had done, what she had told her husband, where she had gone. She spoke with the special propriety that Southern women reserve for matters of death, baptism, and marriage.

"When you learned of his death, did you then drive to Huntsville?" Cook asked.

"Yes."

"Who went with you."

She began to cry again.

"No one went with me," she said. "I went alone."

At this second appearance of tears, a few of the women on the jury sat back, a barely visible set to their jaws.

She told the story of her arrest, then went on in detail about the night of her first and main interrogation. She told how she was hauled here and there in the police car, how they took her to one office but then had to move because someone else needed to use that office.

In the course of this long narrative, Peggy continued to fight back tears, sometimes unsuccessfully. It seemed at some moments as if she was crying about the way she had been treated by the police.

But at the same time, a strange thing was happening to her speech. She told her story by quoting people, and when she quoted the police, she spoke in their voices. She lowered her own voice, put a manly edge to it and used the slang and the epithets that cops use. It was a language and voice she knew well, of course—the language of her father, Wormy Woods. But from the lips of this fastidious Southern belle, in her black suit and demure pearls, the tough cop talk was jarring.

"They told me Mr. White was in the next room, and so was Betty, and they said, 'They've both confessed and they've fingered you.' I said, 'I'd like for him to come in here and tell me that.' And they said, 'You're going to get your wish in a minute, lady. Not only that, we're going to give you a lie detector test, and you ain't going to pass it! That needle's going to go right off the screen! Every bone in little Jackie's body is broken, and it's your fault.' "

The jurors were mesmerized by the beautiful, churchy, tough-talking lady on the stand, whose tears seemed to turn off and on like water.

She told how the police finally released them that night:

"When we got off the elevator, Betty asked if we were under arrest, and he said, 'No, we don't have enough evidence, but we're gonna get it.' Then he pointed upward, I guess to the jail upstairs, and he said, 'When we do, you two gals are gonna land right up there on the ninth floor!' "

Cook took her on through the entire saga of her many subsequent interrogations, a process that took up most of the rest of the morning.

Then he asked her, "Did you ever have sex with James Dennison White?"

"Absolutely not."

The judge adjourned for lunch.

After the break, Cook led Peggy through a telling of her many acts of kindness—the times she and Wayne had adopted wayward teens, brought entire families of needy people to their own home to stay. Cook had her explain how James White had fit into this picture and how his importunings had grown, until his insistent grasping for money finally had exhausted Peggy and Wayne's patience and resources. She told how James had threatened to go back to drinking and how he also threatened suicide if she failed to give him more money.

"I told him I was hearing him say the kinds of things I had heard my sister say—that despondent kind of talk. I said she was a recovering alcoholic, that she had been sober five years. I felt sure if he would join a group the way she had, it would help. Her sobriety had saved her life.

"At the end of April, I started telling him maybe he might want to relocate. I suggested to him that Betty and Jack were having work done in their kitchen. She wanted an island built in her kitchen high enough so she would not have to lean over. Her back hurt her. They were also building on a front porch and a shelter roof over their deck. They wanted to have screened porches like we had as children.

"I said, regardless, we couldn't afford to employ him full-time, but they had plenty of money, and it might give him a chance to relocate. I told Betty about him, and they negotiated a rate of six dollars an hour."

She told how James had called her just as the Guntersville Round-Up was getting under way and had threatened suicide. "I told him, 'I know Betty would help you.' Later Betty called me, and I asked her if she would, and she said, 'You know I will.'

"She said she would put some money in her car for him."

Cook stopped her. "Put some money in her car, how?"

Peggy paused dramatically, as if trying to recall, and then said, "I think she said she'd put it in a book and leave it in her car."

Someone groaned in the back of the room. The courtroom had heard so many versions of the book story that Peggy's mention of it sounded fake, as if she were pretending to be only distantly acquainted with the case. Everyone was sick of the book by now.

"She said she would park her car underneath a light, as close to the entrance as possible. I communicated that to Mr. White."

She told the story of James's late-night call complaining he couldn't get into the park, the arrangements that had to be made, how Betty was paged in the lodge, and how she sent the book down to Mr. White at the gate by courier.

"On Sunday, May seventeenth, I got home from church and ate lunch, and I was getting ready to go for a boat ride, when Betty called. She was very upset. She said, 'Tell me that . . . (Peggy paused in her testimony and blushed, because she was obviously going to have to say a bad word) . . . tell me that so-and-so's number.'

"I said, 'What so-and-so?' Betty said, 'Mr. White. I left the money for him in my car, he had me paged, and I got the money to him, and then he didn't have the courtesy to either stay for the meeting or at least come introduce himself to me.'

"Then later on Mr. White called me and apologized. He said he didn't feel like he belonged there and that was why he didn't stay."

With Cook's help, she continued on through the entire tale of her relationship with White, up to the moment of her arrest, explaining everything that had happened in a way that would strike the jury as plausible—more plausible than the state's story—as long as the jury did not believe she was a Hollywood-grade actress. When Cook finished with her, it was unclear from the jury's faces how they felt on that score.

Jimmy Fry bounded up from his table and said hello to her in the decorously polite manner of a Southern gentleman.

"Ma'am, would you please tell me again how you met Mr. White? He was building some shelves for you and doing some painting?"

"Yes," she said, just a little curtly.

Fry moved on slowly and gently through other matters.

"Why did your sister have a gun?"

"She and Jack had prowlers. I think one night somebody had gone through Trey's truck. That's why she bought a gun."

He questioned her about two calls White had made to her house from the Ramada Inn in Huntsville. She said that she did not remember the calls.

"You just don't remember if you spoke to him that night?"

"That was a long time ago, Mr. Fry."

He turned and looked at the jury blankly for a long moment. Then he moved on.

"Now, your story is that your twin sister, Betty Wilson, wanted to give Mr. White two hundred dollars at the Guntersville State Lodge to help him out with his gas money."

"Yes, sir, and to stay overnight."

"Uh-huh," Fry said. "Well, Miz Lowe, if she wanted to leave him some money, why didn't she just leave it at the desk?"

"She did not want to embarrass Mr. White," she said frostily.

"Oh."

Fry turned toward the jury. "She wanted to give him two hundred dollars for his gas and his motel room, but she didn't want to embarrass him."

"That's right."

"And she had never met this man before, you say?"

"That is correct."

A flicker in the eyes of the jurors indicated that this point had not gone down well with them.

Fry turned back toward Peggy, and now the decorousness was gone from his face and voice.

"Wouldn't it have been pretty simple to make sure Mr. White attended the meeting and to have paid for his room?" he demanded.

He wheeled and turned his back on her again. Now facing the crowd at the back of the room, Fry shouted over his shoulder, "You've got a guy here your sister and you want to help."

"He told me he was fearful of starting to drink," Peggy murmured defensively.

Fry whirled and marched back up into her face. Angry and accusing, he said: "Doesn't it seem a little odd to you that someone who was an alcoholic, who was in Alcoholics Anonymous, would give a drunk money?"

She shook her head, intimidated and floundering. "I . . . I don't know."

Fry snapped his face up toward the judge and waved at Peggy with a dismissive hand.

"I believe that's all."

He walked to his table and sat down with the air of a man who simply could not be bothered with it anymore.

The defense rested. The judge adjourned until morning for the closing statements.

ELEVEN

ON TUESDAY MORNING, MARCH 2, 1993, BETTY CAME down the corridor in chains, smiling, wearing a blue jacket with black collar and cuffs, a peacock-blue top, and a black skirt. She took her seat at the middle of the back of the defense table, facing the bench. Charlie Hooper sat on her right, Marc Sandlin on her left. Jack Drake sat at the front of the table to Betty's left, Cook at the front to her right. They all smiled at each other and made a great show of their ease and confidence.

Across from them, alone at the prosecution table, Jimmy Fry sat staring out a window.

Fry recalled Mickey Brantley as a rebuttal witness to testify that no physical evidence had been found in Betty's BMW because her son Trey had taken the car to the car wash before the Alabama forensic laboratory could get its hands on the car for testing and examination.

For people who had any experience at all with modern forensic techniques and testimony, it was a fairly weak attempt at rebutting a crucial point. Even a very thorough cleaning at the car wash—carried out deliberately to obscure evidence—would almost certainly not be capable of defeating the microscopic and chemical examination the car surely had undergone after being impounded by the Alabama Department of Forensic Sciences.

But the prosecution never had called a witness from the department or the state lab. The defense team could not simply stand up and testify on its own hook that a trip to the car wash was not enough to foil all of modern forensic science. The only way to make that point would be after the prosecution had introduced some kind of forensic testimony by calling its own witness to testify about what was or was not found in the car. And the prosecution had not called anyone.

It was a deeply frustrating point for the defense. The linchpin of White's story—the point at which Betty Wilson was actually physically implicated in the crime—was the matter of the two car rides, one to the scene of the crime and the other away. If that part didn't happen, the rest of White's story was not worth a plug nickel.

Given the harum-scarum nature of the crime itself, as James described it—an unplanned encounter, a savage struggle to the death, tearing off into the woods afterward, thinking better of it, leaping into Betty's BMW when she showed up unexpectedly, and covering up with her new clothes in the backseat—it was inconceivable that a minute scientific examination of the car would have turned up not one iota of physical evidence, car wash or no car wash.

But there was no effective way for the defense to get the point across. Brantley had testified the car had been cleaned. It was true—it had been cleaned for use in the funeral. That fact—and the fact that an experienced police officer like Detective Brantley would offer this point to rebut the absence of physical evidence—might be all the jury would need to wave away its doubts.

What was not explained was why it had not occurred to the defense in time to call the state forensics experts on its own.

Cook tried to hammer away at Brantley as best he could.

"We have been here two weeks, and not a single witness has testified from the state crime lab of Alabama."

Brantley said nothing.

Cook shouted at him: "Is that right?"

"Yes, sir," Brantley said quietly.

A young man on the jury shook his head in distaste when Cook yelled at a police officer.

"You sent Mr. White's clothes to the lab, is that right?"

"Yes, sir."
"Did they find anything?"
"No, sir."
"Any blood?"
"No, sir."
"Hair?"
"No, sir."
"Anything?"
"No, sir."

Cook shook his head. His anger, for a change, seemed unfeigned. He took his seat, and the defense sat back to hear Jimmy Fry's summation.

Fry rose from his table and walked straight to the jury. He leaned on the rail and began speaking to them as if there were no one else in the entire room.

"Something very very important is happening today in Tuscaloosa, Alabama. Most of the evidence you have heard in this trial has come from different places, from Huntsville, Vincent, Talladega, Gadsden. The evidence hasn't come from Tuscaloosa. But we are all citizens of the State of Alabama.

"I am here today on behalf of the state."

He reached out wide with both arms, pulling his blazer apart on the sides of his round stomach.

"Separate stories," he said. "Separate spheres. Separate lives. Distant but brought together."

Turning slowly and walking toward Betty, he said, "Let's begin with the story of a woman who had everything a woman could want."

With each step closer, his voice grew louder and angrier, his arm rising slowly to point at her.

"A maid who even took her furs to the cleaners for her! A Mercedes *and* a BMW! A million-dollar mansion in Huntsville. Worldly goods stacked reaching to the sky. But was it enough?"

He whirled and faced the jury.

"No. More is never enough. No."

Then, so loudly that some jurors flinched, he shouted: "She wanted it *all*!"

"That is why you people are here today. She wanted to take it, wrap herself in it, and roll in it!"

He turned around, walked back over to Betty and, from a few feet away, stared at her as if examining a dead dog by the road.

"What kind of person is this?" he asked in soliloquy.

"That she would bring a stranger, another man, into her husband's house? She had her friends lying for her? What kind of person is this?"

He turned back to the jury, imploring. "She lied to her husband for years. Her life was a lie! The secret life of Betty Wilson!"

He exhaled a long slow breath and then turned toward the window, gazing out sadly. "In the end, she had disassociated herself from Jack."

He came back over to the rail and spoke softly to the jurors.

"Do you know what terrorists do before they get ready to kill somebody? They make them a nonentity."

Fry turned, walked a few paces away, and then turned back toward them from a safe distance.

"That's one story. There's another story here. Way down here in the cellar somewhere. That's the story of James Dennison White."

He looked away. "James Dennison White. James Dennison White has been for some time a wretch."

He looked back quickly at the jurors. "An ugly term. He was broken and downhearted. Maybe a lot of it, maybe most of it was his own fault."

Fry moved back to the rail and spoke to them softly.

"He's the little guy. He's the guy whose dreams will always be bigger than his reach. The guy who wants but never gets.

"In the fall of '91, he was not only down-and-out. He was vulnerable."

Fry shrugged and shook his head to concede a point. "He's not the brightest guy in the world."

Fry lifted a finger and waved it in the air, half turning from the jury. "And then . . . a hope! Maybe more hope than he should have known he could have expected.

"Ask yourself this: What did Betty Wilson and James White have in common? The only thing connecting them is Peggy Lowe. Peggy Lowe yesterday had excellent recall of the events, even of the words people spoke, when her own lawyers asked her questions."

Fry held his palms up in puzzlement. "But when I asked her questions, the answer was, 'That was a long time ago, Mr. Fry.' "

Fry walked out toward the bar separating the sanctuary of the courtroom from the public area. He gazed out over the heads of the people in the public pews, as if looking into the heavens.

"Finally, to complete our story, is the story of a man who loved his wife, who worked hard and long . . ."

As he spoke, Fry turned slowly and stalked back to Betty's face, his voice rising to a shout:

". . . a man who did not deserve to die in a pool of his own blood because of the lust of this woman, beaten pitifully and unmercifully."

She had been striving mightily to control her emotions, but at this moment Betty's hatred of Fry flashed in her eyes. The jurors did not miss it.

Fry turned to a discussion of the state's deal with James.

"James White, like anybody else charged with a crime, was looking for the best deal he could get. He was required by this deal to give evidence which could be corroborated by independent facts. If he lied to the state, then the deal was off."

Fry went through a long laundry list of things James said in his statements that had been proved to be true: He said he went to Guntersville to get money; the guards from the Guntersville State Lodge testified that James had been there when he said he was there; he said he spoke with Peggy many times on the telephone; the phone company records showed that there were many calls from his number to Peggy's number; he said he met Betty at the Chick-Fil-A to get money from her; the manager of Chick-Fil-A testified that he had once employed a woman who met James's description of the woman he said had waited on him. Fry counted his way down through the list to show where each detail of James's testimony had been supported by independent evidence.

Fry hammered at the business with the money in the book. "Why would you give hundreds of dollars to a drunk at an A.A. convention? And why the subterfuge? Why not just leave the money at the desk in a white envelope? What sense does it make?"

Fry went to the evidence table and picked up the library book: *Sleeping Beauty and the Firebird*. "It's just incredible!" he said to the jury. "This book is just incredible.

"May sixteenth. The day James went to Guntersville. It was a big day in this case, because it was the day that ended with a book of fairy tales. She gave him this book, ladies and gentlemen . . . she gave him this book . . . and she said . . . she said, '*Have a good time.*' "

A couple of jurors absentmindedly shook their heads.

Fry moved on through the state's entire case, stopping to emphasize key points. "James White told you about the handoff of the gun. How else would he have known this woman was in Talladega that day? How would he have known that?"

Fry anticipated what the defense would say in its own closing statements:

"James White even described the shoes she was wearing the day Jack was killed. How did he know about that? I know what the defense will tell you. He was stalking her. That's what you're going to hear.

"Well, why? Why would he be stalking her? According to the defense, he didn't even know the woman. So why would he stalk her?"

In one of his few mistakes in the entire trial, Fry referred to a bit of testimony the jury actually had not heard—Betty's statement to the police about why she had returned to the house.

"Her excuse for going home was that she forgot the bank bag," Fry said. "James told you that she had a bank bag with her in the car."

When he was through going over all the instances in which

he said James's testimony had been corroborated, Fry moseyed up to the rail, smiled broadly at the jurors, and made an expansive gesture with one hand.

"Folks, it doesn't take Sherlock Holmes. It doesn't take Columbo. It doesn't take Quincy."

He turned and stared pointedly at Bobby Lee Cook for a moment. Everyone in the room was waiting for him to say, "It doesn't take Matlock," and Fry looked as if he badly wanted to use the line, but he squared himself up and turned back to the jury.

"After what y'all have seen in here in the last week, you can smell what's going on."

Half crouching at the rail, his head flattened against his shoulders and talking in a down and dirty voice, he said, "You can *smell* it.

"As sorry a wretch as James White may be, James White told you a lot of truth."

He straightened up and shrugged. "I'm worn out," he said softly. "I know you are, too. I hope, in trying to match this herd of lawyers on the other side, that I haven't done anything to offend you.

"Y'all will always have a special place in my heart, and I hope I will have a small place in yours."

The two older women on the jury smiled sweetly and nodded to him.

Fry took his seat, and Drake rose.

Drake ran through a series of technical legal issues and questions about testimony. His speech at first was listless and unremarkable, especially on the heels of Fry's remarkable performance. But when Drake had finished taking care of the technical issues on his mind, he set aside his notes, came close to the jury, and his manner changed entirely. The lawyerly cadences dropped from his speech, and he spoke directly, personally, urgently, as if suddenly afraid that all of the law and the lawyering in the world was not going to be enough to make the jury see an essential truth at the center of this whole trial.

"Look. We're dealing with a monster here. He's perfectly capable of calling his brother and having him go plant the clothes that were found under a rock. Look at the gun. He said in his first statements that he took it from the house. So he's working on his story, you see. He's working on a story that not only would be believable but might even be a little bit Hollywood."

Drake surveyed the jurors carefully to make sure they were with him. They seemed to be listening.

"He needed some help with this story. You see? So he got a lawyer. And that gives him something he didn't have before. It gives him access to information."

Leaning on the rail, speaking passionately to the jury, Drake finally was telling them what had happened. The jurors watched and listened more intently with every word Drake spoke.

The problem with Fry's story, even though the jury seemed to love him personally, was that none of it hung together. Examined minutely and a piece at a time, none of the details added up. Why would Betty give James a gun that she knew to be registered in her own name? Why would Betty pass money to James in a library book that she herself had checked out in her own name?

Those pieces of the story, taken one at a time, made sense only if there was no conspiracy. She didn't give him the gun, he stole it. She put the money in a library book because she expected him to come into the lodge, introduce himself, attend a meeting, and return the book.

But if there was no conspiracy, how on earth had James White been able to fashion the fabric of detailed information that he had sold to the police in exchange for his own neck? Now, in the last moments of the trial, after a long desultory showing by the defense team, a member of the team apparently was going to depart from the script and lay it all out for the jury the way it really had happened.

The question was whether Jack Drake was acting in time.

"The lawyer feeds James White information," he said. "And, using that information, James White made the best deal in the history of criminal justice in Alabama," Drake said.

Drake walked the jury through James's changed statements

on several key dates, showing them clearly how James had changed the dates in order to comport with new information being brought to him about what the police were discovering in their investigation.

"In every statement James White made before he came to this courtroom, he said consistently that the handoff on the dam had taken place on May nineteenth, 1992. It was the only time the three of them were together.

"Ladies and gentlemen, we came to court, all of us, prepared to defend that date, and it would have been real easy. You know why? Because, at the time James said Betty was out on Logan Martin dam in Talladega, we knew Betty was over a hundred miles away in Huntsville having dinner with Trey and Jack and going to an A.A. meeting.

"Well, guess what happened when we all showed up for trial? For the first time since we began preparing our case, we learned that Mr. White was prepared to say it had happened on the twentieth.

"How did he know to change it? At the last minute? I'll tell you how."

The jury was now hanging on his words, watching his face closely.

"His lawyer told him to."

Drake backed away slowly, nodding to them. "That's right. He told him to. He said, 'James, Tuesday, May nineteenth, ain't gonna fly, boy. You got to change it.'

"And you all know what old James did next. You know. He did what he did here on the stand. He closed his eyes, and he got those lips to movin', and he said, 'Well, yessir, you know, that's right. I 'member now. It was May twentieth.'

"How do you explain James White?" Drake shrugged. "You can't. He's a demonic monster. He lies. He lies about everything. Why? He can't help himself. He just does.

"So how did James know where Betty went that day and what she wore? I don't know. Know what I think? I think he followed her. Maybe he was mad at Betty, maybe she was the one he was after, maybe he was going to kill Betty.

Drake asked the jury to think about the $2,500 the twins supposedly had given James in cash, $2,200 of it in twenty-dollar bills. How did two such un-clever women—women who gave James a gun registered in Betty's own name and passed the hit money in a library book checked out in Betty's own name—how did these otherwise very bumbling conspirators manage to scrape up $2,500 in cash that the state never had been able to trace or link to them in any way, shape, or form?

"Jimmy Fry came down here with an army," Drake said. "He's got the resources of the entire state of Alabama behind him. So why can't he explain the twenty-five hundred dollars? Where did it come from? He's got subpoena power. He can check the records of any bank in the United States.

"That's one hundred and ten twenty-dollar bills. You have to go to the bank at some point to get that much cash. Yet there are no bank records in evidence in this trial. Why?

"I'll tell you why. It never happened. This is money James already had. He had it around. I suspect James is the kind of boy who didn't put his money in the bank. Somebody might get it. A creditor. James, after all, is a dope dealer."

Drake talked about Betty and her affairs.

"If you believe what some of these witnesses said in this room, if you believe that Dr. Wilson didn't know his wife was having affairs, then he was the only guy in Huntsville who didn't know."

The jurors, especially the women, looked a little nonplussed by this statement. Drake seemed to be saying that Betty not only had cuckolded Jack but had done so openly, perhaps even proudly.

Drake and Fry fell into a brief shouting match when Drake addressed the question of Peggy's scars—scars a lover like James White should have noticed.

"We were prepared to show the scars, the minute the prosecution challenged us on them," Drake said. "But they didn't raise the question, and do you know why? Because they were afraid to."

Fry leaped to his feet, red in the face.

"I'm not afraid of anything!" he shouted.

"You were scared to ask that question!" Drake shouted back.

Judge Younger graveled them down. "Gentlemen, gentlemen, let's get on with this, please."

Drake smoothed his feathers and made a few more remarks about Betty and money, pointing out that if Betty was a greedy woman, then she was already living a quite greedy life when the doctor was alive. Why would she need to kill him for more money?

On this point, he ceded the floor to Bobby Lee Cook.

Cook rose slowly. He spoke slowly and softly.

"We've been here a long time. I don't think there is any necessity for me to tell this jury of your responsibilities and duties. Mr. Fry said a moment ago to my good friend Mr. Jack Drake that he wasn't afraid of anything.

"Well, you're looking at someone who is. In every case I try, I'm afraid there is something that hasn't been done or has been overlooked, something that has been done wrong."

He talked to the jury for a bit about concepts of guilt, the protections afforded citizens by the Bill of Rights, the history of the Constitution. Then, just when it began to seem he had strayed from the matter at hand, Bobby Lee Cook came back to the flaw at the heart of Mickey Brantley's case against the twins:

"Anytime you have a criminal investigation where the result is preordained from the start, it is doomed from the start."

He cited fifty-eight instances in the transcripts of James White's statements and testimony in which White himself later admitted he had lied.

Then Cook walked back to the podium that had been put in place for him in front of the jury. He gripped the sides like a preacher and stared sternly at the jurors. "This is not a case in which Mrs. Wilson was charged with adultery. This is not a case of vanity. It is not a case of Mercedes, maids, clothes, and jewelry.

"There is an old saying. Let him who is without sin cast the first stone."

The eyes of some of the jurors seemed to narrow, as if this was a challenge they might be willing to accept.

Fry was watching the jury keenly as Cook spoke.

Cook went through a long careful list of all the things the state had failed to prove in any way: There was no evidence that Betty was ever in the Chick-Fil-A, that she ever reached Boulder Circle after 5:15 P.M., that anyone had seen White's truck during the long beer-guzzling hours he supposedly waited for Betty on the shopping mall parking lot, or that anyone had ever seen Betty and James together, anywhere, at any time.

He reminded the jury that Brantley had never challenged James, in the early hours of the case, to prove that he knew what Betty looked like.

He hammered at the question of the clothes in the bag. "If these had been the clothes Mr. White had on while murdering this man, stabbing him repeatedly, beating him with a ball bat, how could there not have been blood on the clothes? And yet we have heard not a single witness from the crime lab of the state of Alabama."

Cook came out from behind the podium to get closer to the jury.

Speaking quietly, sharing an amusing secret, he said: "They've got a problem, you see.

"They've got him in the woods. They've got his clothes under a rock. But he doesn't have anything on. He's naked out in the woods!"

The last word in the trial went to Jimmy Fry, who was allowed by the rules to rebut points raised by the defense. He bounded to his feet and approached the jury with fire in his eye.

"Where did the twenty-five hundred dollars come from?" he asked. "Where did it come from? Here you have a woman married to a millionaire, driving a Mercedes, and wearing furs and diamonds! Where did twenty-five hundred dollars come from? I'll tell you where. Her pocket! Twenty-five hundred dollars to this woman is pocket change!"

Fry backed away, turned and walked off a distance, then came back to the jury. "Ladies and gentlemen, if you have a single question left in your minds, you might ask yourselves, 'Why would the defendant do a thing like this?'

"Let me give you a reason. In fact, let me give you millions of reasons. Six million three hundred thousand reasons. The money!

"She didn't want part of it. She wanted *all* of it."

When he said "*all*," Fry hunched down at the waist and made fists of his hands, stooping his knees and thrusting his face forward like a televangelist. The jurors were all wide awake and listening.

"She wanted to be *unfettered* in her *wanton lust* for men, her lust for things, and she wanted to not . . . have . . . to ask old SHITBAG! . . ."

The jurors were frightened by the ferocity of his speech.

". . . to ask old SHITBAG! . . . for another dime! She wanted to move her sister up from Talladega and help her get away from old Wayne.

"I think it must have been like a game to these two women," he said. " 'Let's just kill old Jack . . . the old . . . SHITBAG! . . . the little twerp. He's no good to us. He can't do it. He's no good sexually.'

"To these women, Jack Wilson had already stopped existing. He just stopped existing, as far as they were concerned, until, in the end, he was nobody. A nothing.

"How do you prove a secret? How do you prove a secret? Excuse me for just a moment, will you, ladies and gentlemen? I need to say something to the bailiff here."

Fry cupped his hand to the bailiff's ear and whispered. The bailiff nodded, walked to the prosecution table, poured a glass of water in a white Styrofoam cup, and brought it to Fry. Fry thanked him and sipped the water.

"Now what'd I tell the bailiff?" he said. "You don't know what I told him. It's a secret.

"But you saw what he did! So you know I must have said to him, 'Sir, would you please go over there and bring me a glass of water?'

"How do you prove a secret? You prove it from the surrounding circumstances."

Fry walked off, then returned, started to speak, then paused. Finally he raised both arms in the air, lifting the wings of his jacket high off his bulging girth. "Ladies and gentlemen, I leave you with these words."

In a booming voice, resonating with righteousness and judgment, Jimmy Fry shouted to the rafters: "Like the waters of the River Jordan, let Justice roll!"

Because capital trials are conducted in separate phases in Alabama—the first phase to establish guilt or innocence, the second to decide punishment—no one had been allowed to talk to the jury about the electric chair before the jury withdrew to decide Betty Wilson's fate. That question, whether she would get death or life in prison, would be dealt with after the verdict came in, if the verdict was guilty.

The case went to the jury just before 2:00 P.M. on March 2, 1993. When Deputy Wayne Johnson led them out of the courtroom, the jurors looked dazed and exhausted. None of them even glanced at Betty on the way out.

Peggy, Wayne, and their children waited in their home, seventy miles to the north on the shores of Logan Martin Lake in Talladega. They listened to newscasts on the radio and television and snapped at the telephone when it rang.

Betty waited in the tiny anteroom off the courtroom, surrounded by her sons and her lawyers.

Jack's son Stephen—one of the family members who had struck a deal with the moviemakers for story rights and who stood to inherit the estate if Betty was found guilty—stayed around the courthouse corridors, chatting quietly with some of the media people with whom he had become friendly. His mood seemed serious but calm.

The jurors talked first about Peggy. They all agreed she was unbelievable. The tears had been turned off and on too conveniently; the speech was too pat, her manner too perfect. She should be in Hollywood, they all agreed. They took an early vote and voted ten for conviction, one undecided, and one for acquittal.

The one juror who voted for acquittal, a woman about the age of the twins, was adamant. The state had not proved its case, she said.

For the rest of the afternoon, the other jurors reminded her of instance after instance in which the state had provided hard evidence to corroborate James White's story. What about the cash-register tapes that showed he had gone to the Kmart when he said he did? And what about her shoes? How else would he know about her flowered shoes?

None of them suggested or believed that the core of James Dennison White's story was a lie. If it was a lie, then the police would have been implicated in the lie. And Mr. Fry. And the state of Alabama. None of them believed that was possible.

James White had been a complete success on the stand. The jurors felt sorry for him and believed what he said.

But the holdout juror continued to insist the state had not proved its case completely enough for her to vote to take Betty Wilson's life.

Drake had told reporters he expected an early vote of acquittal. When the jurors reported at the end of the day that they had not yet been able to come to a decision, there was consternation in the camp of the defense team. They didn't admit to the media that they were concerned. But they didn't have to. By then, everyone knew the score.

Jimmy Fry had put Betty Wilson on trial for moral turpitude, for being rich, greedy, dirty-mouthed, flamboyantly unfaithful to her husband, a slut, and a woman who had sexual relations with men outside her race. The defense had countered by agreeing to all of the above and then saying, "But look at her twin! She's not a slut! She's not a potty-mouth! And they're twins. So, if you can't believe the story James White told about Peggy, you can't vote to convict Betty."

Among the court watchers the common theory was that the deliberations would be brief if the defense strategy had been a success. If the jury thought James White's story was a lot of elaboration around a central lie, then there would be no way the jury could even consider sending Betty to the chair or taking away her life by sending her to prison.

On the other hand, if the deliberations went long, it was an indication the jury believed the core of James White's story and was going to spend its time sifting through the corroborative detail, in order to achieve a feeling of due diligence before taking her life. In general, sending someone home is easy, and sending someone to the electric chair or prison for life is difficult.

The more the jurors thought about it, the more they were going to realize they hated Betty.

It had been on their faces throughout the trial. Whenever Jimmy Fry went after Betty's character, his words hit home like insect bites, making the jurors twitch, turn, and nod in tiny signals of emotion.

Fry, who must have seen it himself, had homed in on that part of his message until, by the time he got to the River Jordan, he practically had the jury singing responses.

Betty was a slut. Betty was a bitch.

Betty was a witch.

If they took her life, Betty would be getting her just deserts, one way or another.

If that message had taken root, then Peggy's good character would be nullified. If they believed Betty was a witch, then Peggy, her twin, was merely the witch's alter ego, her public false face.

Judge Younger sent the jury back to its motel for the night. On Wednesday morning they reconvened and took up where they had left off. By now the undecided juror had decided. She wanted to vote for conviction.

Each new detail of the corroborative evidence that the rest of the jury presented to the lone holdout juror was a spoonful of sand, until the sand gradually threatened to suffocate her. The corroboration really meant nothing to her, because she didn't believe the overall story presented by the state. Something in it didn't add up.

But she couldn't point specifically to what it was. And the rest of the jury could continue *ad infinitum* to provide her with things the state had, indeed, proved.

Just before 2:00 P.M. on the second day of deliberations, the holdout juror collapsed. The foreman rushed for a vote. The vote was 12 to 0 to convict.

Betty Wilson blinked back tears as the judge read the counts and the findings of the jury. Her lawyers reached for her to steady her, but she did not feel their hands.

She did not collapse. Something tough in her allowed her to push herself back mentally just an inch behind the surface of these events—far enough away that she could even marvel at them.

So this is how it ends.

She had done nothing. She was guilty of nothing. Worse—there were no villains. That might have made it easier. You couldn't count James White. He was a professional villain. He did what he did. That was his job. There were no surprises in James.

Could you say that Mickey Brantley was the villain? But he might very well never have suspected Betty was innocent. Or Jimmy Fry? In the real world and the here and now, it wasn't truly in the interest of people like Mickey Brantley or Jimmy Fry to ponder too deeply the factual innocence or guilt of a defendant. At some point in a case like this, the civil and political chessmen were in place and it was time for the set-piece battle to begin. The lawyers on all sides, the cops, the expert witnesses, the judge—they were hired to play roles. It was in their interest to speak their lines well and leave it to the jury to decide guilt and innocence.

In this case, the jurors made a wrong decision. They voted on the basis of loathing and envy, fear and ancient superstition—hoary beliefs about women, twins, sex, race. They voted on the basis of a wrong view of humankind. Not truth. They failed to find the truth. They voted to convict an innocent person. In all of this, they were doing what they had been coaxed and urged to do by the state.

It happens. People who go to court with strikes against them—African-American people sitting before white juries, or gay people, or members of religious minorities, physically deformed people—they know all too well how difficult it can be to overcome a jury's predispositions and biases. The only difference is that in this case the victim was a white lady. A rich white lady.

Betty's self-control was not so great that she could keep the thought of death at bay. The lawyers had told her they had conducted a secret conference with Fry during the long hours of waiting. There was some sort of an agreement. Now they and Fry were at the bench, talking to the judge. Sitting alone at the table, waiting to hear whether she would be killed or imprisoned for life, she noticed that her hands were shaking and her back was damp with sweat.

Fry had agreed that it probably would be impossible to win a death sentence, given that Betty was not a physical participant in the murder and given the relatively light sentence that James had won for himself by getting Betty convicted. Both sides agreed to petition the judge jointly: They asked him to waive the penalty trial and levy a sentence of life in prison without possibility of parole. Judge Younger agreed.

One down, one to go.

In the weeks after the verdict, Peggy and Wayne Lowe had to sort out their feelings of grief for Betty from their fear of what lay ahead for them. Betty had been defended by the best lawyers money could buy. Even though Betty could not pay them unless she won acquittal and then inherited Jack's estate, her legal team had been willing to invest hundreds of thousands of dollars' worth of their own time in Betty's case, betting they would win and then be paid.

They had lost. They would not be paid. The money would be tied up in civil courts for years and then most of it probably would go to Jack's sons.

Peggy and Wayne had a combined family income of $50,000

a year and no savings. Every cent they earned went into their home, their lives, their children. The only thing they could offer to lawyers was the national attention the case might bring them, and even that might be a mixed blessing. It was no great boon to a lawyer to take a high-profile case and lose.

Worse, in Peggy's view, was the simple fact that the jury in Tuscaloosa had believed James White. When it came Peggy's turn in the dock, the state would put on precisely the same evidence it had presented in Betty's trial. There was no other evidence. Virtually the same case and the same trial would take place again, only with a different twin sitting at the defense table. If Betty had lost, then there was every reason to believe Peggy might, too.

Every time Betty could get to a pay telephone in the Julia Tutwiler State Penitentiary for Women in Wetumpka, Alabama, she called Peggy, collect. Peggy's phone bill soared to many hundreds of dollars a month. The conversations were long anguishing tortures for Peggy because her heart went out so powerfully to her sister and because the sounds and the shouts she heard in the background were so terrifying. She was hearing Hell, and it was a Hell to which she might soon be consigned herself.

On a wet fall morning, when she needed to be going out the door for work, Peggy hung on the phone with her sister. She paced the length of the kitchen and listened, while Betty spoke to her from an echoing corridor at the Wetumpka state pen.

Every few seconds in the background behind Betty there was a loud electric clacking sound and then the ring of heavy steel on steel—cell-block doors opening and closing.

"What are you going to do today, Betty?"

"I've been sitting on my bunk all day most days. You know I got in the honor block?"

"Yes. Mother told me. Is it better?"

"A little. It's smaller. The lesbians still make love with an audience all around me. And people sit on their bunks all day smoking and thinking up reasons to fight. I try to sit on my bunk and not be noticed."

Driving her spotless red Chrysler LeBaron convertible down

the long winding dirt road out to the paved highway, Peggy noticed that her breath was short and gaspy and her hands were shaking. She pulled over to the side for a moment and waited for the light-headedness to pass. Sitting there, gazing off into the deepness of the Alabama woods, she reflected that being afraid for one's life is like suffering from a chronic illness. After a while, you concentrate on dealing with the symptoms.

But the long weeks and months of preparation for her own trial were gnawing at her in fundamental places, chipping away and changing things inside in ways she could not even measure, let alone control.

There had always been danger in Peggy's life, after all. When she was a small and defenseless child, every homecoming of her brutal drunken father had been an adventure in terror. She had learned how to fend off terror before she had learned how to read.

Always as the hero. The smooth and collected twin. The one who knew how to operate.

It was Betty who had flown into rages and collapsed in tears. Betty was the straightforward one of the pair. And she had suffered for it.

It was Peggy who had learned how to manage the beast in their house, how to watch him and gauge his face, how to say the calming things that would steer him toward a merciful stupor in his La-Z-Boy recliner chair.

It wasn't a hypocritical act. She had devoted her life to building a home and a family in which there was peace, support and love. She lived by the precepts and teachings of her religion without being smug or ascetic, narrow or intolerant or separated in any way from other people by her religion. Her heart went out powerfully to people who suffered, as her heart had gone out to the children of James White.

But the point was that Peggy's way of living and being had always worked. Even as a child, she had brought peace, however tenuous, to the little house on Hoke Street, and she had brought the family honor and respect, with her many social and school successes in the town. She and Wayne had succeeded in making lives for themselves and in raising their own children well.

Now everything that she had ever been was being thrown in her face as accusation. She was not virtuous, according to the jury in Tuscaloosa. She was a liar. A hypocritical slut whose only strength was her acting ability. They were going to get her. Lock her up. And kill her.

TWELVE

IN EVERY HIGH-PROFILE MURDER TRIAL, THERE IS AN element of witch-hunt. It's a necessary ingredient and can even be a force for good. The body politic recognizes a threat to its well-being, and the body reacts to expel the evil from its flesh.

People spy the source of the evil. They pass the word. They move as one to drive it out. And in this process there is always a great deal of pressure on people to line up on the correct side. In gossip, people ask each other who they think did it and why, and when they hear an answer that doesn't conform, they show their displeasure. It gets more difficult to hold out as time goes on. What happened with the jury in Betty's case was only a compressed form of what had been going on in Huntsville, in Talladega, and in all of Alabama in the two years since the murder had occurred. People were lining up.

The wonder of the six-month period between Betty's conviction and the beginning of Peggy's trial was that the people of Peggy's church and town remained steadfast in their support of her. On one occasion they came running out of storefronts and physically chased off a gang of reporters who had come to town to do a story. They did not believe that Peggy could be guilty, and they absolutely did not waver in their conviction. Even though most of the news coverage of the case painted them all either as gullible hicks or as weird hypocrites, they never moved away from her. Whenever she thought the fear and psychological dislocation were going to crush her, it was the strong wall of her community and church that held her up.

Nevertheless, in the late dark hours when she stood at the edge of the lake by herself, gazing over silver ripples, it came home to her: The person she had always been had failed in Tuscaloosa. She was the one who had sent James White to Betty in the first place. She was the one who was supposed to have saved the day in Betty's trial and had not. Now Betty had gone to Hell, and Peggy, the family hero, was not far behind.

Peggy could not afford a high-profile lawyer like Bobby Lee Cook, but she did acquire the services of one David Cromwell Johnson, a middle-aged criminal-defense attorney in Birmingham with a good reputation in local circles. In addition, Johnson was able to bring in Herman "Buck" Watson of Huntsville.

Buck Watson was a silver-maned courtroom master who had represented members of the Dixie Mafia in the old days in Alabama and had taken part in major political trials more recently. He could wrap a witness around his very courtly, very lethal finger and do it so painlessly that the witness would not realize what had happened until someone told him afterward. His addition to the team was a major coup.

The question of who would prosecute was much more complex. Madison County District Attorney Tim Morgan in Huntsville was still bound by his campaign pledge to stay out of the case. He showed no sign of regretting his decision or wanting back in.

Jimmy Fry refused outright. He had taken two months away from the performance of his duties as the elected D.A. in Limestone County. He had won. He had done his share. He made it plain to the Alabama attorney general that he was not at all interested in prosecuting the Peggy trial.

The very first glimmer of hope to reach Peggy's camp since the disaster in Tuscaloosa came indirectly from Jimmy Fry. In his official public pronouncements about the case, Fry was always careful to say he was declining to do the second case because of the press of official duties in his own county. But the word filtering back through the legal grapevine in Alabama was that Jimmy Fry didn't want to take the case because he thought it was a loser.

Betty's case had been winnable for the prosecution for two reasons: because of the slut factor, and because a disjointed defense team had never put together a systematic attack on the police case.

A year and a half of scouring the earth had failed to turn up a single shred of evidence to indicate that Peggy had ever done anything bad in her life. It was going to be difficult, if not impossible, to get any jury to believe that a woman who had led a completely upright and virtuous life fell suddenly into a murder plot and at the same time fell suddenly into love with a nattering, foul-smelling, drunken slob like James Dennison White.

Even more precarious for the state, according to the rumor mill, was the nature of the state's case against the twins. It was the kind of case that might not age well. Given more time and an entire trial record in Tuscaloosa to go by, the second twin's defense team might well be able to do what the Tuscaloosa team had failed to do—that is, show the jury just exactly how the police had channeled information to James, poisoning the well of his testimony.

The word in Alabama was that Jimmy Fry had taken home a trophy from the first trial and was not about to come back to the second one and risk taking home a raspberry. So strong was this story in legal circles, in fact, that Attorney General Jimmy Evans was unable to persuade anyone—not a single county district attorney in the entire state—to take the case. In the end he was forced to assign the case to his own staff, an unusual step which served to persuade Peggy's team that maybe the stories were true.

Maybe, in spite of what had happened to Betty, Peggy might stand a chance.

But every time Peggy allowed herself to entertain hope, she remembered that Betty's lawyers had insisted they would win Betty's case, too, right up until the very moment when the verdict was read.

The trial was moved to Montgomery and set for September 13, 1993.

The land falls gradually from Huntsville, at the tip of the Appalachian chain in northern Alabama, to a place just a few miles north of Montgomery, where it pours out into the rich black plains of South Alabama. Driving down from Birmingham on I-65, one can almost smell the place where the soil changes from red dirt to black, from airy pine and water to the green fullness of deep blue-green cropland.

More than the official capital of Alabama, Montgomery is the state's spiritual and political heart, home to six colleges and universities and a long stretch of emotional history. Big billboards on the freeway outside of town announce proudly: MONTGOMERY! BIRTHPLACE OF THE CONFEDERACY! BIRTHPLACE OF THE CIVIL RIGHTS MOVEMENT!

Even though he had prevailed at the first trial, Huntsville Detective Mickey Brantley came to Montgomery in a less than optimistic frame of mind. In the preceding months, Madison County District Judge William Page, who was presiding over the case, had made it obvious in several hearings that he thought the James Dennison White testimony was extremely suspect, that the signed contract Mo Brooks had given White was outlandish, and that the state had better come up with a whole lot more corroboration than it had shown the jury in Judge Younger's trial in Tuscaloosa if it hoped to prevail in his trial in Montgomery.

Accordingly, and being the good solid cop he was, Mickey Brantley went out and beat the bushes for new corroboration of James's story. He came up with nothing. Neither he nor any other law enforcement investigator in Alabama had ever been able to find a single witness, piece of paper, electronic record, or other shred of evidence that would tend to support the allegation that Betty Wilson had assembled $2,200 in twenty-dollar bills with which to pay off James White.

It was a troubling hole in the evidence, if only because it actually is not all that easy for the average person in today's world to assemble that much cash without leaving a footprint. Where did the 110 twenty-dollar bills come from? If they had come from her own bank, there would be a computer record and possibly even an adding-machine tape to match the transaction. If she wrote a check somewhere else, there would be the record of the check. Even if she had taken other bills and converted them to twenties, there would be a record. If she had always kept a stash of several thousand dollars in twenty-dollar bills around the house, surely someone like Shirley Green would have noticed. And what if she had gone to a merchant for the twenty-dollar bills? This late in the game, after this much publicity, anyone else to whom she had gone for the $2,200 in twenties almost certainly would have come forward.

In months of fevered searching, Brantley had failed to turn up a dollop of physical evidence to back up White's story of the car rides to and from the murder scene. He had failed to turn up a single new eyewitness.

The state would still be totally dependent on Sheila Irby to put James and Betty near the murder scene at roughly the same time. If Peggy's lawyers figured out a way to get around Mrs. Irby's wall of one-liners and cocktail party jokes, her testimony might prove to be of very limited value.

Judge Page had signaled Brantley in unmistakable terms that he had better come up with better evidence to support White's statements. Brantley had tried; he had failed. Only Mickey Brantley could know what that failure meant to Mickey Brantley. Was it enough to cause doubt in his mind, too? With the passage of time and some relief from the immediate political pressure associated with the D.A.'s race, had Mickey Brantley ever had occasion to wonder if a terrible mistake had been made? He kept his own counsel.

But the issue of political pressure surrounding the case was another area of concern. Certainly it would have been political disaster at that point for almost anyone associated with the Madison County Courthouse to admit that the twins might not be guilty. With this much invested in the case—the publicity, the fanfare, the news media hoopla, the books and movies coming—the man or woman who uttered the word "innocent" would risk bringing down the temple.

The problem was that Judge Page didn't care. He was retiring. This would be his last big case. And he was letting everybody know he didn't care. In his statements in preliminary hearings and privately through the courthouse grapevine, the judge had put out the word: He thought James White's testimony stank to high heaven, and if the state didn't put on better evidence than it had shown in Tuscaloosa, Judge William Page didn't care who got what on his or her face. He was going to run a clean straight trial and then clear out his desk and go home.

A short compact man with a genial smile, thin gray hair, and eyes that could turn to steel at the push of a button, Judge Page was a grandfather who hated being away from home.

The opening of the trial in Montgomery was completely different from the opening in Tuscaloosa. The Montgomery County sheriff's deputies who served as bailiffs and courthouse security already had in place a system, devised some time ago for other high-profile trials, by which they made sure the media people would find the seats they needed and not have to bully the general public in the process. There was also a humane and rational system for seeing to it that public onlookers could find a way into the courtroom.

The net effect of Montgomery County's much smoother operation was that the atmosphere in the courtroom and in the corridor outside was, from the opening moments of the trial to the last, quiet, dignified, and somber, where the mood in Tuscaloosa on the worst days had been a cross between a Fourth of July picnic and a KKK trail ride.

Part of the difference, however, was that the news contingent was much smaller and more local or regional. Once Betty was convicted, the national and tabloid media had cooled on the story, figuring the rest would be anticlimactic. The reporters and writers who did come to Montgomery all knew each other, either from their ongoing daily work or at least from the first trial, which tended to make their mood somewhat less canine.

Jury selection—voir dire—was a confusing, apparently formless process, and no one seemed more disconcerted by it than the state's chief prosecutor, Don Valeska. Slim, in his early forties, with glasses in big clear rims and a loose wavy mop of hair, Valeska had a boyish, flappy way of moving around the courtroom. As chief of the attorney general's criminal division, he had successfully prosecuted a number of major criminals and mobsters who had brought very high-dollar legal teams to court with them. Valeska knew a lot about jury selection and was obviously trying hard to see what Peggy's team was up to in the questions they asked prospective jurors and the decisions they made each time it was their term to "shuffle the deck"—to arrange the jury panel in the order of their preference.

But it wasn't easy to see a pattern. The defense team seemed to be allowing in a demographic mishmash of social class and gender. More to the point, the defense lawyers seemed curiously unconcerned by the fact that several potential jurors obviously were aware the defendant's twin sister already had been convicted of murder in the same conspiracy.

Surely the defense realized at this point what the state intended to do in this trial. Since Brantley had come up with none of the new corroboration the judge was going to be looking for in James White's testimony against Peggy, the state was going to put Betty on trial again. Here, at the end of the story, in the final chapter, it was all going to come down again to what had been the central theme back at the very beginning:

Twins.

Betty had been found guilty once already. Getting a second jury to believe she was still guilty wouldn't be rocket science. Of course, it would not be possible to inform this jury of the first jury's verdict. But by reading testimony from the first trial record at this trial, by referring again and again to the record of the first trial, by going over the details of the alleged plot, the prosecution would be able to draw the picture. There was a simple logical deduction for the jury to make: If the first twin had been found innocent, the second twin probably wouldn't be on trial.

But if the defense team accepted jurors on the panel who knew for a fact that Betty had been convicted, then the state's job would be easy, indeed. No matter what the judge told these jurors, the knowledge of Betty's conviction would get around—by wink or nod or something. From that point forward, the rest of it should be a simple matter of stacking the wood.

They were twins. Twins have secrets. Twins are unlike other human beings. They somehow share a single soul. Neither owns a whole conscience.

The defense team could not have failed to figure out that this was the state's plan. In the process of discovery, the state had turned over nothing. They had nothing new. So they would have to go with what they already had—Betty's conviction. Therefore the defense should have been on the alert to keep out any juror who knew that Peggy's twin had already been convicted. But the defense either didn't care or wasn't paying attention.

Valeska watched, scratched his head, and loped around the courtroom, trying to get a bead on David Johnson and his team—the silver-maned Buck Watson and Don Crowder, a tough lawyer with a graying butch haircut, looking somewhat like a bulldog, whom Johnson had brought with him from his firm in Birmingham.

But the defense team was inscrutable. It was impossible to tell whether they were looking for rich or poor, men or women, young or old as jurors.

Only at the end of the day, when the jury had been selected and the jurors filed into the jury box for their instructions, did a certain very noticeable pattern appear.

There were fourteen jurors—twelve regular jurors and two alternates. All of the six men on the jury were African-American. Two of the men were in their twenties, two in their thirties, one in his early forties, and one in his sixties. Five of the eight women on the jury were white. Of those, four were in their sixties and one was in her early twenties. The three black women ranged from early thirties to early fifties.

The major difference between this jury and the one that convicted Betty involved the question of community and history. Tuscaloosa and Montgomery are tangibly different places, and this has everything to do with what happened in their pasts.

During a break in the Montgomery trial one day, a writer stopped a well-dressed businessman on the street downtown and asked him for directions to a newsstand. The businessman wound up taking the writer on a walking tour.

He was a lifelong resident of Montgomery, from a family that had been there for many generations. He was white.

He took the visitor to the steps of the old capitol building and showed him the spot where Jeff Davis had stood to review the Confederate Army when Montgomery was the capital of the Confederacy. So far, the walking tour was turning out to be fairly predictable.

But then the white businessman took the visitor down the hill from the capitol and showed him the steps of the Dexter Avenue Baptist Church, where the congregation sang "We Shall Overcome" after Dr. Martin Luther King, Jr., was acquitted of trumped-up perjury charges. He knew that story as well and told it as proudly as the story of Jefferson Davis on the capitol steps.

In Montgomery, in Selma, Atlanta, and the other Southern cities where there was real organized struggle in the 1950s and '60s, there was also genuine personal change for people, followed by political change. The legacy today is a maturity and frankness between white people and black that is tangible, unmistakable, and unmistakably different from the mood in cities that were passed over by the movement, including cities in the North.

Tuscaloosa was one of the cities where the civil rights years were difficult but inconclusive. Racial division there is still a source of awkwardness, however polite.

Taken all together, it had been a fairly easy opening day in a trial Judge Page had feared was going to be a circus. After the jury was selected, he motioned Deputy Johnson to the bench and whispered something to him. The deputy smiled, nodded, and departed. Judge Page adjourned until morning, hurried to his borrowed chambers in the back, got out of his long black robe, and took the back stairs down to the parking lot, where

Deputy Johnson had his Madison County patrol car fired up and ready. With excited grins on their faces, the two men drove off to Toys "R" Us.

In an impromptu meeting in the back corridor behind the courtroom, Valeska tried to sound out the defense lawyers about whether they had a racial card of some kind in mind. The defense team answered quickly that they would love to have an agreement to keep race strictly out of the trial. In fact, they would agree to allow the state to simply read Errol Fitzpatrick's testimony in court without challenge, if the state would agree not to trot Fitzpatrick himself out in front of the jury again.

Valeska leaped at it. For one thing, making a heavy-handed play with the race card was something a county D.A. like Jimmy Fry could get away with a whole lot more easily politically than could the attorney general of the entire state of Alabama. For another thing, there were an awful lot of black people on this jury. Valeska was clearly delighted to have an agreement to keep race strictly out of the trial. Betty was already guilty without it.

The defense team nodded soberly, and all parties agreed—there would be no mention of race.

Valeska came right out of the chute the next morning with James Dennison White, clad in a crisp white prison jumpsuit again, shackled and scrubbed, looking even healthier than he had in Tuscaloosa. James was every bit as modest and unassuming as he had been there, his voice flat and quiet, his eyes downcast, his manner even and forthright. If there was any change at all from his performance in the first trial, it was that he provided a richer fabric of detail this time.

As they listened to him testify, the jurors kept their faces masked. Without the hubbub and obvious partisanship in the back of the room that had marked the first trial, the jurors in Montgomery seemed much more able to focus on what was being said on the stand.

David Johnson rose for the cross and appeared to circle James from a safe distance, as if wary. Then he began taking James back through his own personal criminal history, before he had ever met Peggy Lowe. The events that Jimmy Fry had successfully conveyed to the first jury as youthful white-trash peccadilloes came across in much more vivid, lurid detail as Johnson worked the story.

An example was a run-in with the law which James had explained away in the first trial as some bad luck he himself had suffered while hitchhiking in Arkansas. In point of fact, James and another man were picked up by a married couple who were traveling with a U-Haul trailer behind their car. James and his companion had locked up the husband in the trailer and were headed off to do Lord knows what to the wife when an army of state troopers surrounded the car with shotguns and forced them out on their bellies. James served five years, escaped, was captured and convicted of dope selling, and was returned to prison where he was charged with sodomy.

While Johnson was running through these events, James interrupted him testily to object that the sodomy had occurred not in prison but while he was in the Talladega County jail awaiting trial on car-theft charges. Johnson acknowledged the error, and James seemed pleased to have shown the court that the prosecutor wasn't so smart after all.

The jurors stared at James without so much as moving their lips.

When he had finished giving the jury a very bracing look at the long criminal career of the state's chief witness, Johnson walked James back through a series of key statements he had made to Mickey Brantley in the early interviews.

James tugged and pulled to resist going where Johnson was leading him, but after an hour or more of worrying the testimony out of him a bit at a time, Johnson had succeeded in painting the first corner of what eventually would become a clear picture for this jury:

James had begun by telling Mickey Brantley the truth—that he had gone to the house on Boulder Circle with no plan at all to kill anyone. "I don't think I was really going to kill the man," James had said again and again, in one form or another.

In the early statements, James said that his struggle with Jack Wilson was the result of a surprise encounter and that Jack was still alive when he left him. The savagery of the attack was attributable to James's drug-addled state of mind. He fled the house not knowing exactly what had happened and ran off through the woods.

Only as Mo Brooks, Mickey Brantley, Harry Renfroe, Jr., and the rest of the law enforcement team became more deeply and publicly invested in the theory of the twins' conspiracy did James's statements begin to mutate.

Gradually, he changed his entire story: It was a plan. He was paid. He went there to kill. He took a length of cord with which to garrote the doctor. He raced out of the house, having completed his mission, and leaped into the backseat of Betty's waiting BMW.

This time, by going over it carefully and in detail, David Johnson was able to get the jury to understand the basic outline of what had happened: James had changed his story from truth to lies in order to get a deal from the cops.

As soon as White was off the stand, Valeska changed plans. Rather than follow White with Mickey Brantley, which would have made logical sense, serving to cement the details of James's story in the jurors' minds, Valeska detoured instead through a long parade of all his best anti-Betty witnesses—the ladies who would sit on the stand and call her a slut and a hypocrite, a bad A.A. member, a castrating bitch.

The state read nearly all of Errol Fitzpatrick's testimony—where and when he and Betty had sex, who paid for the room, whether they had ever discussed love. The jury was impassive—not bored, but impassive, unwilling to show any emotion one way or the other about the sexual affairs of a woman who was not present and not officially on trial.

Toward the end of a full week of trial, Shirley Green, the maid, came back and recited her lurid tales again, including many references to the presence in the house of Errol Fitzpatrick and another man, Nelson Hogg. The ugliest of her stories about Betty's cruelty evinced raised eyebrows from some of the women on the jury—the first inkling of judgment. The men seemed to sit up a little straighter and listen harder when Valeska got to the part where Errol Fitzpatrick testified that he and Betty had engaged in sexual intercourse in the Wilson home.

When Buck Watson rose to cross-examine Shirley Green, he was courtly and kind in his treatment of her. He spoke to her in a voice that was quiet but just barely patronizing. He led her back through the business about Nelson Hogg and Errol Fitzpatrick coming to the house to see Betty.

Then, standing near her, dipping his head to look straight into her eyes, speaking to her sweetly, he said, "And Miz Green, these two men are black, are they not?"

"Yessir," she said quickly.

Valeska, who was just taking a sip of water, got it partway down the wrong pipe. He leaped to his feet, boiling red, eyes popping, choking, both hands flapping at the air.

"Your Honor, I object to this! We had an agreement! This is outrageous! It was the defense that said it was so eager to keep race out of this trial, and now they're the ones who are introducing it!"

Watson stood by with his hands clasped at his chest in an almost angelic pose, watching while Valeska danced and stomped around in front of the bench, objecting to the fact that Watson had just allowed the jurors to know the race of two of Betty's lovers.

The jurors were wide awake and on the edges of their seats. Virtually all of the six black men on the jury turned for the first time in nearly a week of trial and looked at Peggy Lowe at the defense table.

There was nothing for Judge Page to say about it one way or the other. The agreement not to mention race was strictly between the lawyers. It had nothing to do with rules of evidence, the law, or the facts. It was really none of the court's business.

Eventually Valeska regained control of himself and returned to his table. But the rest of the day's action seemed to fly right by him. He allowed assistants to handle most of the remaining witnesses, while he sat at the table and calculated just how badly and totally he had been snookered.

It was a masterful, devastating, brilliant tactic by Johnson and

Watson. By getting the prosecution to agree not to mention race, he had put the prosecution in the position, in the eyes of the jurors, of not wanting the jury to know the race of Betty's lovers. During voir dire, by accepting jurors who knew that Betty had been convicted in Tuscaloosa, Johnson had made sure that Betty's conviction would be discussed in the jury room. He probably had salted the jury with people who had read enough of the coverage to know that the jury in Tuscaloosa was majority white and working class.

And now with a simple, quiet, seemingly offhand question to Shirley Green—"These two men are black, are they not?"—Watson had painted the picture big and bright.

For the rest of the afternoon, the whole physical aspect of the black jurors was different. They watched and listened and gauged what was going on in front of them with a new acuity, and, just as it was obvious that Don Valeska's mind was off somewhere else, doing the calculus, so was it clear from their faces and body language that the jurors were adding things up afresh, from the top of the column all over again to a new bottom line.

Of course. The defendant's twin had been convicted in Tuscaloosa. All of the testimony so far had painted the two women as snakes entwined around the same bloody branch. All of the testimony had painted the other twin as a slut and a bitch. Shirley Green's testimony, the testimony of the rich ladies from Huntsville—all of it had dripped with loathing.

So, if this twin—the one on trial—was a paragon of virtue, how could the other one be a slut and a murderer? Why would people think that of the other one? How could she have been convicted? It had all been a mystery up until the moment when the gray-haired lawyer said, "These two men are black, are they not?"

Sure, times had changed in the Old South. But there were ways in which times had not changed. And it depended on which particular parcel of the Old South you were talking about, almost down to the acre. People in the South, white and black, tend to have a keen sense of precisely where each little town and county stands on a continuum from 1865 to the present.

Montgomery had been through it. It was the eye of the storm, the Big Beginning, the place where the bus boycott happened in 1955. In some ways and on certain terms, Montgomery could claim to have a more advanced and mature attitude toward race than most other cities in the country. On that scale, Montgomery was right at 1993.

Tuscaloosa? More like 1975. Definitely post-sixties. But not all that post.

If the state had told that jury in Tuscaloosa that this rich white lady from Huntsville was spoiled, bad-talked her husband, drank liquor, and then went ahead and had a bunch of successful suit-wearing black men over to her house to have intercourse with her while her sick husband was off working hard, then probably that was all that jury had needed to hear. They would figure she deserved the chair long before the murder ever came up.

Now, here in Montgomery, before this majority black jury, the state had cooked up some kind of secret agreement not to mention the race of Betty Wilson's lovers. And so far the state had spent all its time proving how Peggy must be guilty of murder because her twin sister was.

But maybe her twin sister wasn't guilty of murder. Maybe the only thing she was guilty of was thumbing her nose at the values of the community by sleeping with black men and acting bitchy in public.

From the moment of Buck Watson's disclosure forward, all of the jurors, black and white, were alive with a new and intense curiosity. Buck Watson had told them half of what they needed to know. The other half was the story of Peggy.

Before getting there, however, the trial still had to move through the rest of the state's witnesses. Valeska put Sheila Irby on, and she swished up to the stand even better dressed and more up for it than she had been in Tuscaloosa.

Watson cross-examined her. Again, as he had been with Shirley Green, he was calm, kind, gentlemanly. He always paused for her to make her amusing remarks, and he always smiled at them, in a forbearing kind of way.

Her effect on the jury was just the opposite of what it had been in Tuscaloosa. Where Sheila Irby had been able to bounce her witticisms off the brittle wall of Jack Drake's frustration to the laughter and applause of the gallery in Tuscaloosa, her saucy demeanor landed with a thud in the courtroom in Montgomery.

No one in the back of the room made a sound. The jurors were unamused. Their faces—especially the faces of the black jurors—were plainly disapproving. They didn't like to see this matter treated as a party or a chance for showing off.

Then Watson began patiently walking Sheila Irby back through her testimony in detail. He produced a huge aerial photograph of the area where she claimed she had seen White and Betty Wilson that day. He asked her to tell him again about each and every errand she had run that afternoon with her kids. Every time she named a new destination—the school, the park, the house—Buck Watson placed a pin in the aerial photo.

What emerged was a picture of the loony-tunes logistical nightmare a typical middle-class American mother must survive on an average afternoon—picking the kids up, taking them home, getting them to change clothes, getting one to one game, another to another game, picking up one, picking up the other, taking one here, taking the other there. As the pins multiplied, Watson very patiently asked Sheila Irby to tell him again how long each leg of the trip might have taken her to complete.

Deftly and without ever saying as much, Buck Watson was painting a picture of a woman with a car full of kids driving ninety miles an hour, back and forth, back and forth, here and there, as fast as she could go, all afternoon, on streets she covered every day of her life in this same mad-dash fashion. And then, some weeks later, after seeing the story on TV, after telling an impressive story to her colleagues in the hallway at school, after getting pinned to the wall on it by Mickey Brantley, she had suddenly remembered in vivid and precise detail just whom she had passed at what intersection at precisely what time on that typical day of her life those many weeks previously. And here she was today in court, dressed up and loaded for bear, sticking to her story.

Faint smiles began to appear on the faces of the jurors. By the time Buck Watson thanked Mrs. Irby and passed the witness, few of the jurors were even looking at her.

In the months between trials, David Johnson and his staff had done what the defense team in Tuscaloosa had failed to do with the state's chronology of events and supporting evidence—they had taken it apart, piece by piece, and put it back together themselves. As a result, Johnson was able to take state witnesses and state evidence and make it all work for the defense.

Pam Hide, who had talked to Jack on the telephone barely an hour before his death; John Self, the night clerk at the Ramada; the store clerks, A.A. members, and other people who had seen Betty that day—as Johnson cross-examined them, he distilled out precisely what it was they had to say about the timing of events on the day of the murder—who was where and when.

When he was done, Johnson had accomplished an amazing feat. He was able to use the state's witnesses and the state's evidence to show that the state's version of what had happened was impossible. Betty's time was accounted for, almost minute to minute, by the corroborative evidence. Except for the few minutes when she returned to the house at 5:00 P.M. for the bank bag, there simply were no gaps when she could have driven James to the house and then returned to give him a ride back to his truck. And Dr. Wilson was on the phone chatting with people after the time he would have had to die in order for Betty to have been in on it.

Some of the witnesses who had come to Tuscaloosa to testify against Betty were neutralized in other ways by the defense. The defense team had explained to Euel Dean Cagle, the twins' brother-in-law, why the twins had not been surprised the morning he had wakened them to tell them of White's arrest. Once he understood what had happened, he ceased to be of value to the prosecution. He was not called to testify. Instead, he came to Montgomery and stood around in the corridor outside the courtroom making a great show of his affection and regard for Peggy.

There was no undoing the slut factor. But for every witness Valeska had presented to call Betty Wilson a slut, the defense team presented two to testify to Peggy Lowe's virtue. Some of the stories of Peggy and Wayne's generosity were so moving that the eyes of some of the jurors glistened as the witnesses spoke. Person after person came to the stand to tell how the Lowes, who were people of modest means themselves, had reached out to give succor and support to people in need.

A particular pattern that emerged in the testimony—the core truth, perhaps, of Peggy's own life—was Peggy's inability to turn away from the suffering of a child at the hand of an alcoholic parent or parents. Unwed mothers came to the stand to tell how the Lowes had opened their home to them. Women who had known Peggy for years came to the stand to talk about her reflexive kindness, tolerance, and generosity.

Wayne and Peggy's children came to the stand and spoke convincingly and movingly of the happiness of their homelife. Wayne, who had been painted by the state in both trials as a fool and a cuckold, testified with a frankness, humor, and courage that completely erased the other impression of him. He came across as a strong, responsible man, smart, worldly, a survivor, a moral person, and nobody's fool—the kind of man most women would give a lot for.

But finally it was time for Peggy, the family hero, to take the stand. And all of a sudden, the defense was right back where it had been before Peggy testified in Tuscaloosa. Even with Johnson and Watson's brilliant handling of the racial ploy, with Sheila Irby behind them, the defense team still faced the tricky issue of Peggy's personality. Her overdone, valedictorian persona had backfired in Tuscaloosa, and it could backfire here.

She was going to be the last thing the jury would remember in this trial. And if she came across again as a Hollywood actress, then everything else her lawyers had accomplished would be neutralized—written off by the jury as so much clever lawyering.

The jurors were ready to believe Betty had been framed and convicted for racist reasons. They were certainly ready to believe James White was a liar. They were even willing to entertain the notion that the police had somehow gotten themselves wired up in James White's lies.

But it all depended on what they thought of Peggy. She was the key.

She was not terrified on the day she was to testify. She was not hopeful. Peggy Lowe had spent her life striving away from the dark, and now the dark was upon her, reaching its enveloping wings over her shoulders, moving its cracked lips to her lips, and there seemed to be not one thing she herself could do to stop it.

Just as Bill Wilson had taught little Jackie how to deal with the dark, Peggy had taught herself. All her life she had dealt with darkness by reaching inside and fixing what was wrong, and then the dark retreated.

Now none of that would work. The lawyers had told her that her performance in Tuscaloosa had been too much Goody Two-shoes, too earnest, too candid, to vulnerable. Too much.

But it had been what she was. What she knew how to be. What else could she do?

She wore a pink dress and a single strand of pearls.

David Johnson led her through it. When she spoke, her voice was not at all the voice that had spoken in Tuscaloosa—smooth and confident, fluting and controlled. Instead she spoke in the flatter, more nasal, rough-edged drawl of a girl from Hoke's Bluff at the wrong end of Gadsden. She sounded depressed, defensive, and resigned. She spoke in short choppy sentences and appeared to be having trouble getting her breath.

"My father was a policeman, and he was also a violent alcoholic," she said. "He was physically abusive to my mother and to my two older sisters. He abused my sister Betty one time.

"I got married in 1964. I never drank. My sister became an

alcoholic. I had two children, Angie and Blake. I got divorced."

The jurors were watching her closely. The voice, cringing and flat, didn't seem to match her physical appearance. She was a beautiful woman who obviously had good taste. It seemed strange to hear a woman like this talk in the tones one might expect of a tough character.

She told about her remarriage, going to college, becoming a teacher. She said of Jack, "Jack Wilson was probably one of the most caring, sympathetic, kindhearted men I ever met."

Then she talked about meeting James White. She told how she and Stephanie and Wayne all ate lunch together in her classroom while they prepared it for the first day of classes in the fall. "He started telling Stephie and Wayne and me all about his recent divorce."

Johnson asked her a question, and she had to ask him to repeat it. Her breathing was not regular, which caused her to stumble on her words. She was embarrassed and distracted.

Johnson asked, "Did you have sexual intercourse with James White on this or any other occasion."

She said, "No," and she said it in an angry, bitter, spitting voice. "The first time I ever heard the accusation of sex was at Betty's trial."

The jurors, who had been watching her with squinting intensity up until now, began to relax in small ways, sitting back and folding their hands beneath their chins, the men crossing their legs, the women smoothing their skirts with the backs of their hands.

Johnson asked her why she had referred James White to her sister.

"Mr. White called me. He said he was suicidal. He mentioned a man named Alvin, who I think was the person who had come with him to look at pouring me a new driveway. He said he had tried to kill himself, and Alvin had come in and stopped him."

She explained all of the calls back and forth, White's trip to Guntersville, each and every detail of the state's story. The longer she spoke, the more at ease and accepting the jury became. One by one, they were figuring out what was wrong with her—why the voice didn't match the pearls.

She was a middle-class person, up from humble beginnings, who had led a good life. Now this horror was upon her. Her sister was in prison. And she was terrified.

She wasn't the valedictorian. She wasn't Goody Two-shoes. She wasn't the family hero. She was stripped bare and beaten, and she was terrified for her life.

The jury could accept that.

Finally David Johnson led her through a series of yes or no questions. The jurors listened to each response with the sober, open, respectful faces of believers.

"Did you conspire with your sister to kill Jack Wilson?"

"No."

"Did you give James White twenty-five hundred dollars to kill Jack Wilson?"

"No."

"Did you have sexual intercourse with James White?"

"No."

"Did you take a gun to him?"

"No."

"Are you guilty of the charges against you?"

"No."

The jury deliberated for barely two hours—long enough to elect a foreman, reread the judge's instructions, talk for a while, and then vote.

Peggy Joy Woods Lowe was acquitted on all counts.

EPILOGUE

THE JULIA TUTWILER STATE PENITENTIARY FOR WOMEN in Wetumpka, Alabama, is an unimpressive mound at the top of a hill on Highway 231, half an hour's drive north from Montgomery through forests and bedroom communities. Behind makeshift arrangements of high metal fencing, it is a one-story, 1930s, WPA-style structure, more like a messy, semi-abandoned fairgrounds than a penal colony.

Even though Betty and I were in the office at the front of the prison complex with the door shut, we had to speak loudly in order to hear each other over the clanging of cell-block gates all around us.

She looked good—clear-eyed and trim in her white prison jumpsuit. Her hair was nicely done. Her face had more tone and color than in Tuscaloosa—the last time I had seen her.

Both trials had been concluded. I had spent the better part of two years traveling back and forth to Alabama from my home in Dallas to interview people in the story.

I had reported on and written about crime all of my adult life, during almost thirty years as a reporter, columnist, and author. But this story was a personal experience for me unlike any before.

This time I had started out convinced the people I was going to write about were guilty, and then I had been forced to concede I was wrong. I had discovered something in myself I didn't like in a middle-aged man—that I had trouble admitting error. The phone call to New York from a corridor in the courthouse in Montgomery, two days into Peggy's week-long trial, had been sweaty and defensive.

"She's not going to be convicted," I told my editor.

"Why not?"

"She's not guilty. Neither one of them is. They had nothing to do with it."

"How could that be?"

"Don't ask me. Stuff happens."

But after Peggy's acquittal, everyone else in the media continued on as if both of them had been found guilty. In the relative scale of things, the Alabama twins case had been to Huntsville what the O. J. Simpson case later became to the nation—a fascination so obsessive and huge that it blotted out all other conversation for a time. And yet, after the acquittal in Montgomery, I didn't see or hear a single story in the newspapers or on television or radio examining the premise "What if we were all wrong about them?"

It was as if the second trial had never taken place.

A few months after the second trial, a network television movie painted both Peggy and Betty as fat hillbilly slobs. The movie opened with a long sequence in a swamp in which two men in camouflage gear chased and then shot a dove, against a musical backdrop of ominously twanging mouth harps. There was not even an attempt to tie the scene to the story, except as a mood and scene setter whose purpose was to say: "Somewhere in the depraved *Deliverance*-type bayous of the Incredibly Deep, Faulknerian South . . ."

I'm afraid I also have a good feel for how news media logic works in cases like this. Certain kinds of stories—stories that tend to humble the mighty and bring low the proud—are so irresistible for news editors that it almost doesn't matter how true they are.

Other kinds of stories don't get assigned because they are outside the reach of the genre. You just don't see newspaper stories, for example, about the abuse of rich people.

. . .

When I came home from Montgomery and told people I was going to write a book that would portray the Alabama twins as innocent, they always asked what I suppose was the obvious question: Why?

Why, when everyone else seemed to have agreed that the Alabama twins were guilty, did I want to argue they were not? To be noticed? Or did I have some kind of special proof to offer, something new and shocking, never before made public?

I have come to answer this question as follows:

1. Everyone did not agree that the Alabama twins were guilty. The media did. That's not everyone.
2. There were two trials in this case, but in terms of the evidence presented by the state, the trials were identical. Same evidence. Same arguments. Two times around.

   It was the nature of the state's case against the twins that they both had to be either guilty or innocent. There was no way to believe one of them guilty and the other not.
3. It was the finding of the jury in the second, much more thorough, much more deliberative trial, that Peggy Lowe was innocent. In order to get to that conclusion, the second jury had to believe Peggy Lowe's twin sister, Betty Wilson, was innocent too.

   So my book, and my version of the story, and what I believe in my heart, comports exactly with the finding of the second jury. Therefore my book is not a contradiction of the record. It is a confirmation of it. It is a recitation of the Alabama twins story as the second jury believed it really happened.

As I see it, the real question is not why I would write this book the way I have. The real question is why, after the second trial, the media in Alabama (and the national media that had taken such an interest in the case early on) would not come back to it and try to report the story afresh.

By remaining virtually silent on the implications of the second verdict, the media imply that it was a fluke, that Peggy Lowe somehow got off through trickery or smart lawyering.

Smart lawyering *was* a major element. But were Peggy Lowe's lawyers laboring to hoodwink or trick the jury? I sat through every second of Peggy Lowe's trial, and I didn't see David Cromwell Johnson or Buck Watson do a single thing that would have served to distract the jury from the facts. Instead, they painstakingly laid out the case—who was where, when, doing what, according to whom—so that the jury could see in detail the holes in the state's case.

Even with all of James White's memory alterations, the facts presented by the state itself—the accuser—proved Betty could not have done what the state asserted.

The state's own witnesses accounted for too much of her time. It was not physically possible for Betty to have been driving James White all over Huntsville, as the state claimed, and for her also to have been in all of the other places proved by witnesses.

What David Johnson also did in Montgomery—something the lawyers in Tuscaloosa had failed to do—was show the jury how James White's lies had been woven together over time to present a plausible fabric. All the jury had to do was see how hard it was to get James's story to make sense, and how easy it was for him to change it, and he became worthless as a witness. In an old aphorism of the South: Any man who lied that much would have to get somebody else to call his dog.

If the facts were there in Montgomery, presumably the same facts were there in Tuscaloosa. So why did the first jury believe the twins were guilty?

One reason had to do with simple timing. The defense lawyers in Betty's case had to go first. The lawyers in the second case had the benefit of the first trial and of six intervening months to examine and dissect the state's case.

But the larger factor was Betty herself. Jimmy Fry's real argument against her was based not on the facts of the Jack Wilson murder but on her life, her personal morality before the murder had ever taken place.

The booze, the bitchiness, the infidelity, and in particular, the fact that she regularly had sexual intercourse with African-American men—these were the crimes for which Betty Wilson was sent to prison for life by the jury in Tuscaloosa.

Was it evil of Jimmy Fry to play the race card, subpoenaing Betty Wilson's black lover back from California? Trials are about winning. Our system of jury trials depends on a stiff contest between able champions. Jimmy Fry is a very good lawyer, an able champion of his cause. And I think at this time, in the United States, any lawyer who can play the race card will play it.

It's too good. It's too powerful. It's too efficient a way to sway an American jury. Nobody who really wants to win will walk away from it.

In the twins case, the lawyers in the second trial saw the race card coming because they had seen how it was played in the first trial. They were ready. They played it right back in the state's face.

But they played it.

In addition to race, another critical element in Betty's conviction was her relationship with and treatment of Jack. The images of their sex life that emerged in the media first and then in the trial were as ugly as it gets. Those images were a sort of collective public insult to the modern culture of sex as a semi-public activity intended to take place between pretty people, in a beautiful way, at nice times in a pleasant setting.

But consider this: If the huge, glistening, unlidded eye of the public were lifted to other bedroom windows—if adults generally were to have their sex lives held up in public and judged according to the aesthetic standards of MTV—how many people's sex lives would come off looking picture-perfect?

Life goes on. Life gets less pretty on the outside. But what about the inside?

When Betty and I talked in the warden's office at the prison in Wetumpka, months after her conviction, she spoke of the hope she had held, just before Jack's murder, that they might actually pull it back together.

That was really what their relationship had been about from the beginning—two adults, warts and all, both smart and valuable people, each with terrible shortcomings, fears, flaws, wounds, and anxieties, but both battling bravely to hold on to each other and to extend love. Real love. True love. Not pretty love.

We spoke for almost six hours. It wasn't easy for her. Her world now is frightening and cruel. It requires of her that she be as tough and as cool as she can possibly manage. And I was there asking her to plumb the depths of a pain that was prior to and even deeper than the pain of her imprisonment, more fundamental than the pain of Jack's horrible death. I wanted her to talk about her love for her husband.

In halting phrases, wiping away tears, she told me she had loved Jack dearly. She told me how and why. Weird partners in a stranger life, they were to each other a world entire. They were all they had.

She was convicted for being rich. For being naughty. But more than anything, Betty Wilson was convicted for being ugly. And yet it's hard for me to imagine a love more beautiful than what she and her husband felt for each other.

Betty can't get out of prison just because her sister was found innocent when tried on the same facts. That's not how the law works. Her lawyers must find either new information or mistakes in her trial in order to free her.

But the information that should free her is the same evidence that was presented in her trial. There is no new information. And if the only mistake was the jury's mistake—that they looked at all the right evidence and simply came to the wrong conclusion—then that won't do it.

Betty Wilson may well remain in prison for the rest of her life.

It is understandably embittering for her that James White was allowed to plead to a reduced charge of "simple" murder—that is, not capital murder—and that he will walk out of prison a free man before the year 2000, even though he has admitted his guilt in this terrible, brutal crime.

But what salts the wound is this: The lies for which James White was given this very light sentence he has already recanted.

In a sworn and witnessed affidavit, signed in prison on June 1, 1994, James White confessed that the entire story he had told in court to help get the twins convicted was a lie.

It's quite a document. In the statement of recantation, James White tells what he now says really happened. He says Peggy Lowe helped him find work in 1991. He says he began to think of her in romantic terms. He remembers somehow alluding to these feelings to her, and he says she laughed at him.

But he also says that his memory of this entire period of his life is shrouded in an alcohol-and drug-induced blur, with long stretches of time simply missing.

White claims in the document that Mickey Brantley and other police officers withheld medication from him, threatened him with the electric chair, and browbeat him into saying that Peggy Lowe and Betty Wilson had hired him.

"When I tried to make people on the outside of the jail aware of what I was being pressured into doing to Mrs. Wilson and Mrs. Lowe, the jail administration threatened to punish me and told me that I wouldn't be given my medications until after I testified against Mrs. Wilson and Mrs. Lowe."

James claims in this document to have "found my solution in Christ." He says he finally wants to tell the whole truth about what really happened.

Unfortunately, James tries to say in the same document that he himself really had nothing to do with Jack Wilson's death—a ludicrous claim. His description of cruel, abusive, third-degree–style treatment by the Huntsville police is almost certainly untrue. (In the course of writing this book, one of the people I got to know was Mickey Brantley, and I do not for a minute believe any of James's accusations against him.)

The real point in all this was made by Jimmy Fry, when reporters asked him about James's recantation. Fry responded that the statement was worthless because it was impossible to believe anything James Dennison White said.

Indeed. And when you peel away the other factors—the race

card, the class resentment, the fuss over Betty's sex life—James Dennison White's word was the entire core of the state's case against the twins.

It was a simple accusation case. There was no physical evidence. No eyewitnesses. Nothing except James Dennison White's story. And James Dennison White is a lifelong, medically diagnosed, legally convicted, chronic, self-confessed, and consistent liar. Like everything else James White has ever said in his life, the statement offers a little bit of truth wrapped up in a whole lot of lie.

This was not the story of a conspiracy against the Alabama twins. The law itself has in it all sorts of logic and precedent and justification for the way this case came out.

But as I drove down the hill toward Montgomery, watching the Julia Tutwiler State Penitentiary disappear in my rear-view mirror, I thought this: If the final judgment of the law is that Betty Wilson must spend the rest of her life in prison, then the law is a fool.

INDEX

INDEX

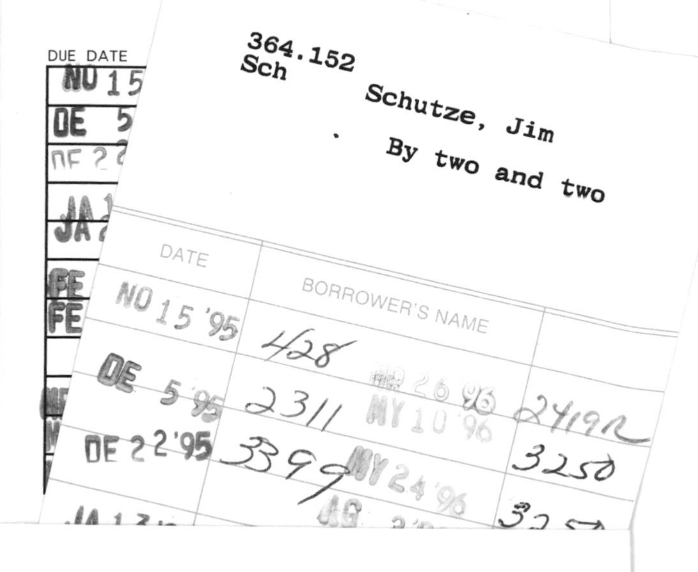
DUE DATE
364.152
Sch
Schutze, Jim
By two and two
DATE
BORROWER'S NAME
NO 15 '95
428
DE 5 '95
2311
MY 10 '96
24192
DE 22 '95
3399
MY 24 '96
3250
SELBYVILLE PUBLIC LIBRARY
SELBYVILLE, DE